The Holy Teaching of Vimalakīrti

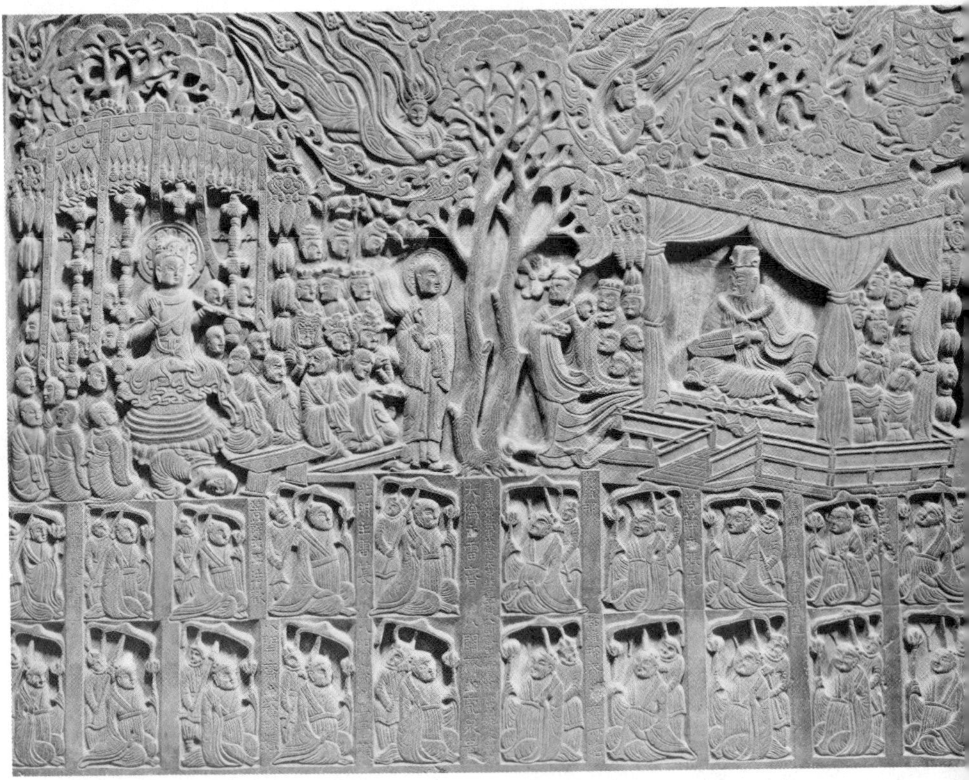

This exquisite Chinese stele suggests the imagination-challenging panorama of the cosmic setting of the events of the Scripture, depicting the main assembly at the house of Vimalakīrti, with attendant hosts. Mañjuśrī is seen in the pavilion on the left, attended by monks, deities, and citizens of Vaiśālī. Vimalakīrti holds forth in the pavilion on the right, surrounded by attendant bodhisattvas. Śāriputra stands on the left of the central tree, faced by the goddess (Chap. 7) who teases him so artfully. The flying figure on the upper right represents the magically incarnated bodhisattva bringing the inexhaustible bowl of ambrosial food from the universe Sarvagandhasugandha (Chap. 10). The figure on the upper left represents one of the bodhisattvas from that other universe about to shower flowers on the assembly out of his delight in the profound teachings. (Photograph courtesy of Metropolitan Museum of Art, Rogers Fund, 1929.)

The Holy Teaching of Vimalakīrti

A Mahāyāna Scripture

Translated by
Robert A. F. Thurman

The Pennsylvania State University Press
University Park, Pennsylvania

Published in cooperation with
The Institute for Advanced Studies of World Religions
New York, N.Y.

Library of Congress Cataloging in Publication Data
Vimalakīrtinirdeśa. English.
The holy teaching of Vimalakīrti.
Includes bibliographical references.
I. Thurman, Robert A. F. II. Title.
BQ2212.E5T47 294.3′8 75-27196
ISBN 0-271-01209-9
ISBN 0-271-00601-3 (Pbk.)

Eighth printing, 1992

Filmset in Hong Kong by Asco Trade Typesetting Limited
Printed in the United States of America

[redacted]

Reverence to Mañjughoṣa,
the ever-young crown prince!

[redacted]

Contents

Preface

Amid the glittering profusion of the jewelry of the Mahāyāna Buddhist Scriptures, The *Holy Teaching of Vimalakīrti* stands out like a masterfully faceted diamond, so located between the heaps of gold, silver, and pearls of the *Transcendent Wisdom* (*Prajñāpāramitā*) *Scriptures* and the array of sapphires, rubies, emeralds, and other gems of the *Garland* (*Avataṃsaka*), or *Inconceivable Liberation* (*Acintyavimokṣa*) *Scriptures* as to refract the radiances of all, beaming them forth to the beholder in a concentrated rainbow-beam of diamond light.

I elaborate upon this traditional metaphor here to convey a sense of the uniqueness of the *Vimalakīrti* among Buddhist Scriptures; its utility for study as containing a quintessence of Mahāyāna doctrines, both of the *profound* and of the *extensive* categories, and its aesthetic virtue as an object of the connoisseur's delight. This helps us understand how a hundred generations of Mahāyāna Buddhists in India, Central Asia, China, Japan, and South East Asia were disposed to study, revere, and enjoy this Scripture, finding enlightenment, inspiration, and the grace of pleasant humor.

Nothing concrete is known about the "original text" of the *Vimalakīrti*. It purports to record events that took place during Gautama Buddha's time (sixth to fifth century B.C.), but no text was apparent in India until after Nāgārjuna (c. first century B.C. to first century A.D.) had revived the Mahāyāna traditions, discovering the Mahāyāna Sanskrit Scriptures, the *Vimalakīrti* text among them. This text was subsequently translated into Chinese seven different times, starting in the third century, the version of Kumārajīva (A.D. 406) being the most popular, and that of Hsüan Tsang (A.D. 650) the most technically accurate. It was translated into Tibetan twice, the definitive version completed in the ninth century by the well-known translator Chos Ñid Tshul Khrims. It was also translated into Sogdian, Khotanese, and Uighur. Unfortunately all basic Sanskrit texts are now lost, except for some fragments found in Mahāyāna philosophical works. The Japanese chose Kumārajīva's version for their translation, and the majority of modern translations have been based on this text. Recently, Dr. E. Lamotte set forth to rectify this situation by basing his fine French translation on the Tibetan and the Hsüan Tsang versions. The history comes full circle finally, as the Rev. E. Bangert first translated the Tibetan into modern Thai and then into current Sanskrit. My translation is based on the Tibetan version, as I am most at home in that language, although at times the simplicity of the Kumārajīva, the psychological precision of Hsüan Tsang, or the elegance of Lamotte may have clarified the Tibetan, provided an alternative, or given me another reference point from which to find a middle way. Any significant departures from the basic Tibetan have been duly noted.

My main goal in this translation is to present the authentic *teaching* of Vimalakīrti, and so my main focus is philosophical rather than philological. Thus, I have taken great pains with the language of the translation, providing the reader with three glossaries, the first for Sanskrit terms and proper names, the second for the numerical categories that abound in Mahāyāna Scriptures, and the third for English Buddhist technical terms that correspond to important Sanskrit concepts, proper understanding of which is crucial for undistorted appreciation of the teaching. Sanskrit terms are given in root form except when they occur in plural or in grammatical combination.

The ultimate inexpressibility of everything is never more keenly felt than when it comes time to express one's gratitude to one's teachers and benefactors for their irrepayable kindness in enabling one to come to the point of serving in such a capacity as this. Nevertheless, silence on this occasion would be like Śāriputra's silence (Chap. 7), not like Vimalakīrti's lion's roar (Chap. 9). First, I must salute the long line of scholars and translators, some mentioned above, from Mañjuśrī to Lamotte, who preserved this teaching over the millennia and made it available to me; I hope this work will contribute to the unending tradition. Second, I avow my heartfelt gratitude to my personal teachers, whom I list in temporal order of my contact with them: Rev. Geshe Wangyal, H. H. the Dalai Lama, Dr. M. Nagatomi, Dr. D. H. H. Ingalls, Dr. V. V. Gokhale, and Lama Anagarika Govinda; I can only hope that this work might please them. Third, I sincerely thank my friend and benefactor, Dr. C. T. Shen, both for his sponsorship of the work and for his most helpful collaboration in the work of comparing the Tibetan and Chinese versions. We were sometimes joined in our round-table discussions by Drs. C. S. George, Tao-Tien Yi, F. S. K. Koo, and T. C. Tsao, whose helpful suggestions I gratefully acknowledge. My thanks also go to Ms. Yeshe Tsomo and Ms. Leah Zahler for their invaluable editorial assistance, and to Ms. Carole Schwager and the staff of The Pennsylvania State University Press. Finally, my very special thanks to Nena, who actually made it all possible, and to Ganden, Uma, and Dechen, who make it all necessary.

If, in spite of all this excellent help, any errors remain undetected, I take full responsibility for them.

Gandendechenay
Shady, New York
August 1975

Robert A. F. Thurman

Introduction

The Message of Vimalakīrti

"Matter is not void because of voidness; voidness is not elsewhere from matter. Matter itself *is* voidness. Voidness itself *is* matter."[1] This statement, common in Mahāyāna Scriptures, expresses the quintessence of the Middle Way (*madhyamapratipat*). It is also fundamental to the message of Vimalakīrti. It is utterly profound, yet so simple it is all too easy to overlook its astounding implications. "Matter" represents the familiar world, the world of relativity, whereas "voidness" represents the goal of spiritual longing, the ultimate, the transcendental, the infinite and eternal. If the two are just the same, what is the purpose of religion? Of philosophy? Of the austerity of spiritual practice? Of this statement or any statement or teaching? Is this not the most blatant form of nihilism?

Indeed, a great many scholars, ancient as well as modern, have mistaken the Middle Way taught by Vimalakīrti, Nāgārjuna, and the Mahāyāna Buddha as leading to the annihilation of all values, mundane and spiritual, and the main purpose of this introduction is to avert this disastrous mistake. The key lies in the concept of "voidness." The word is carefully chosen, and does not mean "nothingness." Thus, the equation of "matter" with "voidness" tells us something about the condition of matter, not that matter does not exist at all. And the equation of "voidness" with "matter" emphasizes the fact that this teaching is, far from being nihilistic, the very cure for nihilism.

Nāgārjuna expounds the same theme in his *Vigrahavyāvartanī*: "I salute the incomparable, perfect Buddha, who made the declaration of the equivalence in meaning of voidness, relativity, and the Middle Way."[2] Here we find, instead of "matter," the term "relativity" (*pratītyasamutpāda*), which is another key term of the Middle Way philosophy. It means that all finite things are interdependent, relative, and mutually conditioned, and implies that there is no possibility of any independent, self-sufficient, permanent thing or entity. An entity exists only in relation to other entities. It must be composed of parts, which came together when it was produced and which separate at the time of its dissolution. All things that can be observed, imagined, or conceived by our finite minds are relative insofar as they are limited at least by having a point of contact, hence a relationship, with our perceptions or imaginations. However, as we make our way through the relative world, our minds are accustomed to constructing pairs of opposites such as "long and short" or "light and dark." Thus we hypothesize an opposite to every finite, dependent, temporal, relative entity we can know or imagine, and we call it infinity, independence, eternity, absolute—that is, usually some etymologically negative term (in-finite = not finite, etc.). This is quite harmless and useful, until we begin to make the unconscious assumption that since most names seem to refer to entities, these must also, and we begin to think of "an independent being" and similar concepts. If we then attach these false notions of ultimate being to whatever we are disposed to value, we fall short of full awareness of thoroughgoing relativity.

So the teachers of the Middle Way use "voidness" to remind us that all such false notions are delusive; that is, they use it to free us from our own conceptualizations. Hence "matter is voidness" does not negate matter as a relative phenomenon; it negates any false notion of matter as an ultimate thing, as having any independent, substantial being, as having any *ultimately* true status. Matter in itself does not need to be felt to have some sort of ultimate, independent substance, to stand in its diverse configurations and undergo its various relative transformations. In fact, were matter to have any sort of independent, ultimate status (such as the true being we tend to attribute to all things because of our habit of confusing name with reality), it would become obstructed in its functional roles of interdependency since, by definition, an independent "thing" cannot be dependent. Therefore, all negative statements in the teachings of the Middle Way, from the Scriptures to the systematic treatises of the Mādhyamika by the great masters such as Nāgārjuna and his successors, do not negate relative things per se but only their ultimate existence, which is initially attributed to them by habitual, delusive, mental constructions.

Most people are so accustomed to such notions that the world might seem impossible if there were no enduring substance in things. In his major work, "Wisdom" (*Prajñā nāma mūlamādhyamakakārikā*),[3] Nāgārjuna quotes a famous objector: "If all this were void, then there would be no creation and no destruction. . . ." And Nāgārjuna's answer comes as a shock at first: "If all this were *not* void, then there would be no creation and no destruction. . . ."[4] Thus voidness, far from annihilating everything, is the *necessary condition* for all relative existence. In other words, voidness here is not "the void" we imagine in microspace or macrospace, a dark nothingness in which galaxies or atoms are contained; nor is it a substratum. It is infinity, which is only a term for the ultimate ineffability of the relative reality to which we can see no ending or beginning.

The difficulty of correct understanding of this principle may lie in its very simplicity. When minds are conditioned to discover truth in subtle complexities, it may become emotionally repugnant to accept a principle so simple that it seems to make intellect obsolete. This principle therefore will not lead to resolution in one's deeper being, unless analytic intellect has succeeded in throwing out every possible alternative. Hence it is as delusive to grasp the principle as a solution in itself as it is delusive to reject it out of hand.

The principle is that the fact that matter *is* voidness is absolutely affirmative of matter, not negative of matter. Indeed, of all theories it is the *only one* that is thus affirmative.

How is this so?

There are basically two kinds of theory about ultimate reality: nihilism and "absolutism." Of course, intellectual history abounds in theories vastly different in detail, but all share one or the other of these basic postulates about reality. They either deny it altogether or they posit some sort of ultimate entity, substratum, or superstratum that serves as foundation, essence, container, or whatever, of the immediate reality. And this absolutism, while appearing to affirm something ultimately, actually negates the immediate reality in favor of the hypostatized ultimate reality. For if "God," "Brahman," the "universe," "the void," "nirvāṇa," "pure mind," "the Tao," "pure being," and so forth, make an ultimate reality beyond the imperfection of our world, the spiritual man must naturally strive to escape this imperfection to reach his ultimate and eternal well-being. However widely the absolutes posited may differ, they all impel us in practice to negate our immediate reality.

Now we may better appreciate the first implication of the statement that the immediate, relative reality *is* the ultimate, perfect reality: that matter is voidness. If it is so, our immediate reality *is* ultimate, cannot be escaped or negated, and must be accepted as it is—at least to start with, before we try to do something about it in a relative way—with no false hope of ever making it ultimate, since it already is so. We are left with the seemingly contradictory tasks of becoming conscious of its ultimacy on the one hand and, on the other hand, of devoting our energies to the improvement of the unavoidable relative situation as best we can. For the successful accomplishment of this dual task we need, respectively, wisdom (*prajñā*) and great compassion (*mahākaruṇā*), and these two functions are the essence of the Great Vehicle (*Mahāyāna*), and of the Middle Way.

Wisdom does not allow us to settle for our habitual involvement with sensory objects (as just being "given" "out there"), and causes us to learn and practice probing beneath the surface of apparent "reality" to gain direct awareness of the ultimate reality of all things. At the same time, great compassion does not allow us to set up any hypostatized "ultimate reality," immerse ourselves in any sort of quietistic trance, or accept any sort of illogical escapism from relativity, but imperatively compels us to act selflessly, as if already enlightened, even when we do not yet feel enlightened. Thus, the correct intellectual understanding of the voidness of matter (*rūpaśūnyatā*), the voidness of consciousness (*vijñāna-śūnyatā*), or even the voidness of voidness (*śūnyatāśūnyatā*) is the indispensable first step in the long meditational cultivation of our tolerance of incomprehensibility (*anupalabdhidharmakṣānti*), as well as the supreme cure for self-defeating selfishness in daily action. And thus the way is difficult, not because of any complexity, but because we cannot grasp matter, we cannot grasp mind, we cannot even grasp any doctrine of the "ungraspability of matter and mind." And still, matter, mind, and ultimate voidness remain before us in ineluctable relativity, like the reflection of the moon in water. It is clear that this subtle, profound, yet simple teaching can be inaccessible or even frightening to those either intellectually or emotionally unprepared, while the gem-like being properly prepared need only hear it, and all mental blocks are instantly shattered.[5]

Thus, this teaching of the Middle Way is not for everyone. And hence the Buddha and the great masters who inherited his teachings devised other teachings intended to develop those who might be overwhelmed by introduction through this teaching, to develop them to a point where they would be ready to confront the "royal reason" equating voidness with relativity. There is the Hinayāna teaching, which teaches a liberation (*nirvāṇa*) that appears to be a release from the relative world short of perfect enlightenment. There is the "mind-only" teaching (*vijñānavāda*), which teaches the reality of pure mind, beyond all miserable phenomena. Nevertheless, in all cases, these teachings serve in the development of an individual only up to a point: the point where he might meet with a Vimalakīrti, who would bring home to him the ultimate message of the Middle Way.

In the words of Nāgārjuna, from the *Ratnāvalī*: "Just as the grammarians make one read the grammar, the Buddha teaches the Dharma according to the tolerance of the disciples. He teaches the Dharma to some people to refrain from sins, to some to accomplish virtue, to some to depend on dualism, and to some to be independent from dualism; finally, to some, he teaches the profound, awe-inspiring practice of enlightenment, whose essence is compassion and voidness."[6]

In keeping with an alternative title of the Scripture ("Inconceivable Liberation"),[7] Vimalakīrti lays great emphasis on the theme of inconceivability, that is, the ultimate incomprehensibility of all things, relative or absolute. He thus spells out the furthest implication of the application of voidness: that the finite, ego-centered mind cannot even conceive of the ultimate nature of things and, hence, as far as such minds are concerned, their ultimate reality is itself inconceivability.

This accords with the degree of attainment of the bodhisattva, so frequently reached by Vimalakīrti's audiences, called "the tolerance of the ultimate birthlessness of all things" (*anutpattika-dharmakṣānti*). It is extremely significant that the term "tolerance" (*kṣānti*) is used here, rather than "conviction," "understanding," or "realization"; it emphasizes the fact that where the ultimate is concerned, the mind is unable to grasp anything in the pattern of dualistic knowledge, for there is no finite object in this case and only relative objects can be grasped with relative certainty in the mundane sense. Yet that is not to say that the student's task is to simply put a label of "inconceivability" on all things and rest complacent with a sense of having reached a high state. Indeed, there are three stages of this tolerance: the verbal (*ghoṣānugā*), conforming (*anulomikī*), and true tolerance of birthlessness. This indicates the difficulty of attainment of true tolerance, which occurs only at the eighth stage of bodhisattvahood.[8] Inconceivability as a verbal concept is only a principle to be applied to the mind, just like the verbal concept of voidness, or even of infinity.

When we reflect intensively on any of these concepts, our minds open gradually in an ever widening sphere whose limits proceed from preconceived limitation to preconceived limitation. We discover to our surprise that there is always something further, and we logically discard the possibility of any limit being ultimate because any limit serves as the near boundary of the next larger space or dimension or time. If we adhere rigorously to this process, we soon find ourselves lost in the stars, as it were, with less and less security about ever having started from anywhere. It takes time for such a process to permeate one's whole being, for this can be a shattering experience to one whose conditioned notions are firmly ingrained and not previously brought into the light of analytic examination. The great master Atiśa once likened the process to a mound of butter melting in a broth, or to an iron pressing smooth the wrinkles in a piece of cotton cloth.

The Buddha gave this type of deepest teaching only to disciples able to deal with it. Nāgārjuna himself rarely spelled it out explicitly, restricting himself to providing the means whereby the disciplined intellect can strip away its own conceptualizations and habitual notions. But Vimalakīrti felt that such a message should be available to a much larger circle of people, for he expressed himself definitively on all occasions, as recorded in this Scripture. Thus I have ventured to follow his example by spelling out the essence of his message in order to insure that his speech would not be utilized falsely as a justification for nihilism or sophistry. Of course it need not be repeated that no formula, no phoneme, and no spelling out can do more than point the way to an understanding beyond words, which, however, includes words as relative things from another point of view. In fact, the very existence of this introduction betrays my inadequacy to live up to Vimalakīrti himself, with his famous silence on the subject of non-duality when questioned by Mañjuśrī.

The Method of Vimalakīrti

The second chapter, "Inconceivable Skill in Liberative Technique," introduces Vimalakīrti as a person who represents the consummate embodiment of skill in liberative technique.[9] This makes even more plain the implication of the Scripture that he is an incarnation (*nirmāṇa*), like Śākyamuni Buddha himself, and, as such, indistinguishable from the Buddha in the ability to do the right thing for each particular person. His eloquence is supreme, his behavior is exemplary, and his miraculous feats are in no way inferior to those of the Buddha himself. Although he is respectful to the Buddha and usually polite with everyone, even the disciples, he is in no way intimidated in the august presence of the Tathāgata, as he proceeds to tell him to his face that he does not really exist.[10]

The main technique Vimalakīrti uses that is of interest here—dichotomy—is found in his discourse, which relates to another alternative title of the Scripture, "Reconciliation of Dichotomies" (*yamakavyātyastāhāra*).[11] This is in keeping with the traditional method of the Middle Way masters, who had great skill in pitting polar opposites against each other to eliminate the fixedness of each and to free the mind of the student who applies himself to the polarities to open into a middle ground of reality beyond concepts. The "Great Sorcerers" (*mahāsiddhas*) of first-millennium India refined this technique to a consummate degree in their songs and extraordinary deeds, and the Great Ch'an and Zen Masters wielded the same "double-edged sword" in their earthshaking statements and their illuminating activities. The singular quality of such teachers' use of dichotomies lies in the fact that they relate them to the actual practice of the hearers, forcing them to integrate them in their minds and actions. Thus, they expect them to be liberated inconceivably, while being totally engaged in the work of helping other living beings.[12] They recommend their full cultivation of great love and great compassion while maintaining total awareness of the total absence of any such thing as a living being, a suffering being, a being in bondage. In short, they show the way to the full nonduality of wisdom and great compassion, the latter being expressed as skill in liberative technique—the integrated approach acknowledged by all the masters as the essence of the Mahāyāna.[13]

This brings out Vimalakīrti's main bone of contention with the disciples, such as Śāriputra, whom he finds to be too complacent in their sense of liberation and superiority of wisdom. It also further emphasizes the positive aspect of the Middle Way in general, which has all too often been overlooked by its Western critics, who have mistaken it for nihilism at worst or at best for a sophistic, dry intellectualism. Vimalakīrti makes it clear that the sole function of wisdom, gnosis, or any state of liberation is its function as a necessary complement to the indispensable great compassion that has no object (*anupalambha*) and is not a sentimentally conceived emotion (*ananūnayadṛṣtimahākaruṇā*). Wisdom as a solitary possession, not integrated with liberative technique, is plainly declared to be bondage;[14] even meditation, trance, concentration, and so on, are declared to be vain unless they aid in reconciliation of the basic dichotomy of world versus liberation, *saṃsāra* versus *nirvāṇa*. That some modern scholars could think that this fundamental point of Vimalakīrti's message, this fundamental procedural basis of the entire Mahāyāna, might have been overlooked or neglected by such masters as Nāgārjuna or Candrakīrti is indeed surprising.

Vimalakīrti's reconciliation of dichotomies is so thoroughgoing that he shocks the disciples by his advocacy of the most horrible things as being part of the bodhisattva's path. The bodhisattva may commit the five deadly sins,[15] may follow the false heterodox teachings, may entertain the sixty-two false views, may consort with all the passions, and so on. Even the Māras, or devils, that plague the various universes are said to be bodhisattvas dwelling in inconceivable liberation[16] —playing the devil, as it were, in order to develop living beings.

This leads to an extraordinary fact that cannot be omitted, as startling as it may be to some because of their historical convictions about the origins of various Buddhist teachings. Vimalakīrti's method in integrating the intellectual and behavioral dichotomies is one of many blatant hints of Tantric ideas in the background of his teaching method. Futher research is needed to determine whether these connections prove the existence of Tantrism at a time earlier than modern scholars generally believe or whether later Tantrics found Vimalakīrti's teachings a source of inspiration. However, in a discussion of Vimalakīrti's method, it must be noted that in the foregoing instances of reconciliation of extreme dichotomies Vimalakīrti is actually teaching pure Tantric doctrine, as can be found in such works as the *Guhyasamājatantra*.[17] The concept of the adept using paths generally considered evil for the attainment of enlightenment and the buddha-qualities is basic in Tantric doctrine and practice. Śākyamuni's revelation of the Sahā world as a jeweled buddha-field accords with Tantric method. That method starts from the premise of Buddhahood, in a sense, as the devotee cultivates his perception of himself as a Buddha, of all living beings as Buddhas and deities, of the world as a pure realm of Tathāgatas, of his own residence as a crystal sky-palace, and so forth.[18] Vimalakīrti's discussion of how a bodhisattva in inconceivable liberation can transfer Mount Sumeru, or an entire universe, into a mustard seed is reminiscent of the yogic practices for transmuting dimensions of time and space found in the *Guhyasamāja*.[19] The description of Vimalakīrti as versed in "esoteric practices";[20] the description of the "Family of the Tathāgatas";[21] Vimalakīrti's verse identifying wisdom as the mother and liberative technique as the father, exactly corresponding with the central Tantric symbolism of male and female as vajra and bell, and the like;[22] the yogic powers ascribed to the bodhisattva in inconceivable liberation, such as the ability to take fire in his stomach;[23] the mention of the appearance of many Tathāgatas—including Akṣobhya, Amitābha, Ratnavyūha, Sarvārthasiddha, and others—in the house of Vimalakīrti, teaching the esotericisms of the Tathāgatas (*tathāgata-guhyaka*);[24] and the culmination of the sūtra in the vision of the Buddha Akṣobhya:[25] All these lend the sūtra a certain aura of Tantra.[26] Whatever the "historical" relationship may be, it is safe to say that Vimalakīrti's method of the reconciliation of dichotomies, as based on the inconceivable liberation of the bodhisattva, forms a Tantra in its own right, that is, a rapid, effective method of simultaneously developing wisdom and great compassion to a high degree. Certainly, there is no doubt that the "Great Sorcerers" (*mahāsiddhas*) of later times would have felt at home in the house of Vimalakīrti.

The Miracles of Vimalakīrti

Vimalakīrti claims inclusion among the "Great Sorcerers" most of all, perhaps, for his generous use of miraculous feats in the course of teaching his fellow men and women. In view of the spirit of modern times, miracles merit some introduction in order to clear the air of prejudice so they may serve their proper function. Actually, modern scholars and the traditional scholars of Tibet, China, and Japan agree, albeit unwittingly, on a fundamental point: Modern scholars do not normally believe in "supernatural" miracles, but neither do they believe the events in the life of Vimalakīrti to be historical. They see the Scripture as a literary creation by an imaginative artist of the Mahāyāna tradition: an allegorical presentation of certain basic philosophical and religious teachings, set in the ancient and hallowed times of the Buddha Śākyamuni and using fictitious Tathāgatas and bodhisattvas to dramatize the doctrines. Traditional scholars do believe in the historicity of Vimalakīrti, the other bodhisattvas, and the Buddha in his Mahāyāna manifestations, as well as in the "science-fictional" world view of interrelated universes or buddha-fields. Nevertheless, because of their technical evaluation of the compassionate motives and miraculous powers of these Buddhas and bodhisattvas, they agree about the allegorical nature of the Scripture. That is, they believe Vimalakīrti to be an emanated incarnation (*nirmāṇakāya*) of the Buddha, a *living allegory*, and a vehicle of the highest teaching; they believe that everything he does and says is solely for the purpose of developing and liberating living beings. Therefore, there is general agreement on the point that the events in the Scripture are allegorical, and we shall leave aside the question of whether they are *living* or *literary* allegory.

This attitude should be maintained to reap the full benefit of the miracles portrayed in the Scripture. Modern and traditional scholars agree that the miracles are not simply displays of magical prowess, either clamoring for belief or challenging disbelief, but rather are intended to stretch the imagination, whether by Vimalakīrti himself, as an artist of life-forms, in their magical accomplishment or by the master literary artist in their creation; they are intended to shake the student's ingrained preconceptions of possibility and impossibility and make him receptive to the message of inconceivability. Certainly the Hwa Yen masters would agree, pointing out the cosmic vision in the jeweled parasol (p. 12), the thrones imported from the universe Merudhvaja (p. 51), the inexhaustible food (p. 81), the miniaturization and display of the universe Abhirati (p. 94), etc., as perfect illustrations of the principle of mutual nonobstruction of phenomena (shih shih wu ai; 事事無碍). Thus Vimalakīrti clearly demonstrates the effective complementarity of the supposed "positive approach" of the *Avataṁsaka* and the "negative approach" of the *Prajñāpāramita*, showing the ultimate miracle to be the utter equivalence of voidness and the dazzling relativity of interpenetrating universes.

As we hear Vimalakīrti's exhortation to strive for tolerance of inconceivability and the inconceivable liberation and as our rigid boundaries for exclusion of possibilities soften and give way before ever expanding frames of reference, our contemplation of the message of Vimalakīrti through opening our mental horizons on the ever widening scope of infinitude will enhance our enjoyment and appreciation of the beauty and splendor of the miraculous displays effected by the Buddha and by Vimalakīrti. Similarly, our imaginative visualization of the mental pictures created by the descriptions of the buddha-fields and by the distortions of dimensions, distances, times, and spaces will contribute to our sensitivity to the profound and subtle implications of Vimalakīrti's eloquent teaching, that we may be so fortunate to come to hear the great lion's roar of his profound silence.

I

Purification of the Buddha-Field[1]

Reverence to all Buddhas, Bodhisattvas, Āryaśrāvakas, and Pratyekabuddhas, in the past, the present, and the future.

Thus have I heard at one time. The Lord Buddha[2] was in residence in the garden of Āmrapālī, in the city of Vaiśālī,[3] attended by a great gathering. Of bhikṣus there were eight thousand, all saints.[4] They were free from impurities and afflictions, and all had attained self-mastery. Their minds were entirely liberated by perfect knowledge. They were calm and dignified, like royal elephants. They had accomplished their work, done what they had to do, cast off their burdens, attained their goals, and totally destroyed the bonds of existence. They all had attained the utmost perfection of every form of mind control.[5]

Of bodhisattvas there were thirty-two thousand, great spiritual heroes[6] who were universally acclaimed. They were dedicated through the penetrating activity of their great superknowledges[7] and were sustained by the grace[8] of the Buddha. Guardians of the city of Dharma, they upheld the true doctrine,[9] and their great teachings resounded like the lion's roar throughout the ten directions. Without having to be asked, they were the natural spiritual benefactors[10] of all living beings. They maintained unbroken the succession of the Three Jewels, conquering devils and foes and overwhelming all critics.

Their mindfulness, intelligence, realization, meditation, incantation,[11] and eloquence all were perfected. They were free of all obscurations and emotional involvements, living in liberation without impediment. They were totally dedicated through the transcendences of generosity, subdued, unwavering, and sincere morality, tolerance, effort, meditation, wisdom, skill in liberative technique, commitment, power, and gnosis.[12] They had attained the intuitive tolerance of the ultimate incomprehensibility of all things.[13] They turned the irreversible wheel of the Dharma.[14] They were stamped with the insignia of signlessness.

They were expert in knowing the spiritual faculties of all living beings. They were brave with the confidence that overawes all assemblies. They had gathered the great stores of merit and of wisdom,[15] and their bodies, beautiful without ornaments, were adorned with all the auspicious signs and marks.[16] They were exalted in fame and glory, like the lofty summit of Mount Sumeru. Their high resolve as hard as diamond, unbreakable in their faith in Buddha, Dharma and Sangha, they showered forth the rain of ambrosia that is released by the light rays of the jewel of the Dharma, which shines everywhere.

Their voices were perfect in diction and resonance, and versatile in speaking all languages. They had penetrated the profound principle of relativity[17] and had destroyed the persistence of the instinctual mental habits underlying all convictions concerning finitude and infinitude.[18] They spoke fearlessly, like lions, sounding the thunder of the magnificent teaching. Unequaled, they surpassed all measure. They were the best captains for the voyage of discovery of the treasures of the Dharma, the stores of merit and wisdom.

They were expert in the way of the Dharma, which is straight, peaceful, subtle, gentle, hard to see, and difficult to realize. They were endowed with the wisdom that is able to understand the thoughts of living beings, as well as their comings and goings. They had been consecrated with the anointment of the peerless gnosis of the Buddha. With their high resolve, they approached the ten powers, the four fearlessnesses, and the eighteen special qualities of the Buddha.[19]

They had crossed the terrifying abyss of the bad migrations,[20] and yet they assumed reincarnation voluntarily in all migrations for the sake of disciplining living beings. Great Kings of medicine, understanding all the sicknesses of passions, they could apply the medicine of the Dharma appropriately.

They were inexhaustible mines of limitless virtues, and they glorified innumerable buddha-fields with the splendor of these virtues. They conferred great benefit when seen, heard, or even approached. Were one to extol them for innumerable hundreds of thousands of myriads of aeons, one still could not exhaust their mighty flood of virtues.

These bodhisattvas were named: Samadarśana, Asamadarśana, Samādhivikurvitarāja, Dharmeśvara, Dharmaketu, Prabhāketu, Prabhāvyūha, Ratnavyūha, Mahāvyūha, Pratibhāṇakūṭa, Ratnakūṭa, Ratnapāṇi, Ratnamudrāhasta, Nityapralambahasta, Nityotkṣiptahasta, Nityatapta, Nityamuditendriya, Prāmodyarāja, Devarāja, Praṇidhānapraveśaprāpta, Prasiddhapratisaṃvitprāpta, Gaganagañja, Ratnolkāparigṛhīta, Ratnaśūra, Ratnapriya, Ratnaśrī, Indrajāla, Jālinīprabha, Nirālambanadhyāna, Prajñākūṭa, Ratnadatta, Mārapramardaka, Vidyuddeva, Vikurvaṇarāja, Kūṭanimittasamatikrānta, Siṃhanādanādin, Giryagrapramardirāja, Gandhahastin, Gandhakuñjaranāga, Nityodyukta, Anikṣiptadhura, Pramati, Sujāta, Padmaśrīgarbha, Padmavyūha, Avalokiteśvara, Mahāsthāmaprāpta, Brahmajāla, Ratnadaṇḍin, Mārakarmavijetā, Kṣetrasamalaṃkāra, Maṇiratnacchattra, Suvarnacūḍa, Maṇicūḍa, Maitreya, Mañjuśrīkumārabhūta, and so forth, with the remainder of the thirty-two thousand.[21]

There were also gathered there ten thousand Brahmās, at their head Brahmā Śikhin,[22] who had come from the Aśoka universe with its four sectors to see, venerate, and serve the Buddha and to hear the Dharma from his own mouth. There were twelve thousand Śakras[23] from various four-sector universes. And there were other powerful gods: Brahmās, Śakras, Lokapālas,[24] devas, nāgas, yakṣas, gandharvas, asuras, garuḍas, kiṃnaras, and mahoragas.[25] Finally, there was the fourfold community, consisting of bhikṣus, bhikṣuṇīs, laymen, and laywomen.[26]

The Lord Buddha, thus surrounded and venerated by these multitudes of many hundreds of thousands of living beings, sat upon a majestic lion-throne and began to teach the Dharma. Dominating all the multitudes, just as Sumeru, the king of mountains, looms high over the oceans, the Lord Buddha shone, radiated, and glittered as he sat upon his magnificent lion-throne.

Thereupon, the Licchavi bodhisattva Ratnākara,[27] with five hundred Licchavi youths, each holding a precious parasol made of seven different kinds of jewels,[28] came forth from the city of Vaiśālī and presented himself at the grove of Āmrapālī. Each approached the Buddha, bowed at his feet, circumambulated him clockwise seven times, laid down his precious parasol in offering, and withdrew to one side.

As soon as all these precious parasols had been laid down, suddenly, by the miraculous power of the Lord, they were transformed into a single precious canopy so great that it formed a covering for this entire billion-world galaxy.[29] The surface of the entire billion-world galaxy was reflected in the interior of the great precious canopy, where the total content of this galaxy could be seen: limitless mansions of suns, moons, and stellar bodies; the realms of the devas, nāgas, yakṣas, gandharvas, asuras, garuḍas, kiṃnaras, and mahoragas, as well as the realms of the four Mahārājas; the king of mountains, Mount Sumeru; Mount Hīmadri, Mount Mucilinda, Mount Mahāmucilinda, Mount Gandhamādana, Mount Ratnaparvata, Mount Kālaparvata, Mount Cakravāḍa, Mount Mahācakravaḍa;[30] all the great oceans, rivers, bays, torrents, streams, brooks, and springs; finally, all the villages, suburbs, cities, capitals, provinces, and wildernesses. All this could be clearly seen by everyone. And the voices of all the Buddhas of the ten directions could be heard proclaiming their teachings of the Dharma in all the worlds, the sounds reverberating in the space beneath the great precious canopy.

At this vision of the magnificent miracle effected by the supernatural power of the Lord Buddha, the entire host was ecstatic, enraptured, astonished, delighted, satisfied, and filled with awe and pleasure. They all bowed down to the Tathāgata, withdrew to one side with palms pressed together, and gazed upon him with fixed attention. The young Licchavi Ratnākara knelt with his right knee on the ground, raised his hands, palms pressed together in salute of the Buddha, and praised him with the following hymn:

Pure are your eyes, broad and beautiful,
  like the petals of a blue lotus.
Pure is your thought, having discovered
  the supreme transcendence of all trances.[31]
Immeasurable is the ocean of your virtues,
  the accumulation of your good deeds.
You affirm the path of peace.
  O Great Ascetic, obeisance to you!

Leader, bull of men,[32] we behold
  the revelation of your miracle.
The superb and radiant fields
  of the Sugatas appear before us,
And your extensive spiritual teachings,
  that lead to immortality[33]
Make themselves heard throughout
  the whole reach of space.

Dharma-King, you rule with the Dharma
  your supreme Dharma-kingdom,
And thereby bestow the treasures of the Dharma
  upon all living beings.
Expert in the deep analysis of things,
  you teach their ultimate meaning.[34]
Sovereign Lord of Dharma, obeisance to you!

All these things arise dependently, from causes,
Yet they are neither existent nor nonexistent.
Therein is neither ego, nor experiencer, nor doer,
Yet no action, good or evil, loses its effects.[35]
  Such is your teaching.

O Sākyamuni, conquering the powerful host of Māra,
You found peace, immortality, and the happiness of that
    supreme enlightenment,

Which is not realized by any among the heterodox,[36]
Though they arrest their feeling, thought, and mental processes.

O Wonderful King of Dharma,
You turned the wheel of Dharma before men and gods,
With its threefold revolution,
its manifold aspects,[37]
Its purity of nature,
and its extreme peace;
And thereby the Three Jewels were revealed.

Those who are well disciplined by your precious Dharma
Are free of vain imaginings and always deeply peaceful.
Supreme doctor, you put an end to birth, decay, sickness, and death.
Immeasurable ocean of virtue, obeisance to you!

Like Mount Sumeru, you are unmoved by honor or scorn.
You love moral beings and immoral beings equally.
Poised in equanimity, your mind is like the sky.
Who would not honor such a precious jewel of a being?[38]

Great Sage, in all these multitudes gathered here,
Who look upon your countenance with hearts sincere in faith,
Each being beholds the Victor, as if just before him.
This is a special quality of the Buddha.[39]

Although the Lord speaks with but one voice,
Those present perceive that same voice differently,
And each understands in his own language according to his own needs.
This is a special quality of the Buddha.[40]

From the Leader's act of speaking in a single voice,
Some merely develop an instinct for the teaching, some gain realization,
Some find pacification of all their doubts.
This is a special quality of the Buddha.

Obeisance to you who command the force of leadership
and the ten powers!
Obeisance to you who are dauntless, knowing no fear!
Obeisance to you, leader of all living beings,
Who fully manifests the special qualities!

Obeisance to you who have cut the bondage of all fetters!
Obeisance to you who, having gone beyond, stand on
firm ground!
Obeisance to you who save the suffering beings!
Obeisance to you who do not remain in the migrations!

You associate with living beings by frequenting their
migrations.
Yet your mind is liberated from all migrations.
Just as the lotus, born of mud, is not tainted thereby,
So the lotus of the Buddha preserves the realization of
voidness.

You nullify all signs in all things everywhere.
You are not subject to any wish for anything at all.[41]
The miraculous power of the Buddhas is inconceivable.
I bow to you, who stand nowhere, like infinite space.

Then, the young Licchavi Ratnākara, having celebrated the Buddha with these verses, further addressed him: "Lord, these five hundred young Licchavis are truly on their way to unexcelled, perfect enlightenment, and they have asked what is the bodhisattvas' purification of the buddha-field.[42] Please, Lord, explain to them the bodhisattvas' purification of the buddha-field!"

Upon this request, the Buddha gave his approval to the young Licchavi Ratnākara: "Good, good, young man! Your question to the Tathāgata about the purification of the buddha-field is indeed good. Therefore, young man, listen well and remember! I will explain to you the purification of the buddha-field of the bodhisattvas."

"Very good, Lord," replied Ratnākara and the five hundred young Licchavis, and they set themselves to listen.

The Buddha said, "Noble sons, a buddha-field of bodhisattvas is a field of living beings. Why so? A bodhisattva embraces a buddha-field to the same extent that he causes the development of living beings. He embraces a buddha-field to the same extent that living beings become disciplined. He embraces a buddha-field to the same extent that, through entrance into a buddha-field, living beings are introduced to the buddha-gnosis. He embraces a buddha-field to the same extent that, through entrance into that buddha-field, living beings increase their holy spiritual faculties.[43] Why so? Noble son, a buddha-field of bodhisattvas springs from the aims of living beings.

"For example, Ratnākara, should one wish to build in empty space, one might go ahead in spite of the fact that it is not possible to build or to adorn anything in empty space. In just the same way, should a bodhisattva, who knows full well that all things are like empty space, wish to build a buddha-field in order to develop living beings, he might go ahead, in spite of the fact that it is not possible to build or to adorn a buddha-field in empty space.[44]

"Yet, Ratnākara, a bodhisattva's buddha-field is a field of positive thought.[45] When he attains enlightenment, living beings free of hypocrisy and deceit will be born in his buddha-field.

"Noble son, a bodhisattva's buddha-field is a field of high resolve. When he attains enlightenment, living beings who have harvested the two stores and have planted the roots of virtue will be born in his buddha-field.

"A bodhisattva's buddha-field is a field of virtuous application. When he attains enlightenment, living beings who live by all virtuous principles will be born in his buddha-field.

"A bodhisattva's buddha-field is the magnificence of the conception of the spirit of enlightenment. When he attains enlightenment, living beings who are actually participating in the Mahāyāna will be born in his buddha-field.[46]

"A bodhisattva's buddha-field is a field of generosity. When he attains enlightenment, living beings who give away all their possessions will be born in his buddha-field.

"A bodhisattva's buddha-field is a field of morality. When he attains enlightenment, living beings who follow the path of the ten virtues with positive thoughts will be born in his buddha-field.

"A bodhisattva's buddha-field is a field of tolerance. When he attains enlightenment, living beings with the transcendences of tolerance, discipline, and the superior trance—hence beautiful with the thirty-two auspicious signs—will be born in his buddha-field.

"A bodhisattva's buddha-field is a field of effort. When he attains enlightenment, living beings who devote their efforts to virtue will be born in his buddha-field.

"A bodhisattva's buddha-field is a field of meditation. When he attains enlightenment, living beings who are evenly balanced through mindfulness and awareness will be born in his buddha-field.

"A bodhisattva's buddha-field is a field of wisdom. When he attains enlightenment, living beings who are destined for the ultimate[47] will be born in his buddha-field.

"A bodhisattva's buddha-field consists of the four immeasurables. When he attains enlightenment, living beings who live by love, compassion, joy, and impartiality will be born in his buddha-field.[48]

"A bodhisattva's buddha-field consists of the four means of unification. When he attains enlightenment, living beings who are held together by all the liberations will be born in his buddha-field.

"A bodhisattva's buddha-field is skill in liberative technique. When he attains enlightenment, living beings skilled in all liberative techniques and activities will be born in his buddha-field.

"A bodhisattva's buddha-field consists of the thirty-seven aids to enlightenment, living beings who devote their efforts to the four foci of mindfulness, the four right efforts, the four bases of magical power, the five spiritual faculties, the five strengths, the seven factors of enlightenment, and the eight branches of the holy path will be born in his buddha-field.

"A bodhisattva's buddha-field is his mind of total dedication. When he attains enlightenment, the ornaments of all virtues will appear in his buddha-field.

"A bodhisattva's buddha-field is the doctrine that eradicates the eight adversities. When he attains enlightenment, the three bad migrations will cease, and there will be no such thing as the eight adversities in his buddha-field.

"A bodhisattva's buddha-field consists of his personal observance of the basic precepts[49] and his restraint in blaming others for their transgressions. When he attains enlightenment, even the word 'crime' will never be mentioned in his buddha-field.

"A bodhisattva's buddha-field is the purity of the path of the ten virtues. When he attains enlightenment, living beings who are secure in long life, great in wealth, chaste in conduct, enhanced by true speech, soft-spoken, free of divisive intrigues and adroit in reconciling factions, enlightening in their conversations,[50] free of envy, free of malice, and endowed with perfect views will be born in his buddha-field.

"Thus, noble son, just as is the bodhisattva's production of the spirit of enlightenment, so is his positive thought. And just as is his positive thought, so is his virtuous application.

"His virtuous application is tantamount to his high resolve, his high resolve is tantamount to his determination, his determination is tantamount to his practice, his practice is tantamount to his total dedication, his total dedication is tantamount to his liberative technique, his liberative technique is tantamount to his development of living beings, and his development of living beings[51] is tantamount to the purity of his buddha-field.

"The purity of his buddha-field reflects the purity of living beings; the purity of the living beings reflects the purity of his gnosis; the purity of his gnosis reflects the purity of his doctrine; the purity of his doctrine reflects the purity of his transcendental practice;[52] and the purity of his transcendental practice reflects the purity of his own mind."

Thereupon, magically influenced by the Buddha, the venerable Śāriputra[53] had this thought: "If the buddha-field is pure only to the extent that the mind of the bodhisattva is pure, then, when Śākyamuni Buddha was engaged in the career of the bodhisattva, his mind must have been impure. Otherwise, how could this buddha-field appear to be so impure?"

The Buddha, knowing telepathically the thought of venerable Śāriputra, said to him, "What do you think, Śāriputra? Is it because the sun and moon are impure that those blind from birth do not see them?"

Śāriputra replied, "No, Lord. It is not so. The fault lies with those blind from birth, and not with the sun and moon."

The Buddha declared, "In the same way, Śāriputra, the fact that some living beings do not behold the splendid display of virtues of the buddha-field of the Tathāgata is due to their own ignorance. It is not the fault of the Tathāgata. Śāriputra, the buddha-field of the Tathāgata is pure, but you do not see it."

Then, the Brahmā Śikhin said to the venerable Śāriputra, "Reverend Śāriputra, do not say that the buddha-field of the Tathāgata is impure. Reverend Śāriputra, the buddha-field of the Tathāgata is pure. I see the splendid expanse of the buddha-field of the Lord Śākyamuni as equal to the splendor of, for example, the abodes of the highest deities."[54]

Then the venerable Śāriputra said to the Brahmā Śikhin, "As for me, O Brahmā, I see this great earth, with its highs and lows, its thorns, its precipices, its peaks, and its abysses, as if it were entirely filled with ordure."

Brahmā Śikhin replied, "The fact that you see such a buddha-field as this as if it were so impure, reverend Śāriputra, is a sure sign that there are highs and lows in your mind and that your positive thought in regard to the buddha-gnosis is not pure either. Reverend Śāriputra, those whose minds are impartial toward all living beings and whose positive thoughts toward the buddha-gnosis are pure see this buddha-field as perfectly pure."

Thereupon the Lord touched the ground of this billion-world-galactic universe with his big toe, and suddenly it was transformed into a huge mass of precious jewels, a magnificent array of many hundreds of thousands of clusters of precious gems, until it resembled the universe of the Tathāgata Ratnavyūha, called

Anantaguṇaratnavyūha.[55] Everyone in the entire assembly was filled with wonder, each perceiving himself seated on a throne of jeweled lotuses.

Then, the Buddha said to the venerable Śāriputra, "Śāriputra, do you see this splendor of the virtues of the buddha-field?"

Śāriputra replied, "I see it, Lord! Here before me is a display of splendor such as I never before heard of or beheld!"

The Buddha said, "Śāriputra, this buddha-field is always thus pure, but the Tathāgata makes it appear to be spoiled by many faults, in order to bring about the maturity of inferior living beings. For example, Śāriputra, the gods of the Trayastriṃśa heaven[56] all take their food from a single precious vessel, yet the nectar which nourishes each one differs according to the differences of the merits each has accumulated. Just so, Śāriputra, living beings born in the same buddha-field see the splendor of the virtues of the buddha-fields of the Buddhas according to their own degrees of purity."

When this splendor of the beauty of the virtues of the buddha-field shone forth, eighty-four thousand beings conceived the spirit of unexcelled perfect enlightenment, and the five hundred Licchavi youths who had accompanied the young Licchavi Ratnākara all attained the conformative tolerance of ultimate birthlessness.[57]

Then, the Lord withdrew his miraculous power and at once the buddha-field was restored to its usual appearance. Then, both men and gods who subscribed to the disciple-vehicle[58] thought, "Alas! All constructed things are impermanent."

Thereby, thirty-two thousand living beings purified their immaculate, undistorted Dharma-eye[59] in regard to all things. The eight thousand bhikṣus were liberated from their mental defilements, attaining the state of nongrasping. And the eighty-four thousand living beings who were devoted to the grandeur of the buddha-field, having understood that all things are by nature but magical creations, all conceived in their own minds the spirit of unexcelled, totally perfect enlightenment.[60]

2

Inconceivable Skill in Liberative Technique

At that time, there lived in the great city of Vaiśālī a certain Licchavi, Vimalakīrti by name. Having served the ancient Buddhas, he had generated the roots of virtue by honoring them and making offerings to them. He had attained tolerance as well as eloquence. He played with the great superknowledges. He had attained the power of incantations and the fearlessnesses.[1] He had conquered all demons and opponents. He had penetrated the profound way of the Dharma. He was liberated through the transcendence of wisdom. Having integrated his realization with skill in liberative technique, he was expert in knowing the thoughts and actions of living beings. Knowing the strength or weakness of their faculties, and being gifted with unrivaled eloquence, he taught the Dharma appropriately to each. Having applied himself energetically to the Mahāyāna, he understood it and accomplished his tasks with great finesse. He lived with the deportment of a Buddha, and his superior intelligence was as wide as an ocean. He was praised, honored, and commended by all the Buddhas and was respected by Indra, Brahmā, and all the Lokapālas. In order to develop living beings with his skill in liberative technique, he lived in the great city of Vaiśālī.

His wealth was inexhaustible for the purpose of sustaining the poor and the helpless. He observed a pure morality in order to protect the immoral. He maintained tolerance and self-control in order to reconcile beings who were angry, cruel, violent, and brutal. He blazed with energy in order to inspire people who were lazy. He maintained concentration, mindfulness, and meditation in order to sustain the mentally troubled. He attained decisive wisdom in order to sustain the foolish.[2]

He wore the white clothes of the layman, yet lived impeccably like a religious devotee. He lived at home, but remained aloof from the realm of desire, the realm of pure matter, and the immaterial realm.[3] He had a son, a wife, and female attendants,[4] yet always maintained continence. He appeared to be surrounded by servants, yet lived in solitude. He appeared to be adorned with ornaments, yet always was endowed with the auspicious signs and marks. He seemed to eat and drink, yet always took nourishment from the taste of meditation. He made his appearance at the fields of sports and in the casinos, but his aim was always to mature those people who were attached to games and gambling. He visited the fashionable heterodox teachers, yet always kept unswerving loyalty to the Buddha. He understood the mundane and transcendental sciences and esoteric practices,[5] yet always took pleasure in the delights of the Dharma. He mixed in all crowds, yet was respected as foremost of all.[6]

In order to be in harmony with people, he associated with elders, with those of middle age, and with the young, yet always spoke in harmony with the Dharma.[7] He engaged in all sorts of businesses, yet had no interest in profit or possessions. To train living beings, he would appear at crossroads and on street corners, and to protect them he participated in government. To turn people away from the Hinayāna and to engage them in the Mahāyāna, he appeared among listeners and teachers of the Dharma. To develop children, he visited all the schools. To demonstrate the evils of desire, he even entered the brothels. To establish drunkards in correct mindfulness, he entered all the cabarets.

He was honored as the businessman among businessmen because he demonstrated the priority of the Dharma. He was honored as the landlord among landlords because he renounced the aggressiveness of ownership. He was honored as the warrior among warriors because he cultivated endurance, determination, and fortitude. He was honored as the aristocrat among aristocrats because he suppressed pride, vanity, and arrogance. He was honored as the official among officials because he regulated the functions of government according to the Dharma. He was honored as the prince of princes because he reversed their attachment to royal pleasures and sovereign power.[8] He was honored as a eunuch in the royal harem because he taught the young ladies according to the Dharma.

He was compatible with ordinary people because he appreciated the excellence of ordinary merits. He was honored as the Indra among Indras because he showed them the temporality[8a] of their lordship. He was honored as the Brahmā among Brahmās because he showed them the special excellence of gnosis. He was honored as the Lokapāla among Lokapālas because he fostered the development of all living beings.

Thus lived the Licchavi Vimalakīrti in the great city of Vaiśālī, endowed with an infinite knowledge of skill in liberative techniques.

At that time, out of this very skill in liberative technique, Vimalakīrti manifested himself as if sick. To inquire after his health, the king, the officials, the lords, the youths, the aristocrats, the householders, the businessmen, the townfolk, the countryfolk, and thousands of other living beings came forth from the great city of Vaiśālī and called on the invalid. When they arived, Vimalakīrti taught them the Dharma, beginning his discourse from the actuality of the four main elements:

"Friends, this body is so impermanent, fragile, unworthy of confidence, and feeble. It is so insubstantial, perishable, short-lived, painful, filled with diseases, and subject to changes. Thus, my friends, as this body is only a vessel of many sicknesses, wise men do not rely on it. This body is like a ball of foam, unable to bear any pressure. It is like a water bubble, not remaining very long. It is like a mirage, born from the appetites of the passions. It is like the trunk of the plantain tree, having no core. Alas! This body is like a machine, a nexus of bones and tendons. It is like a magical illusion, consisting of falsifications.[9] It is like a dream, being an unreal vision. It is like a reflection, being the image of former actions. It is like an echo, being dependent on conditioning. It is like a cloud, being characterized by turbulence and dissolution. It is like a flash of lightning, being unstable, and decaying every moment. The body is ownerless, being the product of a variety of conditions.

"This body is inert, like the earth; selfless, like water; lifeless, like fire; impersonal, like the wind; and nonsubstantial, like space. This body is unreal, being a collocation of the four main elements. It is void, not existing as self or as self-possessed. It is inanimate, being like grass, trees, walls, clods of earth, and hallucinations. It is insensate, being driven like a windmill. It is filthy, being an agglomeration of pus and excrement. It is false, being fated to be broken and destroyed, in spite of being anointed and massaged. It is afflicted by the four hundred and four diseases.[10] It is like an ancient well, constantly overwhelmed by old age. Its duration is never certain—certain only is its end in death. This body is a combination of aggregates, elements, and sense-media,[11] which are comparable to murderers, poisonous snakes, and an empty town, respectively. Therefore, you should be revulsed by such a body. You should despair of it and should arouse your admiration for the body of the Tathāgata.

"Friends, the body of a Tathāgata is the body of Dharma,[12] born of gnosis. The body of a Tathāgata is born of the stores of merit and wisdom.[13] It is born of morality, of meditation, of wisdom, of the liberations, and of the knowledge and vision of liberation.[14] It is born of love, compassion, joy, and impartiality. It is born of charity, discipline, and self-control. It is born of the path of ten virtues. It is born of patience and gentleness. It is born of the roots of virtue planted by solid efforts. It is born of the concentrations, the liberations, the meditations, and the absorptions. It is born of learning, wisdom, and liberative technique. It is born of the thirty-seven aids to enlightenment. It is born of mental quiescence and transcendental analysis.[15] It is born of the ten powers, the four fearlessnesses, and the eighteen special qualities. It is born of all the transcendences. It is born from sciences and superknowledges. It is born of the abandonment of all evil qualities, and of the collection of all good qualities. It is born of truth. It is born of reality. It is born of conscious awareness.[16]

"Friends, the body of a Tathāgata is born of innumerable good works. Toward such a body you should turn your aspirations, and, in order to eliminate the sicknesses of the passions of all living beings, you should conceive the spirit of unexcelled, perfect enlightenment."

While the Licchavi Vimalakīrti thus taught the Dharma to those who had come to inquire about his sickness, many hundreds of thousands of living beings conceived the spirit of unexcelled, perfect enlightenment.

3

The Disciples' Reluctance to Visit Vimalakīrti[1]

Then, the Licchavi Vimalakīrti thought to himself, "I am sick, lying on my bed in pain, yet the Tathāgata, the saint, the perfectly accomplished Buddha, does not consider me or take pity upon me, and sends no one to inquire after my illness."

The Lord knew this thought in the mind of Vimalakīrti and said to the venerable Śāriputra, "Śāriputra, go to inquire after the illness of the Licchavi Vimalakīrti."

Thus having been addressed, the venerable Śāriputra answered the Buddha, "Lord, I am indeed reluctant[2] to go to ask the Licchavi Vimalakīrti about his illness. Why? I remember one day, when I was sitting at the foot of a tree in the forest, absorbed in contemplation, the Licchavi Vimalakīrti came to the foot of that tree and said to me, 'Reverend Śāriputra, this is not the way to absorb yourself in contemplation. You should absorb yourself in contemplation so that neither body nor mind appear anywhere in the triple world.[3] You should absorb yourself in contemplation in such a way that you can manifest all ordinary behavior without forsaking cessation.[4] You should absorb yourself in contemplation in such a way that you can manifest the nature of an ordinary person without abandoning your cultivated spiritual nature. You should absorb yourself in contemplation so that the mind neither settles within nor moves without toward external forms. You should absorb yourself in contemplation in such a way that the thirty-seven aids to enlightenment are manifest without deviation toward any convictions. You should absorb yourself in contemplation in such a way that you are released in liberation without abandoning the passions that are the province of the world.[5]

"'Reverend Śāriputra, those who absorb themselves in contemplation in such a way are declared by the Lord to be truly absorbed in contemplation.'

"Lord, when I heard this teaching, I was unable to reply and remained silent.

Therefore, I am reluctant to go to ask that good man about his sickness."

Then, the Buddha said to the venerable Mahāmaudgalyāyana, "Maudgalyāyana, go to the Licchavi Vimalakīrti to inquire about his illness."[6]

Maudgalyāyana replied, "Lord, I am indeed reluctant to go to the Licchavi Vimalakīrti to inquire about his illness. Why? I remember one day when I was teaching the Dharma to the householders in a square in the great city of Vaiśālī, and the Licchavi Vimalakīrti came along and said to me, 'Reverend Maudgalyāyana, that is not the way to teach the Dharma to the householders in their white clothes. The Dharma must be taught according to reality.

"'Reverend Maudgalyāyana, the Dharma is without living beings, because it is free of the dust of living beings. It is selfless, because it is free of the dust of desire. It is lifeless, because it is free of birth and death. It is without personalities, because it dispenses with past origins and future destinies.

"'The Dharma is peace and pacification, because it is free from desire. It does not become an object, because it is free of words and letters; it is inexpressible, and it transcends all movement of mind.[7]

"'The Dharma is omnipresent, because it is like infinite space. It is without color, mark, or shape, because it is free of all process. It is without the concept of "mine," because it is free of the habitual notion of possession. It is without ideation, because it is free of mind, thought, or consciousness. It is incomparable, because it has no antithesis. It is without presumption of conditionality, because it does not conform to causes.

"'It permeates evenly all things, because all are included in the ultimate realm.[8] It conforms to reality by means of the process of nonconformity. It abides at the reality-limit,[9] for it is utterly without fluctuation. It is immovable, because it is independent of the six objects of sense. It is without coming and going, for it never stands still. It is comprised by voidness, is remarkable through signlessness, and is free of presumption and repudiation, because of wishlessness. It is without establishment and rejection, without birth or destruction. It is without any fundamental consciousness, transcending the range of eye, ear, nose, tongue, body, and thought. It is without highness and lowness. It abides without movement or activity.[10]

"'Reverend Mahāmaudgalyāyana, how could there be a teaching in regard to such a Dharma? Reverend Mahāmaudgalyāyana, even the expression "to teach the Dharma" is presumptuous, and those who listen to it listen to presumption. Reverend Maudgalyāyana, where there are no presumptuous words, there is no teacher of the Dharma, no one to listen, and no one to understand. It is as if an illusory person were to teach the Dharma to illusory people.

"'Therefore, you should teach the Dharma by keeping your mind on this.

You should be adept in regard to the spiritual faculties of living beings. By means of the correct vision of the wisdom-eye, manifesting the great compassion, acknowledging the benevolent activity of the Buddha, purifying your intentions, understanding the definitive expressions[11] of the Dharma, you should teach the Dharma in order that the continuity of the Three Jewels may never be interrupted.'

"Lord, when Vimalakīrti had discoursed thus, eight hundred householders in the crowd conceived the spirit of unexcelled, perfect enlightenment, and I myself was speechless. Therefore, Lord, I am indeed reluctant to go to this good man to inquire about his illness."

Then, the Buddha said to the venerable Mahākāśyapa,[12] "Mahākāśyapa, you go to the Licchavi Vimalakīrti to inquire about his illness."

"Lord, I am indeed reluctant to go to the Licchavi Vimalakīrti to inquire about his illness. Why? I remember one day, when I was in the street of the poor begging for my food, the Licchavi Vimalakīrti came along and said to me, 'Reverend Mahākāśyapa, to avoid the houses of the wealthy, and to favor the houses of the poor—this is partiality in benevolence.[13] Reverend Mahākāśyapa, you should dwell on the fact of the equality of things, and you should seek alms with consideration for all living beings at all times. You should beg your food in awareness of the ultimate nonexistence of food. You should seek alms for the sake of eliminating the materialism[14] of others. When you enter a town, you should keep in mind its actual voidness, yet you should proceed through it in order to develop men and women. You should enter homes as if entering the family of the Buddha.[15] You should accept alms by not taking anything. You should see form like a man blind from birth, hear sounds as if they were echoes, smell scents as if they were winds, experience tastes without any discrimination, touch tangibles in awareness of the ultimate lack of contact in gnosis, and know things with the consciousness of an illusory creature. That which is without intrinsic substance and without imparted substance does not burn. And what does not burn will not be extinguished.[16]

"'Elder Mahākāśyapa, if, equipoised in the eight liberations without transcending the eight perversions,[17] you can enter the equanimity of reality by means of the equanimity of perversion, and if you can make a gift to all living beings and an offering to all the saints and Buddhas out of even a single measure of alms, then you yourself may eat. Thus, when you eat, after offering, you should be neither affected by passions nor free of passions, neither involved in concentration nor free from concentration, neither living in the world nor abiding in liberation. Furthermore, those who give such alms, reverend, have neither great merit nor small merit, neither gain nor loss. They should follow the way of the Buddhas, not the way of the disciples. Only in this way, Elder Mahākāśyapa, is the practice of eating by alms meaningful.'

"Lord, when I heard this teaching, I was astonished and thought: 'Reverence to all bodhisattvas! If a lay bodhisattva may be endowed with such eloquence, who is there who would not conceive the spirit of unexcelled, perfect enlightenment?' From that time forth, I no longer recommend the vehicles of the disciples and of the solitary sages but recommend the Mahāyāna. And thus, Lord, I am reluctant to go to this good man to inquire about his illness."

Then, the Buddha said to the venerable Subhūti,[18] "Subhūti, go to the Licchavi Vimalakīrti to inquire about his illness."

Subhūti replied, "Lord, I am indeed reluctant to go to this good man to inquire about his illness. Why? My Lord, I remember one day, when I went to beg my food at the house of the Licchavi Vimalakīrti in the great city of Vaiśālī, he took my bowl and filled it with some excellent food and said to me, 'Reverend Subhūti, take this food if you understand the equality of all things, by means of the equality of material objects, and if you understand the equality of all the attributes of the Buddha, by means of the equality of all things. Take this food if, without abandoning desire, hatred, and folly, you can avoid association with them; if you can follow the path of the single way without ever disturbing the egoistic views;[19] if you can produce the knowledges and liberations without conquering ignorance and the craving for existence; if, by the equality of the five deadly sins,[20] you reach the equality of liberation; if you are neither liberated nor bound; if you do not see the Four Holy Truths,[21] yet are not the one who "has not seen the truth"; if you have not attained any fruit, yet are not the one who "has not attained";[22] if you are an ordinary person, yet have not the qualities of an ordinary person; if you are not holy, yet are not unholy; if you are responsible for all things, yet are free of any notion concerning anything.

"'Take this food, reverend Subhūti, if, without seeing the Buddha, hearing the Dharma, or serving the Saṅgha, you undertake the religious life under the six heterodox masters; namely, Purāṇa Kāśyapa, Māskārin Gośāliputra, Saṃjāyin Vairaṭiputra, Kakuda Kātyāyana, Ajita Keśakambala, and Nirgrantha Jñātiputra,[23] and follow the ways they prescribe.

"'Take this food, reverend Subhūti, if, entertaining all false views, you find neither extremes nor middle; if, bound up in the eight adversities, you do not obtain favorable conditions; if, assimilating the passions, you do not attain purification; if the dispassion[24] of all living beings is your dispassion, reverend; if those who make offerings to you are not thereby purified;[25] if those who offer you food, reverend, still fall into the three bad migrations; if you associate with all Māras; if you entertain all passions; if the nature of passions is the nature of a reverend; if you have hostile feelings toward all living beings; if you despise all the Buddhas; if you criticize all the teachings of the Buddha; if you do not rely on the Saṅgha; and finally, if you never enter ultimate liberation.'

"Lord, when I heard these words of the Licchavi Vimalakīrti, I wondered what I should say and what I should do, but I was totally in the dark. Leaving the bowl, I was about to leave the house when the Licchavi Vimalakīrti said to me, 'Reverend Subhūti, do not fear these words, and pick up your bowl. What do you think, reverend Subhūti? If it were an incarnation[26] created by the Tathāgata who spoke thus to you, would you be afraid?'

"I answered, 'No indeed, noble sir!' He then said, 'Reverend Subhūti, the nature of all things is like illusion, like a magical incarnation. So you should not fear them. Why? All words also have that nature, and thus the wise are not attached to words, nor do they fear them. Why? All language does not ultimately exist, except as liberation. The nature of all things is liberation.'[27]

"When Vimalakīrti had discoursed in this way, two hundred gods obtained the pure doctrinal vision in regard to all things, without obscurity or defilement, and five hundred gods obtained the conformative tolerance. As for me, I was speechless and unable to respond to him. Therefore, Lord, I am reluctant to go to this good man to inquire about his illness."

Then, the Buddha said to the venerable Pūrṇamaitrāyaṇīputra,[28] "Pūrṇa, go to the Licchavi Vimalakīrti to inquire about his illness."

Pūrṇa replied, "Lord, I am indeed reluctant to go to this good man to inquire about his illness. Why? Lord, I remember one day, when I was teaching the Dharma to some young monks in the great forest, the Licchavi Vimalakīrti came there and said to me, 'Reverend Pūrṇa, first concentrate yourself, regard the minds of these young bhikṣus, and then teach them the Dharma! Do not put rotten food into a jeweled bowl! First understand the inclinations of these monks, and do not confuse priceless sapphires with glass beads!

"'Reverend Pūrṇa, without examining the spiritual faculties of living beings, do not presume upon the one-sidedness of their faculties; do not wound those who are without wounds; do not impose a narrow path upon those who aspire to a great path; do not try to pour the great ocean into the hoof-print of an ox; do not try to put Mount Sumeru into a grain of mustard; do not confuse the brilliance of the sun with the light of a glowworm; and do not expose those who admire the roar of a lion to the howl of a jackal!

"'Reverend Pūrṇa, all these monks were formerly engaged in the Mahāyāna but have forgotten the spirit of enlightenment. So do not instruct them in the disciple-vehicle. The disciple-vehicle is not ultimately valid, and you disciples are like men blind from birth, in regard to recognition of the degrees of the spiritual faculties of living beings.'

"At that moment, the Licchavi Vimalakīrti entered into such a concentration that those monks were caused to remember their various former existences, in which they had produced the roots of virtue by serving five hundred Buddhas for the sake of perfect enlightenment. As soon as their own spirits of enlightenment had become clear to them, they bowed at the feet of that good man and pressed their palms together in reverence. He taught them the Dharma, and they all attained the stage of irreversibility[29] from the spirit of unexcelled, perfect enlightenment. It occurred to me then, 'The disciples, who do not know the thoughts or the inclinations of others, are not able to teach the Dharma to anyone. Why? These disciples are not expert in discerning the superiority and inferiority of the spiritual faculties of living beings, and they are not always in a state of concentration like the Tathāgata, the Saint, the perfectly accomplished Buddha.'

"Therefore, Lord, I am reluctant to go to that good man to inquire about his health."

The Buddha then said to the venerable Mahākātyāyana,[30] "Kātyāyana, go to the Licchavi Vimalakīrti to inquire about his illness."

Kātyāyana replied, "Lord, I am indeed reluctant to go to that good man to inquire about his illness. Why? Lord, I remember one day when, after the Lord had given some brief instruction to the monks, I was defining the expressions of that discourse by teaching the meaning of impermanence, suffering, selflessness, and peace;[31] the Licchavi Vimalakīrti came there and said to me, 'Reverend Mahākātyāyana, do not teach an ultimate reality endowed with activity, production, and destruction! Reverend Mahākātyāyana, nothing was ever destroyed, is destroyed, or will ever be destroyed. Such is the meaning of "impermanence." The meaning of the realization of birthlessness, through the realization of the voidness of the five aggregates, is the meaning of "suffering."[32] The fact of the nonduality of self and selflessness is the meaning of "selflessness." That which has no intrinsic substance and no other sort of substance does not burn, and what does not burn is not extinguished;[33] such lack of extinction is the meaning of "peace."'

"When he had discoursed thus, the minds of the monks were liberated from their defilements and entered a state of nongrasping. Therefore, Lord, I am reluctant to go to that good man to inquire about his illness."

The Buddha then said to the venerable Aniruddha,[34] "Aniruddha, go to the Licchavi Vimalakīrti to inquire about his illness."

"My Lord, I am indeed reluctant to go to that good man to inquire about his illness. Why? I remember, Lord, one day when I was taking a walk, the great Brahmā named Śubhavyūha and the ten thousand other Brahmās who accompanied him illuminated the place with their radiance and, having bowed their heads at my feet, withdrew to one side and asked me, 'Reverend Aniruddha, you have been proclaimed by the Buddha to be the foremost among those who possess the divine eye.[35] To what distance does the divine vision of the venerable Aniruddha extend?' I answered, 'Friends, I see the entire billion-world-galactic universe of the Lord Śākyamuni just as plainly as a man of ordinary vision sees a myrobalan nut on the palm of his hand.' When I had said these words, the Licchavi Vimalakīrti came there and, having bowed his head at my feet, said to me, 'Reverend Aniruddha, is your divine eye compounded in nature? Or is it uncompounded in nature? If it is compounded in nature, it is the same as the superknowledges[36] of the heterodox. If it is uncompounded in nature, then it is not constructed and, as such, is incapable of seeing.[37] Then, how do you see, O elder?'

"At these words, I became speechless, and Brahmā also was amazed to hear this teaching from that good man. Having bowed to him, he said, 'Who then, in the world, possesses the divine eye?'

"Vimalakīrti answered, 'In the world, it is the Buddhas who have the divine eye. They see all the buddha-fields without even leaving their state of concentration and without being affected by duality.'

"Having heard these words, the ten thousand Brahmās were inspired with high resolve and conceived the spirit of unexcelled, perfect enlightenment. Having paid homage and respect both to me and to that good man, they disappeared. As for me, I remained speechless, and therefore I am reluctant to go to that good man to inquire about his illness."

The Buddha then said to the venerable Upāli,[38] "Upāli, go to the Licchavi Vimalakīrti to inquire about his illness."

Upāli replied, "Lord, I am indeed reluctant to go to that good man to inquire about his illness. Why? Lord, I remember that one day there were two monks who had committed some infraction and were too ashamed to appear before the Lord, so they came to me and said, 'Reverend Upāli, we have both committed an infraction but are too ashamed to appear before the Buddha. Venerable Upāli, kindly remove our anxieties by absolving us of these infractions.'[39]

"Lord, while I was giving those two monks some religious discourse, the Licchavi Vimalakīrti came there and said to me, 'Reverend Upāli, do not aggravate further the sins of these two monks. Without perplexing them, relieve their remorse. Reverend Upāli, sin is not to be apprehended within, or without, or between the two. Why? The Buddha has said, "Living beings are afflicted by the passions of thought, and they are purified by the purification of thought."

"'Reverend Upāli, the mind is neither within nor without, nor is it to be apprehended between the two. Sin is just the same as the mind, and all things are just the same as sin. They do not escape this same reality.

"'Reverend Upāli, this nature of the mind, by virtue of which your mind, reverend, is liberated—does it ever become afflicted?'[40]

"'Never,' I replied.

"'Reverend Upāli, the minds of all living beings have that very nature. Reverend Upāli, passions consist of conceptualizations. The ultimate non-existence of these conceptualizations and imaginary fabrications—that is the purity that is the intrinsic nature of the mind.[41] Misapprehensions are passions. The ultimate absence of misapprehensions is the intrinsic nature of the mind. The presumption of self is passion. The absence of self is the intrinsic nature of the mind. Reverend Upāli, all things are without production, destruction, and duration, like magical illusions, clouds, and lightning; all things are evanescent, not remaining even for an instant; all things are like dreams, hallucinations, and unreal visions; all things are like the reflection of the moon in water and like a mirror-image; they are born of mental construction. Those who know this are called the true upholders of the discipline,[42] and those disciplined in that way are indeed well disciplined.'"

"Then the two monks said, 'This householder is extremely well endowed with wisdom. The reverend Upāli, who was proclaimed by the Lord as the foremost of the upholders of the discipline, is not his equal.'

"I then said to the two monks, 'Do not entertain the notion that he is a mere householder! Why? With the exception of the Tathāgata himself, there is no disciple or bodhisattva capable of competing with his eloquence or rivaling the brilliance of his wisdom.'

"Thereupon, the two monks, delivered from their anxieties and inspired with a high resolve, conceived the spirit of unexcelled, perfect enlightenment. Bowing down to that good man, they made the wish: 'May all living beings attain eloquence such as this!' Therefore, I am reluctant to go to that good man to inquire about his illness."

The Buddha then said to the venerable Rāhula,[43] "Rāhula, go to the Licchavi Vimalakīrti to inquire about his illness."

Rāhula replied, "Lord, I am indeed reluctant to go to that good man to inquire about his illness. Why? Lord, I remember that one day many young Licchavi gentlemen came to the place where I was and said to me, 'Reverend Rāhula, you are the son of the Lord, and, having renounced a kingdom of a universal monarch, you have left the world. What are the virtues and benefits you saw in leaving the world?'

"As I was teaching them properly the benefits and virtues of renouncing the world, the Licchavi Vimalakīrti came there and, having greeted me, said, 'Reverend Rāhula, you should not teach the benefits and virtues of renunciation in the way that you do. Why? Renunciation is itself the very absence of virtues and benefits. Reverend Rāhula, one may speak of benefits and virtues in regard to compounded things, but renunciation is uncompounded, and there can be no question of benefits and virtues in regard to the uncompounded. Reverend Rāhula, renunciation is not material but is free of matter. It is free of the extreme views of beginning and end.[44] It is the path of liberation. It is praised by the wise, embraced by the saints, and causes the defeat of all Māras. It liberates from the five states of existence, purifies the five eyes, cultivates the five powers, and supports the five spiritual faculties. Renunciation is totally harmless to others and is not adulterated with evil things. It disciplines the heterodox, transcending all denominations. It is the bridge over the swamp of desire, without grasping, and free of the habits of "I" and "mine." It is without attachment and without disturbance, eliminating all commotion. It disciplines one's own mind and protects the minds of others. It favors mental quiescence and stimulates transcendental analysis. It is irreproachable in all respects and so is called renunciation. Those who leave the mundane in this way are called "truly renunciant." Young men, renounce the world in the light of this clear teaching! The appearance of the Buddha is extremely rare. Human life endowed with leisure and opportunity is very hard to obtain. To be a human being is very precious.'[45]

"The young men complained: 'But, householder, we have heard the Tathāgata declare that one should not renounce the world without the permission of one's parents.'

"Vimalakīrti answered: 'Young men, you should cultivate yourselves intensively to conceive the spirit of unexcelled, perfect enlightenment. That in itself will be your renunciation and high ordination!'[46]

"Thereupon, thirty-two[47] of the Licchavi youths conceived the spirit of unexcelled, perfect enlightenment. Therefore, Lord, I am reluctant to go to that good man to inquire about his illness."

The Buddha then said to the venerable Ānanda,[48] "Ānanda, go to the Licchavi Vimalakīrti to inquire about his illness."

Ānanda replied, "Lord, I am indeed reluctant to go to that good man to inquire about his illness. Why? Lord, I remember one day when the body of the Lord manifested some indisposition and he required some milk; I took the bowl and went to the door of the mansion of a great Brahman family.[49] The Licchavi Vimalakīrti came there, and, having saluted me, said, 'Reverend Ānanda, what are you doing on the threshold of this house with your bowl in your hand so early in the morning?'

"I replied: 'The body of the Lord manifests some indisposition, and he needs some milk. Therefore, I have come to fetch some.'

"Vimalakīrti then said to me, 'Reverend Ānanda, do not say such a thing! Reverend Ānanda, the body of the Tathāgata is tough as a diamond, having eliminated all the instinctual traces of evil and being endowed with all goodness. How could disease or discomfort affect such a body?

"'Reverend Ānanda, go in silence, and do not belittle the Lord. Do not say such things to others. It would not be good for the powerful gods or for the bodhisattvas coming from the various buddha-fields to hear such words.

"'Reverend Ānanda, a universal monarch, who is endowed only with a small root of virtue, is free of diseases. How then could the Lord, who has an infinite root of virtue, have any disease? It is impossible.

"'Reverend Ānanda, do not bring shame upon us, but go in silence, lest the heterodox sectarians[50] should hear your words. They would say, "For shame! The teacher of these people cannot even cure his own sicknesses. How then can he cure the sicknesses of others?" Reverend Ānanda, go then discreetly so that no one observes you.

"'Reverend Ānanda, the Tathāgatas have the body of the Dharma—not a body that is sustained by material food. The Tathāgatas have a transcendental body that has transcended all mundane qualities. There is no injury to the body of a Tathāgata, as it is rid of all defilements. The body of a Tathāgata is uncompounded and free of all formative activity. Reverend Ānanda, to believe there can be illness in such a body is irrational and unseemly!'

"When I had heard these words, I wondered if I had previously misheard and misunderstood the Buddha, and I was very much ashamed. Then I heard a voice from the sky: 'Ānanda! The householder speaks to you truly. Nevertheless, since the Buddha has appeared during the time of the five corruptions, he disciplines living beings by acting lowly and humble. Therefore, Ānanda, do not be ashamed, and go and get the milk!'[51]

"Lord, such was my conversation[52] with the Licchavi Vimalakīrti, and therefore I am reluctant to go to that good man to inquire about his illness."

In the same way, the rest of the five hundred disciples were reluctant to go to the Licchavi Vimalakīrti, and each told the Buddha his own adventure, recounting all his conversations with the Licchavi Vimalakīrti.

4

The Reluctance of the Bodhisattvas

Then, the Buddha said to the bodhisattva Maitreya,[1] "Maitreya, go to the Licchavi Vimalakīrti to inquire about his illness."

Maitreya replied, "Lord, I am indeed reluctant to go to that good man to inquire about his illness. Why? Lord, I remember that one day I was engaged in a conversation with the gods of the Tuṣita heaven,[2] the god Saṃtuṣita and his retinue, about the stage of nonregression of the great bodhisattvas. At that time, the Licchavi Vimalakīrti came there and addressed me as follows:

"'Maitreya, the Buddha has prophesied that only one more birth stands between you and unexcelled, perfect enlightenment. What kind of birth does this prophecy concern, Maitreya? Is it past? Is it future? Or is it present? If it is a past birth, it is already finished. If it is a future birth, it will never arrive. If it is a present birth, it does not abide. For the Buddha has declared, "Bhikṣus, in a single moment, you are born, you age, you die, you transmigrate, and you are reborn."

"'Then might the prophecy concern birthlessness? But birthlessness applies to the stage of destiny for the ultimate,[3] in which there is neither prophecy nor attainment of perfect enlightenment.

"'Therefore, Maitreya, is your reality from birth? Or is it from cessation? Your reality as prophesied is not born and does not cease, nor will it be born nor will it cease.[4] Furthermore, your reality is just the same as the reality of all living beings, the reality of all things, and the reality of all the holy ones. If your enlightenment can be prophesied in such a way, so can that of all living beings. Why? Because reality does not consist of duality or of diversity. Maitreya, whenever you attain Buddhahood, which is the perfection of enlightenment, at the same time all living beings will also attain Buddhahood. Why? Enlightenment consists of the realizations of all living beings. Maitreya, at the moment when you attain ultimate liberation, all living beings will also attain ultimate liberation. Why? The Tathāgatas do not enter ultimate liberation until all living beings have entered ultimate liberation. For, since all living beings are utterly liberated, the Tathāgatas see them as having the nature of ultimate liberation.

" 'Therefore, Maitreya, do not fool and delude these deities! No one abides in, or regresses from, enlightenment. Maitreya, you should introduce these deities to the repudiation of all discriminative constructions concerning enlightenment.[5]

" 'Enlightenment is perfectly realized neither by the body nor by the mind. Enlightenment is the eradication of all marks. Enlightenment is free of presumptions concerning all objects. Enlightenment is free of the functioning of all intentional thoughts. Enlightenment is the annihilation of all convictions. Enlightenment is free from all discriminative constructions. Enlightenment is free from all vacillation, mentation, and agitation. Enlightenment is not involved in any commitments. Enlightenment is the arrival at detachment, through freedom from all habitual attitudes. The ground of enlightenment is the ultimate realm.[6] Enlightenment is realization of reality. Enlightenment abides at the limit of reality.[7] Enlightenment is without duality, since therein are no minds and no things. Enlightenment is equality, since it is equal to infinite space.

" 'Enlightenment is unconstructed, because it is neither born nor destroyed, neither abides nor undergoes any transformation. Enlightenment is the complete knowledge of the thoughts, deeds, and inclinations of all living beings. Enlightenment is not a door for the six media of sense.[8] Enlightenment is unadulterated, since it is free of the passions of the instinctually driven succession of lives. Enlightenment is neither somewhere nor nowhere, abiding in no location or dimension. Enlightenment, not being contained in anything, does not stand in reality. Enlightenment is merely a name and even that name is unmoving. Enlightenment, free of abstention and undertaking, is energyless. There is no agitation in enlightenment, as it is utterly pure by nature. Enlightenment is radiance, pure in essence. Enlightenment is without subjectivity and completely without object. Enlightenment, which penetrates the equality of all things, is undifferentiated. Enlightenment, which is not shown by any example, is incomparable. Enlightenment is subtle, since it is extremely difficult to realize. Enlightenment is all-pervasive, as it has the nature of infinite space. Enlightenment cannot be realized, either physically or mentally. Why? The body is like grass, trees, walls, paths, and hallucinations. And the mind is immaterial, invisible, baseless, and unconscious.'[9]

"Lord, when Vimalakīrti had discoursed thus, two hundred of the deities in that assembly attained the tolerance of birthlessness. As for me, Lord, I was rendered speechless. Therefore, I am reluctant to go to that good man to inquire about his illness."

The Buddha then said to the young Licchavi Prabhāvyūha,[10] "Prabhāvyūha, go to the Licchavi Vimalakīrti to inquire about his illness."

Prabhāvyūha replied, "Lord, I am indeed reluctant to go to that good man to inquire about his illness. Why? Lord, I remember one day, when I was going out of the great city of Vaiśāli, I met the Licchavi Vimalakīrti coming in. He greeted me, and I then addressed him: 'Householder, where do you come from?' He replied, 'I come from the seat of enlightenment.'[11] I then inquired, 'What is meant by "seat of enlightenment"?' He then spoke the following words to me, 'Noble son, the seat of enlightenment is the seat of positive thought because it is without artificiality. It is the seat of effort, because it releases energetic activities. It is the seat of high resolve, because its insight is superior. It is the seat of the great spirit of enlightenment, because it does not neglect anything.

"'It is the seat of generosity, because it has no expection of reward. It is the seat of morality, because it fulfills all commitments. It is the seat of tolerance, because it is free of anger toward any living being. It is the seat of effort, because it does not turn back. It is the seat of meditation, because it generates fitness of mind. It is the seat of wisdom, because it sees everything directly.[12]

"'It is the seat of love, because it is equal to all living beings. It is the seat of compassion, because it tolerates all injuries. It is the seat of joy, because it is joyfully devoted to the bliss of the Dharma. It is the seat of equanimity, because it abandons affection and aversion.[13]

"'It is the seat of paranormal perception,[14] because it has the six super-knowledges. It is the seat of liberation, because it does not intellectualize. It is the seat of liberative technique, because it develops living beings. It is the seat of the means of unification,[15] because it brings together living beings. It is the seat of learning, because it makes practice of the essence. It is the seat of decisiveness,[16] because of its precise discrimination. It is the seat of the aids to enlightenment,[17] because it eliminates the duality of the compounded and the uncompounded. It is the seat of truth, because it does not deceive anyone.

"'It is the seat of interdependent origination, because it proceeds from the exhaustion of ignorance to the exhaustion of old age and death.[18] It is the seat of eradication of all passions, because it is perfectly enlightened about the nature of reality. It is the seat of all living beings, because all living beings are without intrinsic identity. It is the seat of all things, because it is perfectly enlightened with regard to voidness.

"'It is the seat of the conquest of all devils, because it never flinches. It is the seat of the triple world, because it is free of involvement. It is the seat of the heroism that sounds the lion's roar, because it is free of fear and trembling. It is the seat of the strengths, the fearlessnesses, and all the special qualities of the Buddha, because it is irreproachable in all respects. It is the seat of the three knowledges, because in it no passions remain. It is the seat of instantaneous, total understanding of all things, because it realizes fully the gnosis of omniscience.

"'Noble son, when bodhisattvas are thus endowed with the transcendences, the roots of virtue, the ability to develop living beings, and the incorporation of the holy Dharma,[19] whether they lift up their feet or put them down, they all come from the seat of enlightenment. They come from the qualities of the Buddha, and stand on the qualities of the Buddha.'

"Lord, when Vimalakīrti had explained this teaching, five hundred gods and men conceived the spirit of enlightenment, and I became speechless. Therefore, Lord, I am reluctant to go to that good man to inquire about his illness."

The Buddha then said to the bodhisattva Jagatīṃdhara,[20] "Jagatīṃdhara, go to the Licchavi Vimalakīrti to inquire about his illness."

"Jagatīṃdhara replied, "My Lord, I am indeed reluctant to go to that good man to inquire about his illness. Why? Lord, I remember that one day, when I was at home, the wicked Māra, disguised as Indra and surrounded with twelve thousand heavenly maidens, approached me with the sounds of music and singing. Having saluted me by touching my feet with his head, he withdrew with his retinue to one side. I then, thinking he was Śakra, the king of the gods, said to him, 'Welcome, O Kauśikā![21] You should remain consciously aware in the midst of the pleasures of desire. You should often think on impermanence and strive to utilize the essential in body, life, and wealth.'

"Māra then said to me, 'Good sir, accept from me these twelve thousand divine maidens and make them your servants.'

"I replied, 'O Kauśikā, do not offer me, who am religious and a son of the Śākya,[22] things which are not appropriate. It is not proper for me to have these maidens.'

"No sooner had I said these words than the Licchavi Vimalakīrti came there and said to me, 'Noble son, do not think that this is Indra! This is not Indra but the evil Māra, who has come to ridicule you.'

"Then the Licchavi Vimalakīrti said to Māra, 'Evil Māra, since these heavenly maidens are not suitable for this religious devotee, a son of the Śākya, give them to me.'

"Then Māra was terrified and distressed, thinking that the Licchavi Vimalakīrti had come to expose him. He tried to make himself invisible, but, try as he might with all his magical powers, he could not vanish from sight. Then a voice resounded in the sky, saying, 'Evil One, give these heavenly maidens to the good man Vimalakīrti, and only then will you be able to return to your own abode.'

"Then Māra was even more frightened and, much against his will, gave the heavenly maidens.

"The Licchavi Vimalakīrti, having received the goddesses, said to them, 'Now that you have been given to me by Māra, you should all conceive the spirit of unexcelled, perfect enlightenment.'[23]

"He then exhorted them with discourse suitable for their development toward enlightenment, and soon they conceived the spirit of enlightenment. He then said to them, 'You have just conceived the spirit of enlightenment. From now on, you should devote yourselves to find joy in pleasures of the Dharma, and should take no pleasure in desires.'

"They then asked him, 'What is "joy in the pleasures of the Dharma"?'

"He declared, 'It is the joy of unbreakable faith in the Buddha, of wishing to hear the Dharma, of serving the Saṅgha and honoring the spiritual benefactors without pride. It is the joy of renunciation of the whole world, of not being fixed in objects, of considering the five aggregates to be like murderers, of considering the elements to be like venomous serpents, and of considering the sense-media to be like an empty town.[24] It is the joy of always guarding the spirit of enlightenment, of helping living beings, of sharing through generosity, of not slackening in morality, of control and tolerance in patience, of thorough cultivation of virtue by effort, of total absorption in meditation, and of absence of passions in wisdom. It is the joy of extending enlightenment, of conquering the Māras, of destroying the passions, and of purifying the buddha-field. It is the joy of accumulating all virtues, in order to cultivate the auspicious marks and signs. It is the joy of the liberation of nonintimidation[25] when hearing the profound teaching. It is the joy of exploration of the three doors of liberation, and of the realization of liberation. It is the joy of being an ornament of the seat of enlightenment, and of not attaining liberation at the wrong time. It is the joy of serving those of equal fortune, of not hating or resenting those of superior fortune, of serving the spiritual benefactors, and of avoiding sinful friends. It is the joy of the superior gladness of faith and devotion to the Dharma. It is the joy of acquiring liberative techniques and of the conscious cultivation of the aids to enlightenment. Thus, the bodhisattva admires and finds joy in the delights of the Dharma.'

"Thereupon, Māra said to the goddesses, 'Now come along and let us return home.'

"They said, 'You gave us to this householder. Now we should enjoy the delights of the Dharma and should no longer enjoy the pleasures of desires.'

"Then Māra said to the Licchavi Vimalakīrti, 'If it is so that the bodhisattva, the spiritual hero, has no mental attachment, and gives away all his possessions, then, householder, please give me these goddesses.'

"Vimalakīrti replied, 'They are given, Māra. Go home with your retinue. May you fulfill the religious aspirations of all living beings!'

"Then the goddesses, saluting Vimalakīrti, said to him, 'Householder, how should we live in the abode of the Māras?'

"Vimalakīrti replied, 'Sisters, there is a door of the Dharma[26] called "The Inexhaustible Lamp." Practice it! What is it? Sisters, a single lamp may light hundreds of thousands of lamps without itself being diminished. Likewise, sisters, a single bodhisattva may establish many hundreds of thousands of living beings in enlightenment without his mindfulness being diminished. In fact, not only does it not diminish, it grows stronger. Likewise, the more you teach and demonstrate virtuous qualities to others, the more you grow with respect to these virtuous qualities. This is the door of the Dharma called "The Inexhaustible Lamp." When you are living in the realm of Māra, inspire innumerable gods and goddesses with the spirit of enlightenment. In such a way, you will repay the kindness[27] of the Tathāgata, and you will become the benefactors of all living beings.'

"Then, those goddesses bowed at the feet of the Licchavi Vimalakīrti and departed in the company of Māra. Thus, Lord, I saw the supremacy of the magical power, wisdom, and eloquence of the Licchavi Vimalakīrti, and therefore I am reluctant to go to that good man to inquire about his illness."

The Buddha then said to the merchant's son, Sudatta,[28] "Noble son, go to the Licchavi Vimalakīrti to inquire about his illness."

Sudatta replied, "Lord, I am indeed reluctant to go to that good man to inquire about his illness. Why? Lord, I remember one day in my father's house when, in order to celebrate a great sacrifice,[29] I was bestowing gifts upon religious devotees, brahmans, the poor, the wretched, the unfortunate, beggars, and all the needy. On the seventh and final day of this great sacrifice, the Licchavi Vimalakīrti came there and said, 'Merchant's son, you should not celebrate a sacrifice in this way. You should celebrate a Dharma-sacrifice. What is the use of the sacrifice of material things?'

"I then asked him, 'How does one give a Dharma-sacrifice?'

"He replied, 'A Dharma-sacrifice is that which develops living beings without beginning or end, giving gifts to them all simultaneously.[30] What is that? It consists of the great love which is consummated in enlightenment; of the great compassion which is consummated in the concentration of the holy Dharma on the liberation of all living beings;[31] of the great joy which is consummated in the awareness of the supreme happiness of all living beings;[32] and of the great equanimity which is consummated in concentration through knowledge.

"'The Dharma-sacrifice consists of the transcendence of generosity, which is consummated in peacefulness and self-discipline; of the transcendence of morality, which is consummated in the moral development of immoral beings; of the transcendence of tolerance, consummated through the principle of selflessness; of the transcendence of effort, consummated in initiative toward enlightenment; of the transcendence of meditation, consummated in the solitude of body and mind; and of the transcendence of wisdom, consummated in the omniscient gnosis.

"'The Dharma-sacrifice consists of the meditation of voidness, consummated in effectiveness in the development of all living beings; of the meditation of signlessness, consummated in the purification of all compounded things; and of the meditation of wishlessness, consummated in voluntarily assuming rebirths.

"'The Dharma-sacrifice consists of heroic strength, consummated in the upholding of the holy Dharma; of the power of life,[33] consummated in the means of unification; of the absence of pride, consummated in becoming the slave and the disciple of all living beings; of the gain of body, health, and wealth, consummated by the extraction of essence from the essenceless;[34] of mindfulness, consummated by the six remembrances; of positive thought, consummated through the truly enjoyable Dharma; of purity of livelihood, consummated by correct spiritual practice; of the respect of saints, consummated by joyful and faithful service; of soberness of mind, consummated by absence of dislike for ordinary people; of high resolve, consummated by renunciation; of skill in erudition, consummated by religious practice; of retirement in solitary retreats, consummated by understanding things free of passions; of introspective meditation, consummated by attainment of the Buddha-gnosis; of the stage of the practice of yoga, consummated by the yoga of liberating all living beings from their passions.[35]

"'The Dharma-sacrifice consists of the store of merit which is consummated by the auspicious signs and marks, the ornaments of the buddha-fields, and all other means of development of living beings; of the store of knowledge which is consummated in the ability to teach the Dharma according to the thoughts and actions of all living beings; of the store of wisdom, which is consummated in the uniform gnosis free of acceptance and rejection in regard to all things; of the store of all roots of virtue, consummated in the abandonment of all passions, obscurations, and unvirtuous things; and of the attainment of all the aids to enlightenment, consummated in the realization of the gnosis of omniscience as well as in accomplishment of all virtue.

"'That, noble son, is the Dharma-sacrifice. The bodhisattva who lives by this Dharma-sacrifice is the best of sacrificers, and, through his extreme sacrifice, is himself worthy of offerings from all people, including the gods.'

"Lord, as soon as the householder had discoursed thus, two hundred brahmans among the crowd of brahmans present conceived the spirit of unexcelled, perfect enlightenment. And I, full of astonishment, having saluted this good man by touching his feet with my head, took from around my neck a necklace of pearls worth one hundred thousand pieces of gold and offered it to him.[36] But he would not accept it. I then said to him, 'Please accept, good man, this necklace of pearls, out of compassion for me, and give it to whomsoever you wish.'

"Then, Vimalakīrti took the pearls and divided them into two halves. He gave one half of them to the lowliest poor of the city, who had been disdained by those present at the sacrifice. The other half he offered to the Tathāgata Duṣprasāha. And he performed a miracle such that all present beheld the universe called Marīci and the Tathāgata Duṣprasāha. On the head of the Tathāgata Duṣprasāha, the pearl necklace took the form of a pavilion, decorated with strings of pearls, resting on four bases, with four columns, symmetrical, well constructed, and lovely to behold. Having shown such a miracle, Vimalakīrti said, 'The giver who makes gifts to the lowliest poor of the city, considering them as worthy of offering as the Tathāgata himself, the giver who gives without any discrimination, impartially, with no expectation of reward, and with great love—this giver, I say, totally fulfills the Dharma-sacrifice.'

"Then the poor of the city, having seen that miracle and having heard that teaching, conceived the spirit of unexcelled, perfect enlightenment. Therefore, Lord, I am reluctant to go to that good man to inquire about his illness."

In the same way, all the bodhisattvas, great spiritual heroes, told the stories of their conversations with Vimalakīrti and declared their reluctance to go to him.

5

The Consolation of the Invalid

Then, the Buddha said to the crown prince, Mañjuśrī,[1] "Mañjuśrī, go to the Licchavi Vimalakīrti to inquire about his illness."

Mañjuśrī replied, "Lord, it is difficult to attend upon the Licchavi Vimalakīrti. He is gifted with marvelous eloquence concerning the law of the profound. He is extremely skilled in full expressions and in the reconciliation of dichotomies.[2] His eloquence is inexorable, and no one can resist his imperturbable intellect. He accomplishes all the activities of the bodhisattvas. He penetrates all the secret mysteries of the bodhisattvas and the Buddhas. He is skilled in civilizing all the abodes of devils. He plays with the great superknowledges. He is consummate in wisdom and liberative technique. He has attained the supreme excellence of the indivisible, nondual sphere of the ultimate realm. He is skilled in teaching the Dharma with its infinite modalities within the uniform ultimate. He is skilled in granting means of attainment in accordance with the spiritual faculties of all living beings. He has thoroughly integrated his realization with skill in liberative technique. He has attained decisiveness with regard to all questions. Thus, although he cannot be withstood by someone of my feeble defenses, still, sustained by the grace of the Buddha, I will go to him and will converse with him as well as I can."

Thereupon, in that assembly, the bodhisattvas, the great disciples, the Śakras, the Brahmās, the Lokapālas, and the gods and goddesses, all had this thought: "Surely the conversations of the young prince Mañjuśrī and that good man will result in a profound teaching of the Dharma."

Thus, eight thousand bodhisattvas, five hundred disciples, a great number of Śakras, Brahmās, Lokapālas, and many hundreds of thousands of gods and goddesses, all followed the crown prince Mañjuśrī to listen to the Dharma. And the crown prince Mañjuśrī, surrounded and followed by these bodhisattvas, disciples, Śakras, Brahmās, Lokapālas, gods, and goddesses, entered the great city of Vaiśālī.

Meanwhile, the Licchavi Vimalakīrti thought to himself, "Mañjuśrī, the crown prince, is coming here with numerous attendants. Now, may this house be transformed into emptiness!"

Then, magically his house became empty. Even the doorkeeper disappeared. And, except for the invalid's couch upon which Vimalakīrti himself was lying, no bed or couch or seat could be seen anywhere.

Then, the Licchavi Vimalakīrti saw the crown prince Mañjuśrī and addressed him thus: "Mañjuśrī! Welcome, Mañjuśrī! You are very welcome! There you are, without any coming. You appear, without any seeing. You are heard, without any hearing."

Mañjuśrī declared, "Householder, it is as you say. Who comes, finally comes not. Who goes, finally goes not. Why? Who comes is not known to come. Who goes is not known to go. Who appears is finally not to be seen.[3]

"Good sir, is your condition tolerable? Is it livable? Are your physical elements not disturbed? Is your sickness diminishing? Is it not increasing? The Buddha asks about you—if you have slight trouble, slight discomfort, slight sickness, if your distress is light, if you are cared for, strong, at ease, without self-reproach, and if you are living in touch with the supreme happiness.

"Householder, whence came this sickness of yours? How long will it continue? How does it stand? How can it be alleviated?"

Vimalakīrti replied, "Mañjuśrī, my sickness comes from ignorance and the thirst for existence and it will last as long as do the sicknesses of all living beings. Were all living beings to be free from sickness, I also would not be sick. Why? Mañjuśrī, for the bodhisattva, the world consists only of living beings, and sickness is inherent in living in the world. Were all living beings free of sickness, the bodhisattva also would be free of sickness. For example, Mañjuśrī, when the only son of a merchant is sick, both his parents become sick on account of the sickness of their son. And the parents will suffer as long as that only son does not recover from his sickness. Just so, Mañjuśrī, the bodhisattva loves all living beings as if each were his only child. He becomes sick when they are sick and is cured when they are cured. You ask me, Mañjuśrī, whence comes my sickness; the sicknesses of the bodhisattvas arise from great compassion."

Mañjuśrī: Householder, why is your house empty? Why have you no servants?

Vimalakīrti: Mañjuśrī, all buddha-fields are also empty.

Mañjuśrī: What makes them empty?

Vimalakīrti: They are empty because of emptiness.[4]

Mañjuśrī: What is "empty" about emptiness?[5]

Vimalakīrti: Constructions are empty, because of emptiness.[6]

Mañjuśrī: Can emptiness be conceptually constructed?[7]

Vimalakīrti: Even that concept is itself empty, and emptiness cannot construct emptiness.[8]

Mañjuśrī: Householder, where should emptiness be sought?

Vimalakīrti: Mañjuśrī, emptiness should be sought among the sixty-two convictions.[9]

Mañjuśrī: Where should the sixty-two convictions be sought?

Vimalakīrti: They should be sought in the liberation of the Tathāgatas.

Mañjuśrī: Where should the liberation of the Tathāgatas be sought?

Vimalakīrti: It should be sought in the prime mental activity of all living beings.

Mañjuśrī, you ask me why I am without servants, but all Māras and opponents are my servants. Why? The Māras advocate this life of birth and death and the bodhisattva does not avoid life. The heterodox opponents advocate convictions, and the bodhisattva is not troubled by convictions. Therefore, all Māras and opponents are my servants.

Mañjuśrī: Householder, of what sort is your sickness?

Vimalakīrti: It is immaterial and invisible.

Mañjuśrī: Is it physical or mental?

Vimalakīrti: It is not physical, since the body is insubstantial in itself. It is not mental, since the nature of the mind is like illusion.

Mañjuśrī: Householder, which of the four main elements is disturbed: earth, water, fire, or air?

Vimalakīrti: Mañjuśrī, I am sick only because the elements of living beings are disturbed by sicknesses.[10]

Mañjuśrī: Householder, how should a bodhisattva console another bodhisattva who is sick?

Vimalakīrti: He should tell him that the body is impermanent, but should not exhort him to renunciation or disgust. He should tell him that the body is miserable, but should not encourage him to find solace in liberation; that the body is selfless, but that living beings should be developed; that the body is peaceful, but not to seek any ultimate calm. He should urge him to confess his evil deeds, but not for the sake of absolution.[11] He should encourage his empathy for all living beings on account of his own sickness, his remembrance of suffering experienced from beginningless time, and his consciousness of working for the welfare of living beings. He should encourage him not to be distressed, but to manifest the roots of virtue, to maintain the primal purity and the lack of craving, and thus to always strive to become the king of healers, who can cure all sicknesses. Thus should a bodhisattva console a sick bodhisattva, in such a way as to make him happy.

Mañjuśrī asked, "Noble sir, how should a sick bodhisattva control his own mind?"

Vimalakīrti replied, "Mañjuśrī, a sick bodhisattva should control his own mind with the following consideration: Sickness arises from total involvement in the process of misunderstanding from beginningless time.[12] It arises from the passions that result from unreal mental constructions, and hence ultimately nothing is perceived which can be said to be sick. Why? The body is the issue of the four main elements, and in these elements there is no owner and no agent. There is no self in this body, and, except for arbitrary insistence on self, ultimately no "I" which can be said to be sick can be apprehended. Therefore, thinking '"I" should not adhere to any self, and "I" should rest in the knowledge of the root of illness,' he should abandon the conception of himself as a personality and produce the conception of himself as a thing, thinking 'This body is an aggregate of many things; when it is born, only things are born; when it ceases, only things cease; these things have no awareness or feeling of each other; when they are born, they do not think, "I am born." When they cease, they do not think, "I cease."'

"Furthermore, he should understand thoroughly the conception of himself as a thing by cultivating the following consideration: 'Just as in the case of the conception of "self," so the conception of "thing" is also a misunderstanding, and this misunderstanding is also a grave sickness; I should free myself from this sickness and should strive to abandon it.'[13]

"What is the elimination of this sickness? It is the elimination of egoism and possessiveness. What is the elimination of egoism and possessiveness? It is the freedom from dualism. What is freedom from dualism? It is the absence of involvement with either the external or the internal. What is absence of involvement with either external or internal? It is nondeviation, nonfluctuation, and nondistraction from equanimity. What is equanimity? It is the equality of everything from self to liberation. Why? Because both self and liberation are void. How can both be void? As verbal designations, they both are void, and neither is established in reality. Therefore, one who sees such equality makes no difference between sickness and voidness; his sickness is itself voidness, and that sickness as voidness is itself void.[14]

"The sick bodhisattva should recognize that sensation is ultimately nonsensation, but he should not realize the cessation of sensation. Although both pleasure and pain are abandoned when the buddha-qualities are fully accomplished, there is then no sacrifice of the great compassion for all living beings living in the bad migrations. Thus, recognizing in his own suffering the infinite sufferings of these living beings,[15] the bodhisattva correctly contemplates these living beings and resolves to cure all sicknesses. As for these living beings, there is nothing to be applied, and there is nothing to be removed; one has only to teach them the

Dharma for them to realize the basis from which sicknesses arise. What is this basis? It is object-perception.[16] Insofar as apparent objects are perceived, they are the basis of sickness. What things are perceived as objects? The three realms of existence are perceived as objects. What is the thorough understanding of the basic, apparent object? It is its nonperception, as no objects exist ultimately. What is nonperception? The internal subject and the external object are not perceived dualistically. Therefore, it is called nonperception.[17]

"Mañjuśrī, thus should a sick bodhisattva control his own mind in order to overcome old age, sickness, death, and birth. Such, Mañjuśrī, is the sickness of the bodhisattva. If he takes it otherwise, all his efforts will be in vain. For example, one is called 'hero' when one overcomes all enemies. Just so, one is called 'bodhisattva' when one conquers the miseries of aging, sickness, and death.[18]

"The sick bodhisattva should tell himself: 'Just as my sickness is unreal and nonexistent, so the sicknesses of all living beings are unreal and nonexistent.' Through such considerations, he arouses the great compassion toward all living beings without falling into any sentimental compassion.[19] The great compassion that strives to eliminate the accidental passions does not conceive of any life in living beings. Why? Because great compassion that falls into sentimentally purposive views only exhausts the bodhisattva in his reincarnations. But the great compassion which is free of involvement with sentimentally purposive views does not exhaust the bodhisattva in all his reincarnations.[20] He does not reincarnate through involvement with such views but reincarnates with his mind free of involvement. Hence, even his reincarnation is like a liberation. Being reincarnated as if being liberated, he has the power and ability to teach the Dharma which liberates living beings from their bondage. As the Lord declares: 'It is not possible for one who is himself bound to deliver others from their bondage. But one who is himself liberated is able to liberate others from their bondage.' Therefore, the bodhisattva should participate in liberation and should not participate in bondage.

"What is bondage? And what is liberation? To indulge in liberation from the world without employing liberative technique is bondage for the bodhisattva. To engage in life in the world with full employment of liberative technique is liberation for the bodhisattva. To experience the taste of contemplation, meditation, and concentration without skill in liberative technique is bondage. To experience the taste of contemplation and meditation with skill in liberative technique is liberation. Wisdom not integrated with liberative technique is bondage, but wisdom integrated with liberative technique is liberation. Liberative technique not integrated with wisdom is bondage, but liberative technique integrated with wisdom is liberation.

"How is wisdom not integrated with liberative technique a bondage? Wisdom not integrated with liberative technique consists of concentration on voidness, signlessness, and wishlessness, and yet, being motivated by sentimental compassion,[21] failure to concentrate on cultivation of the auspicious signs and marks, on the adornment of the buddha-field, and on the work of development of living beings—and it is bondage.

"How is wisdom integrated with liberative technique a liberation? Wisdom integrated with liberative technique consists of being motivated by the great compassion[22] and thus of concentration on cultivation of the auspicious signs and marks, on the adornment of the buddha-field, and on the work of development of living beings, all the while concentrating on deep investigation of voidness, signlessness, and wishlessness—and it is liberation.

"What is the bondage of liberative technique not integrated with wisdom? The bondage of liberative technique not integrated with wisdom consists of the bodhisattva's planting of the roots of virtue without dedicating them for the sake of enlightenment, while living in the grip of dogmatic convictions, passions, attachments, resentments, and their subconscious instincts.[23]

"What is the liberation of liberative technique integrated with wisdom? The liberation of liberative technique integrated with wisdom consists of the bodhisattva's dedication of his roots of virtue for the sake of enlightenment, without taking any pride therein, while forgoing all convictions, passions, attachments, resentments, and their subconscious instincts.[24]

"Mañjuśrī, thus should the sick bodhisattva consider things. His wisdom is the consideration of body, mind, and sickness as impermanent, miserable, empty, and selfless. His liberative technique consists of not exhausting himself by trying to avoid all physical sickness, and of applying himself to accomplish the benefit of living beings, without interrupting the cycle of reincarnations. Furthermore, his wisdom lies in understanding that body, mind, and sickness are neither new nor old, both simultaneously and sequentially. And his liberative technique lies in not seeking cessation of body, mind, or sicknesses.

"That, Mañjuśrī, is the way a sick bodhisattva should concentrate his mind; he should live neither in control of his mind, nor in indulgence of his mind. Why? To live by indulging the mind is proper for fools and to live in control of the mind is proper for the disciples. Therefore, the bodhisattva should live neither in control nor in indulgence of his mind. Not living in either of the two extremes is the domain of the bodhisattva.

"Not the domain of the ordinary individual and not the domain of the saint, such is the domain of the bodhisattva.[25] The domain of the world yet not the domain of the passions, such is the domain of the bodhisattva. Where one understands liberation, yet does not enter final and complete liberation, there is the domain of the bodhisattva. Where the four Māras manifest, yet where all the works of Māras are transcended, there is the domain of the bodhisattva. Where one seeks the gnosis of omniscience, yet does not attain this gnosis at the wrong time, there is the domain of the bodhisattva. Where one knows the Four Holy Truths, yet does not realize those truths at the wrong time, there is the domain of the bodhisattva. A domain of introspective insight, wherein one does not arrest voluntary reincarnation in the world, such is the domain of the bodhisattva. A domain where one realizes birthlessness, yet does not become destined for the ultimate, such is the domain of the bodhisattva. Where one sees relativity without entertaining any convictions, there is the domain of the bodhisattva. Where one associates with all beings, yet keeps free of all afflictive instincts, there is the domain of the bodhisattva. A domain of solitude with no place for the exhaustion of body and mind, such is the domain of the bodhisattva. The domain of the triple world, yet indivisible from the ultimate realm, such is the domain of the bodhisattva. The domain of voidness, yet where one cultivates all types of virtues, such is the domain of the bodhisattva. The domain of signlessness, where one keeps in sight the deliverance of all living beings, such is the domain of the bodhisattva. The domain of wishlessness, where one voluntarily manifests lives in the world, such is the domain of the bodhisattva.

"A domain essentially without undertaking, yet where all the roots of virtue are undertaken without interruption, such is the domain of the bodhisattva. The domain of the six transcendences, where one attains the transcendence[26] of the thoughts and actions of all living beings, such is the domain of the bodhisattva. The domain of the six superknowledges,[27] wherein defilements are not exhausted, such is the domain of the bodhisattva. The domain of living by the holy Dharma, without even perceiving any evil paths, such is the domain of the bodhisattva. The domain of the four immeasurables, where one does not accept rebirth in the heaven of Brahmā, such is the domain of the bodhisattva. The domain of the six remembrances, unaffected by any sort of defilement, such is the domain of the bodhisattva. The domain of contemplation, meditation, and concentration, where one does not reincarnate in the formless realms by force of these meditations and concentrations,[28] such is the domain of the bodhisattva. The domain of the four foci of mindfulness, where body, sensation, mind, and things are not ultimately of concern, such is the domain of the bodhisattva. The domain of the four right efforts, where the duality of good and evil is not apprehended, such is the domain of the bodhisattva. The domain of the four bases of magical powers, where they are effortlessly mastered, such is the domain of the bodhisattva. The domain of the five spiritual faculties, where one knows the degrees of the spiritual faculties of living beings, such is the domain of the bodhisattva. The domain of living with the five powers, where one delights in the ten powers of the Tathāgata, such is the domain of the bodhisattva. The domain of perfection of the seven factors of enlightenment, where one is skilled in the knowledge of fine intellectual distinctions, such is the domain of the bodhisattva. The domain of the holy eightfold path, where one delights in the unlimited path of the Buddha, such is the domain of the bodhisattva.[29] The domain of the cultivation of the aptitude for mental quiescence and transcendental analysis, where one does not fall into extreme quietism, such is the domain of the bodhisattva. The domain of the realization of the unborn nature of all things, yet of the perfection of the body, the auspicious signs and marks, and the ornaments of the Buddha, such is the domain of the bodhisattva. The domain of manifesting the attitudes of the disciples and the solitary sages without sacrificing the qualities of the Buddha, such is the domain of the bodhisattva. The domain of conformity to all things utterly pure in nature while manifesting behavior that suits the inclinations of all living beings, such is the domain of the bodhisattva. A domain where one realizes that all the buddha-fields are indestructible and uncreatable, having the nature of infinite space, yet where one manifests the establishment of the qualities of the buddha-fields in all their variety and magnitude, such is the domain of the bodhisattva. The domain where one turns the wheel of the holy Dharma and manifests the magnificence of ultimate liberation, yet never forsakes the career of the bodhisattva, such is the domain of the bodhisattva!"[30]

When Vimalakīrti had spoken this discourse, eight thousand of the gods in the company of the crown prince Mañjuśrī conceived the spirit of unexcelled, perfect enlightenment.

6

The Inconceivable Liberation

Thereupon, the venerable Śāriputra had this thought: "There is not even a single chair in this house. Where are these disciples and bodhisattvas going to sit?"

The Licchavi Vimalakīrti read the thought of the venerable Śāriputra and said, "Reverend Śāriputra, did you come here for the sake of the Dharma? Or did you come here for the sake of a chair?"

Śāriputra replied, "I came for the sake of the Dharma, not for the sake of a chair."

Vimalakīrti continued, "Reverend Śāriputra, he who is interested in the Dharma is not interested even in his own body, much less in a chair. Reverend Śāriputra, he who is interested in the Dharma has no interest in matter, sensation, intellect, motivation, or consciousness.[1] He has no interest in these aggregates, or in the elements, or in the sense-media.[2] Interested in the Dharma, he has no interest in the realm of desire, the realm of matter, or the immaterial realm. Interested in the Dharma, he is not interested in attachment to the Buddha, attachment to the Dharma, or attachment to the Saṅgha. Reverend Śāriputra, he who is interested in the Dharma is not interested in recognizing suffering, abandoning its origination, realizing its cessation, or practicing the path.[3] Why? The Dharma is ultimately without formulation and without verbalization. Who verbalizes: 'Suffering should be recognized, origination should be eliminated, cessation should be realized, the path should be practiced,' is not interested in the Dharma but is interested in verbalization.[4]

"Reverend Śāriputra, the Dharma is calm and peaceful. Those who are engaged in production and destruction are not interested in the Dharma, are not interested in solitude, but are interested in production and destruction.[5]

"Furthermore, reverend Śāriputra, the Dharma is without taint and free of defilement. He who is attached to anything, even to liberation, is not interested in the Dharma but is interested in the taint of desire. The Dharma is not an object. He who pursues objects is not interested in the Dharma but is interested in objects. The Dharma is without acceptance or rejection. He who holds on to things or lets go of things is not interested in the Dharma but is interested in holding and letting go. The Dharma is not a secure refuge. He who enjoys a secure refuge is not interested in the Dharma but is interested in a secure refuge. The Dharma is without sign. He whose consciousness pursues signs is not interested in the Dharma but is interested in signs. The Dharma is not a society. He who seeks to associate with the Dharma is not interested in the Dharma but is interested in association. The Dharma is not a sight, a sound, a category, or an idea. He who is involved in sights, sounds, categories, and ideas is not interested in the Dharma but is interested in sights, sounds, categories, and ideas. Reverend Śāriputra, the Dharma is free of compounded things and uncompounded things. He who adheres to compounded things and uncompounded things is not interested in the Dharma but is interested in adhering to compounded things and uncompounded things.

"Thereupon, reverend Śāriputra, if you are interested in the Dharma, you should take no interest in anything."[6]

When Vimalakīrti had spoken this discourse, five hundred gods obtained the purity of the Dharma-eye in viewing all things.

Then, the Licchavi Vimalakīrti said to the crown prince, Mañjuśrī, "Mañjuśrī, you have already been in innumerable hundreds of thousands of buddha-fields throughout the universes of the ten directions.[7] In which buddha-field did you see the best lion-thrones with the finest qualities?"

Mañjuśrī replied, "Noble sir, if one crosses the buddha-fields to the east, which are more numerous than all the grains of sand of thirty-two Ganges rivers, one will discover a universe called Merudhvaja. There dwells a Tathāgata called Merupradīparāja. His body measures eighty-four hundred thousand leagues in height, and the height of his throne is sixty-eight hundred thousand leagues. The bodhisattvas there are forty-two hundred thousand leagues tall and their own thrones are thirty-four hundred thousand leagues high. Noble sir, the finest and most superb thrones exist in that universe Merudhvaja, which is the buddha-field of the Tathāgata Merupradīparāja."

At that moment, the Licchavi Vimalakīrti, having focused himself in concentration, performed a miraculous feat such that the Lord Tathāgata Merupradīparāja, in the universe Merudhvaja, sent to this universe thirty-two hundred thousand thrones. These thrones were so tall, spacious, and beautiful that the bodhisattvas, great disciples, Śakras, Brahmās, Lokapālas, and other gods had never before seen the like. The thrones descended from the sky and came to rest in the house of the Licchavi Vimalakīrti. The thirty-two hundred thousand thrones arranged themselves without crowding and the house seemed to enlarge itself accordingly. The great city of Vaiśālī did not become obscured; neither did the land of Jambudvīpa,[8] nor the world of four continents. Everything else appeared just as it was before.

Then, the Licchavi Vimalakīrti said to the young prince Mañjuśrī, "Mañjuśrī, let the bodhisattvas be seated on these thrones, having transformed their bodies to a suitable size!"[9]

Then, those bodhisattvas who had attained the superknowledges transformed their bodies to a height of forty-two hundred thousand leagues and sat upon the thrones. But the beginner bodhisattvas were not able to transform themselves to sit upon the thrones. Then, the Licchavi Vimalakīrti taught these beginner bodhisattvas a teaching that enabled them to attain the five superknowledges, and, having attained them, they transformed their bodies to a height of forty-two hundred thousand leagues and sat upon the thrones. But still the great disciples were not able to seat themselves upon the thrones.

The Licchavi Vimalakīrti said to the venerable Śāriputra, "Reverend Śāriputra, take your seat upon a throne."

He replied, "Good sir, the thrones are too big and too high, and I cannot sit upon them."

Vimalakīrti said, "Reverend Śāriputra, bow down to the Tathāgata Merupradīparāja, and you will be able to take your seat."

Then, the great disciples bowed down to the Tathāgata Merupradīparāja and they were seated upon the thrones.

Then, the venerable Śāriputra said to the Licchavi Vimalakīrti, "Noble sir, it is astonishing that these thousands of thrones, so big and so high, should fit into such a small house and that the great city of Vaiśālī, the villages, cities, kingdoms, capitals of Jambudvīpa, the other three continents, the abodes of the gods, the nāgas, the yakṣas, the gandharvas, the asuras, the garuḍas, the kiṃnaras, and the mahoragas—that all of these should appear without any obstacle, just as they were before!"

The Licchavi Vimalakīrti replied, "Reverend Śāriputra, for the Tathāgatas and the bodhisattvas, there is a liberation called 'Inconceivable.'[10] The bodhisattva who lives in the inconceivable liberation can put the king of mountains, Sumeru, which is so high, so great, so noble, and so vast, into a mustard seed. He can perform this feat without enlarging the mustard seed and without shrinking Mount Sumeru. And the deities of the assembly of the four Mahārājas and of the Trayastriṃśā heavens do not even know where they are.[11] Only those beings who are destined to be disciplined by miracles[12] see and understand the putting of the king of mountains, Sumeru, into the mustard seed. That, reverend Śāriputra, is an entrance to the domain of the inconceivable liberation of the bodhisattvas.

"Furthermore, reverend Śāriputra, the bodhisattva who lives in the inconceivable liberation can pour into a single pore of his skin all the waters of the four great oceans, without injuring the water-animals such as fish, tortoises, crocodiles, frogs, and other creatures, and without the nāgas, yakṣas, gandharvas, and asuras even being aware of where they are. And the whole operation is visible without any injury or disturbance to any of those living beings.

"Such a bodhisattva can pick up with his right hand this billion-world-galactic universe as if it were a potter's wheel and, spinning it round, throw it beyond universes as numerous as the sands of the Ganges, without the living beings therein knowing their motion or its origin, and he can catch it and put it back in its place, without the living beings suspecting their coming and going; and yet the whole operation is visible.

"Furthermore, reverend Śāriputra, there are beings who become disciplined after an immense period of evolution, and there are also those who are disciplined after a short period of evolution. The bodhisattva who lives in the inconceivable liberation, for the sake of disciplining those living beings who are disciplined through immeasurable periods of evolution, can make the passing of a week seem like the passing of an aeon, and he can make the passing of an aeon seem like the passing of a week for those who are disciplined through a short period of evolution. The living beings who are disciplined through an immeasurable period of evolution actually perceive a week to be the passing of an aeon, and those disciplined by a short period of evolution actually perceive an aeon to be the passing of a week.[13]

"Thus, a bodhisattva who lives in the inconceivable liberation can manifest all the splendors of the virtues of all the buddha-fields within a single buddha-field. Likewise, he can place all living beings in the palm of his right hand and can show them with the supernatural speed of thought all the buddha-fields without ever leaving his own buddha-field. He can display in a single pore all the offerings ever offered to all the Buddhas of the ten directions, and the orbs of all the suns, moons, and stars of the ten directions. He can inhale all the hurricanes of the cosmic wind-atmospheres[14] of the ten directions into his mouth without harming his own body and without letting the forests and the grasses of the buddha-fields be flattened. He can take all the masses of fire of all the supernovas that ultimately consume all the universes of all the buddha-fields into his stomach without interfering with their functions. Having crossed buddha-fields as numerous as the sands of the Ganges downward, and having taken up a buddha-field, he can rise up through buddha-fields as numerous as the sands of the Ganges and place it on high, just as a strong man may pick up a jujube leaf on the point of a needle.

"Thus, a bodhisattva who lives in the inconceivable liberation can magically transform any kind of living being into a universal monarch, a Lokapāla, a Śakra, a Brahmā, a disciple, a solitary sage, a bodhisattva, and even into a Buddha. The bodhisattva can transform miraculously all the cries and noises, superior, mediocre, and inferior, of all living beings of the ten directions, into the voice of the Buddha, with the words of the Buddha, the Dharma, and the Saṅgha, having them proclaim, 'Impermanent! Miserable! Empty! Selfless!' And he can cause them to recite the words and sounds of all the teachings taught by all the Buddhas of the ten directions.

"Reverend Śāriputra, I have shown you only a small part of the entrance into the domain of the bodhisattva who lives in the inconceivable liberation. Reverend Śāriputra, to explain to you the teaching of the full entrance into the domain of the bodhisattva who lives in the inconceivable liberation would require more than an aeon, and even more than that."[15]

Then, the patriarch Mahākāśyapa, having heard this teaching of the inconceivable liberation of the bodhisattvas, was amazed, and he said to the venerable Śāriputra, "Venerable Śāriputra, if one were to show a variety of things to a person blind from birth, he would not be able to see a single thing. Likewise, venerable Śāriputra, when this door of the inconceivable liberation is taught, all the disciples and solitary sages are sightless, like the man blind from birth, and cannot comprehend even a single cause of the inconceivable liberation. Who is there among the wise who, hearing about this inconceivable liberation, does not conceive the spirit of unexcelled, perfect enlightenment? As for us, whose faculties are deteriorated, like a burned and rotten seed, what else can we do if we do not become receptive to this great vehicle? We, all the disciples and solitary sages, upon hearing this teaching of the Dharma, should utter a cry of regret that would shake this billion-world-galactic universe![16] And as for the bodhisattvas, when they hear this inconceivable liberation they should be as joyful as a young crown prince when he takes the diadem and is anointed, and they should increase to the utmost their devotion to this inconceivable liberation. Indeed, what could the entire host of Māras ever do to one who is devoted to this inconceivable liberation?"

When the patriarch Mahākāśyapa had uttered this discourse, thirty-two thousand gods conceived the spirit of unexcelled, perfect enlightenment.

Then, the Licchavi Vimalakīrti said to the patriarch Mahākāśyapa, "Reverend Mahākāśyapa, the Māras who play the devil in the innumerable universes of the ten directions are all bodhisattvas dwelling in the inconceivable liberation, who are playing the devil in order to develop living beings through their skill in liberative technique. Reverend Mahākāśyapa, all the miserable beggars who come to the bodhisattvas of the innumerable universes of the ten directions to ask for a hand, a foot, an ear, a nose, some blood, muscles, bones, marrow, an eye, a torso, a head, a limb, a member, a throne, a kingdom, a country, a wife, a son, a daughter, a slave, a slave-girl, a horse, an elephant, a chariot, a cart, gold, silver, jewels, pearls, conches, crystal, coral, beryl, treasures, food, drink, elixirs, and clothes—these demanding beggars are usually bodhisattvas living in the inconceivable liberation who, through their skill in liberative technique, wish to test and thus demonstrate the firmness of the high resolve of the bodhisattvas. Why? Reverend Mahākāśyapa, the bodhisattvas demonstrate that firmness by means of terrible austerities. Ordinary persons have no power to be thus demanding of bodhisattvas, unless they are granted the opportunity. They are not capable of killing and depriving in that manner without being freely given the chance.

"Reverend Mahākāśyapa, just as a glowworm cannot eclipse the light of the sun, so, reverend Mahākāśyapa, it is not possible without special allowance that an ordinary person can thus attack and deprive a bodhisattva. Reverend Mahākāśyapa, just as a donkey could not muster an attack on a wild elephant, even so, reverend Mahākāśyapa, one who is not himself a bodhisattva cannot harass a bodhisattva. Only one who is himself a bodhisattva can harass another bodhisattva, and only a bodhisattva can tolerate the harassment of another bodhisattva. Reverend Mahākāśyapa, such is the introduction to the power of the knowledge of liberative technique of the bodhisattvas who live in the inconceivable liberation."[17]

7

The Goddess

Thereupon, Mañjuśrī, the crown prince, addressed the Licchavi Vimalakīrti: "Good sir, how should a bodhisattva regard all living beings?"

Vimalakīrti replied, "Mañjuśrī, a bodhisattva should regard all living beings as a wise man regards the reflection of the moon in water or as magicians regard men created by magic. He should regard them as being like a face in a mirror; like the water of a mirage; like the sound of an echo; like a mass of clouds in the sky; like the previous moment of a ball of foam; like the appearance and disappearance of a bubble of water; like the core of a plantain tree; like a flash of lightning; like the fifth great element; like the seventh sense-medium; like the appearance of matter in an immaterial realm; like a sprout from a rotten seed; like a tortoise-hair coat; like the fun of games for one who wishes to die; like the egoistic views[1] of a stream-winner; like a third rebirth of a once-returner; like the descent of a nonreturner into a womb; like the existence of desire, hatred, and folly in a saint; like thoughts of avarice, immorality, wickedness, and hostility in a bodhisattva who has attained tolerance; like the instincts of passions in a Tathāgata; like the perception of color in one blind from birth; like the inhalation and exhalation of an ascetic absorbed in the meditation of cessation; like the track of a bird in the sky; like the erection of a eunuch; like the pregnancy of a barren woman; like the unproduced passions of an emanated incarnation of the Tathāgata; like dream-visions seen after waking; like the passions of one who is free of conceptualizations; like fire burning without fuel; like the reincarnation of one who has attained ultimate liberation.

"Precisely thus, Mañjuśrī, does a bodhisattva who realizes ultimate selflessness consider all beings."[2]

Mañjuśrī then asked further, "Noble sir, if a bodhisattva considers all living beings in such a way, how does he generate the great love[3] toward them?"

Vimalakīrti replied, "Mañjuśrī, when a bodhisattva considers all living beings in this way, he thinks: 'Just as I have realized the Dharma, so should I teach it to living beings.'[4] Thereby, he generates the love that is truly a refuge for all living beings; the love that is peaceful because free of grasping; the love that is not feverish, because free of passions; the love that accords with reality because it is equanimous in all three times; the love that is without conflict because free of the violence of the passions; the love that is nondual because it is involved neither with the external nor with the internal; the love that is imperturbable because totally ultimate.

"Thereby he generates the love that is firm, its high resolve unbreakable, like a diamond; the love that is pure, purified in its intrinsic nature; the love that is even, its aspirations being equal; the saint's love that has eliminated its enemy;[5] the bodhisattva's love that continuously develops living beings; the Tathāgata's love that understands reality; the Buddha's love that causes living beings to awaken from their sleep; the love that is spontaneous because it is fully enlightened spontaneously;[6] the love that is enlightenment because it is unity of experience; the love that has no presumption because it has eliminated attachment and aversion; the love that is great compassion because it infuses the Mahāyāna with radiance; the love that is never exhausted because it acknowledges voidness and selflessness; the love that is giving because it bestows the gift of Dharma free of the tight fist of a bad teacher; the love that is morality because it improves immoral living beings; the love that is tolerance because it protects both self and others; the love that is effort because it takes responsibility for all living beings; the love that is contemplation because it refrains from indulgence in tastes; the love that is wisdom because it causes attainment at the proper time;[7] the love that is liberative technique because it shows the way everywhere; the love that is without formality because it is pure in motivation; the love that is without deviation because it acts from decisive motivation; the love that is high resolve because it is without passions; the love that is without deceit because it is not artificial; the love that is happiness because it introduces living beings to the happiness of the Buddha. Such, Mañjuśrī, is the great love of a bodhisattva."

Mañjuśrī: What is the great compassion of a bodhisattva?

Vimalakīrti: It is the giving of all accumulated roots of virtue to all living beings.

Mañjuśrī: What is the great joy of the bodhisattva?

Vimalakīrti: It is to be joyful and without regret in giving.

Mañjuśrī: What is the equanimity of the bodhisattva?

Vimalakīrti: It is what benefits both self and others.[8]

Mañjuśrī: To what should one resort when terrified by fear of life?[9]

Vimalakīrti: Mañjuśrī, a bodhisattva who is terrified by fear of life should resort to the magnanimity of the Buddha.

Mañjuśrī: Where should he who wishes to resort to the magnanimity of the Buddha take his stand?

Vimalakīrti: He should stand in equanimity toward all living beings.[10]

Mañjuśrī: Where should he who wishes to stand in equanimity toward all living beings take his stand?

Vimalakīrti: He should live for the liberation of all living beings.[11]

Mañjuśrī: What should he who wishes to liberate all living beings do?

Vimalakīrti: He should liberate them from their passions.

Mañjuśrī: How should he who wishes to eliminate passions apply himself?

Vimalakīrti: He should apply himself appropriately.

Mañjuśrī: How should he apply himself, to "apply himself appropriately"?

Vimalakīrti: He should apply himself to productionlessness and to destructionlessness.

Mañjuśrī: What is not produced? And what is not destroyed?

Vimalakīrti: Evil is not produced and good is not destroyed.

Mañjuśrī: What is the root of good and evil?

Vimalakīrti: Materiality[12] is the root of good and evil.

Mañjuśrī: What is the root of materiality?

Vimalakīrti: Desire is the root of materiality.

Mañjuśrī: What is the root of desire and attachment?

Vimalakīrti: Unreal construction is the root of desire.

Mañjuśrī: What is the root of unreal construction?

Vimalakīrti: The false concept is its root.

Mañjuśrī: What is the root of the false concept?

Vimalakīrti: Baselessness.

Mañjuśrī: What is the root of baselessness?

Vimalakīrti: Mañjuśrī, when something is baseless, how can it have any root? Therefore, all things stand on the root which is baseless.[13]

Thereupon, a certain goddess who lived in that house, having heard this teaching of the Dharma of the great heroic bodhisattvas, and being delighted, pleased, and overjoyed, manifested herself in a material body and showered the great spiritual heroes, the bodhisattvas, and the great disciples with heavenly flowers. When the flowers fell on the bodies of the bodhisattvas, they fell off on the floor, but when they fell on the bodies of the great disciples, they stuck to them and did not fall. The great disciples shook the flowers and even tried to use their magical powers, but still the flowers would not shake off. Then, the goddess said to the venerable Śāriputra, "Reverend Śāriputra, why do you shake these flowers?"

Śāriputra replied, "Goddess, these flowers are not proper for religious persons[14] and so we are trying to shake them off."

The goddess said, "Do not say that, reverend Śāriputra. Why? These flowers are proper indeed! Why? Such flowers have neither constructual thought nor discrimination. But the elder Śāriputra has both constructual thought and discrimination.

"Reverend Śāriputra, impropriety for one who has renounced the world for the discipline of the rightly taught Dharma consists of constructual thought and discrimination, yet the elders are full of such thoughts. One who is without such thoughts is always proper.

"Reverend Śāriputra, see how these flowers do not stick to the bodies of these great spiritual heroes, the bodhisattvas! This is because they have eliminated constructual thoughts and discriminations.

"For example, evil spirits have power over fearful men but cannot disturb the fearless. Likewise, those intimidated by fear of the world are in the power of forms, sounds, smells, tastes, and textures, which do not disturb those who are free from fear of the passions inherent in the constructive world. Thus, these flowers stick to the bodies of those who have not eliminated their instincts for the passions and do not stick to the bodies of those who have eliminated their instincts. Therefore, the flowers do not stick to the bodies of these bodhisattvas, who have abandoned all instincts."[15]

Then the venerable Śāriputra said to the goddess, "Goddess, how long have you been in this house?"

The goddess replied, "I have been here as long as the elder has been in liberation."

Śāriputra said, "Then, have you been in this house for quite some time?"

The goddess said, "Has the elder been in liberation for quite some time?"

At that, the elder Śāriputra fell silent.

The goddess continued, "Elder, you are 'foremost of the wise!' Why do you not speak? Now, when it is your turn, you do not answer the question."

Śāriputra: Since liberation is inexpressible, goddess, I do not know what to say.

Goddess: All the syllables pronounced by the elder have the nature of liberation. Why? Liberation is neither internal nor external, nor can it be apprehended apart from them.[16] Likewise, syllables are neither internal nor external, nor can they be apprehended anywhere else. Therefore, reverend Śāriputra, do not point to liberation by abandoning speech![17] Why? The holy liberation is the equality of all things!

Śāriputra: Goddess, is not liberation the freedom from desire, hatred, and folly?

Goddess: "Liberation is freedom from desire, hatred, and folly"—that is the teaching for the excessively proud.[18] But those free of pride are taught that the very nature of desire, hatred, and folly is itself liberation.

Śāriputra: Excellent! Excellent, goddess! Pray, what have you attained, what have you realized, that you have such eloquence?

Goddess: I have attained nothing, reverend Śāriputra. I have no realization. Therefore I have such eloquence. Whoever thinks, "I have attained! I have realized!" is overly proud in the discipline of the well taught Dharma.

Śāriputra: Goddess, do you belong to the disciple-vehicle, to the solitary-vehicle, or to the great vehicle?[19]

Goddess: I belong to the disciple-vehicle when I teach it to those who need it. I belong to the solitary-vehicle when I teach the twelve links of dependent origination to those who need them. And, since I never abandon the great compassion, I belong to the great vehicle, as all need that teaching to attain ultimate liberation.[20]

Nevertheless, reverend Śāriputra, just as one cannot smell the castor plant in a magnolia wood, but only the magnolia flowers, so, reverend Śāriputra, living in this house, which is redolent with the perfume of the virtues of the Buddha-qualities, one does not smell the perfume of the disciples and the solitary sages. Reverend Śāriputra, the Śakras, the Brahmās, the Lokapālas, the devas, nāgas, yakṣas, gandharvas, asuras, garuḍas, kiṃnaras, and mahoragas who live in this house hear the Dharma from the mouth of this holy man and, enticed by the perfume of the virtues of the Buddha-qualities, proceed to conceive the spirit of enlightenment.

Reverend Śāriputra, I have been in this house for twelve years, and I have heard no discourses concerning the disciples and solitary sages but have heard only those concerning the great love, the great compassion, and the inconceivable qualities of the Buddha.

Reverend Śāriputra, eight strange and wonderful things manifest themselves constantly in this house. What are these eight?

A light of golden hue shines here constantly, so bright that it is hard to distinguish day and night; and neither the moon nor the sun shines here distinctly. That is the first wonder of this house.

Furthermore, reverend Śāriputra, whoever enters this house is no longer troubled by his passions from the moment he is within. That is the second strange and wonderful thing.[21]

Furthermore, reverend Śāriputra, this house is never forsaken by Śakra, Brahmā, the Lokapālas, and the bodhisattvas from all the other buddha-fields. That is the third strange and wonderful thing.

Furthermore, reverend Śāriputra, this house is never empty of the sounds of the Dharma, the discourse on the six transcendences, and the discourses of the irreversible wheel of the Dharma. That is the fourth strange and wonderful thing.

Furthermore, reverend Śāriputra, in this house one always hears the rhythms, songs, and music of gods and men, and from this music constantly resounds the sound of the infinite Dharma of the Buddha. That is the fifth strange and wonderful thing.

Furthermore, reverend Śāriputra, in this house there are always four inexhaustible treasures,[22] replete with all kinds of jewels, which never decrease, although all the poor and wretched may partake to their satisfaction. That is the sixth strange and wonderful thing.

Furthermore, reverend Śāriputra, at the wish of this good man, to this house come the innumerable Tathāgatas of the ten directions, such as the Tathāgatas Śākyamuni, Amitābha, Akṣobhya, Ratnaśrī, Ratnārcis, Ratnacaṇdra, Ratnavyūha, Duṣprasāha, Sarvārthasiddha, Ratnabahula, Siṁhakīrti, Siṃhasvara, and so forth; and when they come they teach the door of Dharma called the "Secrets of the Tathāgatas" and then depart.[23] That is the seventh strange and wonderful thing.

Furthermore, reverend Śāriputra, all the splendors of the abodes of the gods and all the splendors of the fields of the Buddhas shine forth in this house. That is the eighth strange and wonderful thing.

Reverend Śāriputra, these eight strange and wonderful things are seen in this house. Who then, seeing such inconceivable things, would believe the teaching of the disciples?

Śāriputra: Goddess, what prevents you from transforming yourself out of your female state?[24]

Goddess: Although I have sought my "female state" for these twelve years, I have not yet found it. Reverend Śāriputra, if a magician were to incarnate a woman by magic, would you ask her, "What prevents you from transforming yourself out of your female state?"

Śāriputra: No! Such a woman would not really exist, so what would there be to transform?

Goddess: Just so, reverend Śāriputra, all things do not really exist. Now, would you think, "What prevents one whose nature is that of a magical incarnation from transforming herself out of her female state?"

Thereupon, the goddess employed her magical power to cause the elder Śāriputra to appear in her form and to cause herself to appear in his form. Then the goddess, transformed into Śāriputra, said to Śāriputra, transformed into a goddess, "Reverend Śāriputra, what prevents you from transforming yourself out of your female state?"

And Śāriputra, transformed into the goddess, replied, "I no longer appear in the form of a male! My body has changed into the body of a woman! I do not know what to transform!"

The goddess continued, "If the elder could again change out of the female state, then all women could also change out of their female states. All women appear in the form of women in just the same way as the elder appears in the form of a woman. While they are not women in reality, they appear in the form of women. With this in mind, the Buddha said, 'In all things, there is neither male nor female.'"

Then, the goddess released her magical power and each returned to his ordinary form. She then said to him, "Reverend Śāriputra, what have you done with your female form?"

Śāriputra: I neither made it nor did I change it.

Goddess: Just so, all things are neither made nor changed, and that they are not made and not changed, that is the teaching of the Buddha.[25]

Śāriputra: Goddess, where will you be born when you transmigrate after death?

Goddess: I will be born where all the magical incarnations of the Tathāgata are born.

Śāriputra: But the emanated incarnations of the Tathāgata do not transmigrate nor are they born.

Goddess: All things and living beings are just the same; they do not transmigrate nor are they born!

Śāriputra: Goddess, how soon will you attain the perfect enlightenment of Buddhahood?

Goddess: At such time as you, elder, become endowed once more with the qualities of an ordinary individual, then will I attain the perfect enlightenment of Buddhahood.

Śāriputra: Goddess, it is impossible that I should become endowed once more with the qualities of an ordinary individual.

Goddess: Just so, reverend Śāriputra, it is impossible that I should attain the perfect enlightenment of Buddhahood! Why? Because perfect enlightenment stands upon the impossible. Because it is impossible, no one attains the perfect enlightenment of Buddhahood.

Śāriputra: But the Tathāgata has declared: "The Tathāgatas, who are as numerous as the sands of the Ganges, have attained perfect Buddhahood, are attaining perfect Buddhahood, and will go on attaining perfect Buddhahood."

Goddess: Reverend Śāriputra, the expression, "the Buddhas of the past, present and future," is a conventional expression made up of a certain number of syllables. The Buddhas are neither past, nor present, nor future. Their enlightenment transcends the three times! But tell me, elder, have you attained sainthood?

Śāriputra: It is attained, because there is no attainment.

Goddess: Just so, there is perfect enlightenment because there is no attainment of perfect enlightenment.

Then the Licchavi Vimalakīrti said to the venerable elder Śāriputra, "Reverend Śāriputra, this goddess has already served ninety-two million billion Buddhas. She plays with the superknowledges. She has truly succeeded in all her vows. She has gained the tolerance of the birthlessness of things. She has actually attained irreversibility. She can live wherever she wishes on the strength of her vow to develop living beings."

8

The Family of the Tathāgatas[1]

Then, the crown prince Mañjuśrī said to the Licchavi Vimalakīrti, "Noble sir, how does the bodhisattva follow the way to attain the qualities of the Buddha?"

Vimalakīrti replied, "Mañjuśrī, when the bodhisattva follows the wrong way, he follows the way to attain the qualities of the Buddha."

Mañjuśrī continued, "How does the bodhisattva follow the wrong way?"

Vimalakīrti replied, "Even should he enact the five deadly sins, he feels no malice, violence, or hate. Even should he go into the hells, he remains free of all taint of passions. Even should he go into the states of the animals, he remains free of darkness and ignorance. When he goes into the states of the asuras, he remains free of pride, conceit, and arrogance. When he goes into the realm of the lord of death, he accumulates the stores of merit and wisdom. When he goes into the states of motionlessness and immateriality, he does not dissolve therein.

"He may follow the ways of desire, yet he stays free of attachment to the enjoyments of desire. He may follow the ways of hatred, yet he feels no anger to any living being. He may follow the ways of folly, yet he is ever conscious with the wisdom of firm understanding.

"He may follow the ways of avarice, yet he gives away all internal and external things without regard even for his own life. He may follow the ways of immorality, yet, seeing the horror of even the slightest transgressions, he lives by the ascetic practices and austerities. He may follow the ways of wickedness and anger, yet he remains utterly free of malice and lives by love. He may follow the ways of laziness, yet his efforts are uninterrupted as he strives in the cultivation of roots of virtue. He may follow the ways of sensuous distraction, yet, naturally concentrated, his contemplation is not dissipated. He may follow the ways of false wisdom, yet, having reached the transcendence of wisdom, he is expert in all mundane and transcendental sciences.

"He may show the ways of sophistry and contention, yet he is always conscious of ultimate meanings and has perfected the use of liberative techniques. He may show the ways of pride, yet he serves as a bridge and a ladder for all people. He may show the ways of the passions, yet he is utterly dispassionate and naturally pure. He may follow the ways of the Māras, yet he does not really accept their authority in regard to his knowledge of the qualities of the Buddha. He may follow the ways of the disciples, yet he lets living beings hear the teaching they have not heard before.[2] He may follow the ways of the solitary sages, yet he is inspired with great compassion in order to develop all living beings.

"He may follow the ways of the poor, yet he holds in his hand a jewel of inexhaustible wealth.[3] He may follow the ways of cripples, yet he is beautiful and well adorned with the auspicious signs and marks. He may follow the ways of those of lowly birth, yet, through his accumulation of the stores of merit and wisdom, he is born in the family of the Tathāgatas. He may follow the ways of the weak, the ugly, and the wretched, yet he is beautiful to look upon, and his body is like that of Nārāyana.

"He may manifest to living beings the ways of the sick and the unhappy, yet he has entirely conquered and transcended the fear of death.

"He may follow the ways of the rich, yet he is without acquisitiveness and often reflects upon the notion of impermanence. He may show himself engaged in dancing with harem girls, yet he cleaves to solitude, having crossed the swamp of desire.

"He follows the ways of the dumb and the incoherent, yet, having acquired the power of incantations, he is adorned with a varied eloquence.[4]

"He follows the ways of the heterodox without ever becoming heterodox. He follows the ways of all the world, yet he reverses all states of existence. He follows the way of liberation without ever abandoning the progress of the world.

"Mañjuśrī, thus does the bodhisattva follow the wrong ways, thereby following the way to the qualities of the Buddha."

Then, the Licchavi Vimalakīrti said to the crown prince Mañjuśrī, "Mañjuśrī, what is the 'family of the Tathāgatas'?"

Mañjuśrī replied, "Noble sir, the family of the Tathāgatas consists of all basic egoism; of ignorance and the thirst for existence; of lust, hate, and folly; of the four misapprehensions, of the five obscurations, of the six media of sense, of the seven abodes of consciousness, of the eight false paths, of the nine causes of irritation, of the paths of ten sins.[5] Such is the family of the Tathāgatas. In short, noble sir, the sixty-two kinds of convictions constitute the family of the Tathāgatas!"

Vimalakīrti: Mañjuśri, with what in mind do you say so?

Mañjuśrī: Noble sir, one who stays in the fixed determination of the vision of the uncreated is not capable of conceiving the spirit of unexcelled perfect enlightenment. However, one who lives among created things, in the mines of passions, without seeing any truth, is indeed capable of conceiving the spirit of unexcelled perfect enlightenment.

Noble sir, flowers like the blue lotus, the red lotus, the white lotus, the water lily, and the moon lily do not grow on the dry ground in the wilderness, but do grow in the swamps and mud banks. Just so, the Buddha-qualities do not grow in living beings certainly destined for the uncreated but do grow in those living beings who are like swamps and mud banks of passions. Likewise, as seeds do not grow in the sky but do grow in the earth, so the Buddha-qualities do not grow in those determined for the absolute but do grow in those who conceive the spirit of enlightenment, after having produced a Sumeru-like mountain of egoistic views.[6]

Noble sir, through these considerations one can understand that all passions constitute the family of the Tathāgatas. For example, noble sir, without going out into the great ocean, it is impossible to find precious, priceless pearls. Likewise, without going into the ocean of passions, it is impossible to obtain the mind of omniscience.

Then, the elder Mahākāśyapa applauded the crown prince Mañjuśrī: "Good! Good, Mañjuśrī! This is indeed well spoken! This is right! The passions do indeed constitute the family of the Tathāgatas. How can such as we, the disciples, conceive the spirit of enlightenment, or become fully enlightened in regard to the qualities of the Buddha? Only those guilty of the five deadly sins can conceive the spirit of enlightenment and can attain Buddhahood, which is the full accomplishment of the qualities of the Buddha!

"Just as, for example, the five desire objects[7] have no impression or effect on those bereft of faculties, even so all the qualities of the Buddha have no impression or effect on the disciples, who have abandoned all adherences. Thus, the disciples can never appreciate those qualities.[8]

"Therefore, Mañjuśrī, the ordinary individual is grateful to the Tathāgata, but the disciples are not grateful. Why? The ordinary individuals, upon learning of the virtues of the Buddha, conceive the spirit of unexcelled perfect enlightenment, in order to insure the uninterrupted continuity of the heritage of the Three Jewels; but the disciples, although they may hear of the qualities, powers, and fearlessnesses of the Buddha until the end of their days, are not capable of conceiving the spirit of unexcelled perfect enlightenment."

Thereupon, the bodhisattva Sarvarūpasaṃdarśana, who was present in that assembly, addressed the Licchavi Vimalakīrti: "Householder, where are your father and mother, your children, your wife, your servants, your maids, your laborers, and your attendants? Where are your friends, your relatives, and your kinsmen? Where are your servants, your horses, your elephants, your chariots, your bodyguards, and your bearers?"

Thus addressed, the Licchavi Vimalakīrti spoke the following verses to the bodhisattva Sarvarūpasaṃdarśana:

Of the true bodhisattvas,
The mother is the transcendence of wisdom,
The father is the skill in liberative techique;[9]
The Leaders are born of such parents.

Their wife is the joy in the Dharma,
Love and compassion are their daughters,
The Dharma and the truth are their sons;
And their home is deep thought on the meaning of voidness.

All the passions are their disciples,
Controlled at will.
Their friends are the aids to enlightenment;[10]
Thereby they realize supreme enlightenment.

Their companions, ever with them,
Are the six transcendences.
Their consorts are the means of unification,[11]
Their music is the teaching of the Dharma.

The incantations make their garden,
Which blossoms with the flowers of the factors of enlightenment,
With trees of the great wealth of the Dharma,[12]
And fruits of the gnosis of liberation.

Their pool consists of the eight liberations,
Filled with the water of concentration,
Covered with the lotuses of the seven purities[13]—
Who bathes therein becomes immaculate.

Their bearers are the six superknowledges,
Their vehicle is the unexcelled Mahāyāna,
Their driver is the spirit of enlightenment,
And their path is the eightfold peace.

Their ornaments are the auspicious signs,
And the eighty marks;
Their garland[14] is virtuous aspiration,
And their clothing is good conscience and consideration.

Their wealth is the holy Dharma,
And their business is its teaching,
Their great income is pure practice,
And it is dedicated to the supreme enlightenment.

Their bed[15] consists of the four contemplations,
And its spread is the pure livelihood,
And their awakening consists of gnosis,
Which is constant learning and meditation.

Their food is the ambrosia of the teachings,[16]
And their drink is the juice of liberation.
Their bath is pure aspiration,
And morality their unguent and perfume.

Having conquered the enemy passions,
They are the invincible heroes.
Having subdued the four Māras,
They raise their standard on the field of enlightenment.

They manifest birth voluntarily,
Yet they are not born, nor do they originate.
They shine in all the fields of the Buddhas,
Just like the rising sun.

Though they worship Buddhas by the millions,
With every conceivable offering,
They never dwell upon the least difference
Between the Buddhas and themselves.

They journey through all Buddha-fields
In order to bring benefit to living beings,
Yet they see those fields as just like empty space,
Free of any conceptual notions of "living beings."[17]

The fearless bodhisattvas can manifest,
All in a single instant,
The forms, sounds, and manners of behavior
Of all living beings.[18]

Although they recognize the deeds of Māras,
They can get along even with these Māras;
For even such activities may be manifested
By those perfected in liberative technique.

They play with illusory manifestations
In order to develop living beings,
Showing themselves to be old or sick,
And even manifesting their own deaths.[19]

They demonstrate the burning of the earth
In the consuming flames of the world's end,
In order to demonstrate impermanence
To living beings with the notion of permanence.[20]

Invited by hundreds of thousands of living beings,
All in the same country,
They partake of offerings at the homes of all,
And dedicate all for the sake of enlightenment.[21]

They excel in all esoteric sciences,
And in the many different crafts,
And they bring forth the happiness
Of all living beings.[22]

By devoting themselves as monks
To all the strange sects of the world,
They develop all those beings
Who have attached themselves to dogmatic views.[23]

They may become suns or moons,
Indras, Brahmās, or lords of creatures,
They may become fire or water
Or earth or wind.[24]

During the short aeons of maladies,
They become the best holy medicine;
They make beings well and happy,
And bring about their liberation.[25]

During the short aeons of famine,
They become food and drink.
Having first alleviated thirst and hunger,
They teach the Dharma to living beings.[26]

During the short aeons of swords,
They meditate on love,
Introducing to nonviolence
Hundreds of millions of living beings.[27]

In the middle of great battles
They remain impartial to both sides;
For bodhisattvas of great strength
Delight in reconciliation of conflict.[28]

In order to help the living beings,
They voluntarily descend into
The hells which are attached
To all the inconceivable buddha-fields.[29]

They manifest their lives
In all the species of the animal kingdom,
Teaching the Dharma everywhere.
Thus they are called "Leaders."[30]

They display sensual enjoyment to the worldlings,
And trances to the meditative.
They completely conquer the Māras,
And allow them no chance to prevail.[31]

Just as it can be shown that a lotus
Cannot exist in the center of a fire,
So they show the ultimate unreality
Of both pleasures and trances.[32]

They intentionally become courtesans
In order to win men over,
And, having caught them with the hook of desire,
They establish them in the buddha-gnosis.[33]

In order to help living beings,
They always become chieftains,
Captains, priests, and ministers,
Or even prime ministers.[34]

For the sake of the poor,
They become inexhaustible treasures,
Causing those to whom they give their gifts
To conceive the spirit of enlightenment.[35]

They become invincible champions,
For the sake of the proud and the vain,
And, having conquered all their pride,
They start them on the quest for enlightenment.[36]

They always stand at the head
Of those terrified with fright,
And, having bestowed fearlessness upon them,
They develop them toward enlightenment.[37]

They become great holy men,
With the superknowledges and pure continence,
And thus induce living beings to the morality
Of tolerance, gentleness, and discipline.[38]

Here in the world, they fearlessly behold
Those who are masters to be served,
And they become their servants or slaves,
Or serve as their disciples.[39]

Well trained in liberative technique,
They demonstrate all activities,
Whichever possibly may be a means
To make beings delight in the Dharma.[40]

Their practices are infinite;
  And their spheres of influence are infinite;
Having perfected an infinite wisdom,
  They liberate an infinity of living beings.[41]

Even for the Buddhas themselves,
  During a million aeons,
Or even a hundred million aeons,
  It would be hard to express all their virtues.[42]

Except for some inferior living beings,
  Without any intelligence at all,
Is there anyone with any discernment
  Who, having heard this teaching,
Would not wish for the supreme enlightenment?

9

The Dharma-Door of Nonduality

Then, the Licchavi Vimalakīrti asked those bodhisattvas, "Good sirs, please explain how the bodhisattvas enter the Dharma-door of nonduality!"[1]

The bodhisattva Dharmavikurvaṇa[2] declared, "Noble sir, production and destruction are two, but what is not produced and does not occur cannot be destroyed. Thus the attainment of the tolerance of the birthlessness of things[3] is the entrance into nonduality."

The bodhisattva Śrīgandha declared, "'I' and 'mine' are two. If there is no presumption of a self, there will be no possessiveness. Thus, the absence of presumption is the entrance into nonduality."

The bodhisattva Śrīkūṭa declared, "'Defilement' and 'purification' are two. When there is thorough knowledge of defilement, there will be no conceit about purification. The path leading to the complete conquest of all conceit is the entrance into nonduality."

The bodhisattva Bhadrajyotis declared, "'Distraction' and 'attention' are two. When there is no distraction, there will be no attention, no mentation, and no mental intensity. Thus, the absence of mental intensity is the entrance into nonduality."

The bodhisattva Subāhu declared, "'Bodhisattva-spirit' and 'disciple-spirit' are two. When both are seen to resemble an illusory spirit, there is no bodhisattva-spirit, nor any disciple-spirit. Thus, the sameness of natures of spirits is the entrance into nonduality."

The bodhisattva Animiṣa declared, "'Grasping' and 'nongrasping' are two. What is not grasped is not perceived, and what is not perceived is neither presumed nor repudiated.[4] Thus, the inaction and noninvolvement of all things is the entrance into nonduality."

The bodhisattva Sunetra declared, "'Uniqueness' and 'characterlessness' are two. Not to presume or construct something is neither to establish its uniqueness nor to establish its characterlessness. To penetrate the equality of these two is to enter nonduality."[5]

The bodhisattva Tiṣya declared, "'Good' and 'evil' are two. Seeking neither good nor evil, the understanding of the nonduality of the significant and the meaningless is the entrance into nonduality."

The bodhisattva Siṃha declared, "'Sinfulness' and 'sinlessness' are two. By means of the diamond-like wisdom that pierces to the quick, not to be bound or liberated is the entrance into nonduality."

The bodhisattva Siṃhamati declared, "To say, 'This is impure' and 'This is immaculate' makes for duality. One who, attaining equanimity, forms no conception of impurity or immaculateness, yet is not utterly without conception, has equanimity without any attainment of equanimity—he enters the absence of conceptual knots. Thus, he enters into nonduality."

The bodhisattva Śuddhādhimukti declared, "To say, 'This is happiness' and 'That is misery' is dualism. One who is free of all calculations, through the extreme purity of gnosis—his mind is aloof, like empty space; and thus he enters into nonduality."[6]

The bodhisattva Nārāyana declared, "To say, 'This is mundane' and 'That is transcendental' is dualism. This world has the nature of voidness, so there is neither transcendence nor involvement, neither progress nor standstill. Thus, neither to transcend nor to be involved, neither to go nor to stop— this is the entrance into nonduality."

The bodhisattva Dāntamati declared, "'Life' and 'liberation'[7] are dualistic. Having seen the nature of life, one neither belongs to it nor is one utterly liberated from it. Such understanding is the entrance into nonduality."

The bodhisattva Pratyakṣadarśana declared, "'Destructible' and 'indestructible' are dualistic. What is destroyed is ultimately destroyed. What is ultimately destroyed does not become destroyed; hence, it is called 'indestructible.' What is indestructible is instantaneous, and what is instantaneous is indestructible. The experience of such is called 'the entrance into the principle of nonduality.'"[8]

The bodhisattva Parigūḍha declared, "'Self' and 'selflessness' are dualistic. Since the existence of self cannot be perceived, what is there to be made 'selfless'? Thus, the nondualism of the vision of their nature is the entrance into nonduality."

The bodhisattva Vidyuddeva declared, "'Knowledge' and 'ignorance' are dualistic. The natures of ignorance and knowledge are the same, for ignorance is undefined, incalculable, and beyond the sphere of thought. The realization of this is the entrance into nonduality."

The bodhisattva Priyadarśana declared, "Matter itself is void. Voidness does not result from the destruction of matter, but the nature of matter is itself voidness. Therefore, to speak of voidness on the one hand, and of matter, or of sensation, or of intellect, or of motivation, or of consciousness on the other—is entirely dualistic. Consciousness itself is voidness. Voidness does not result from the destruction of consciousness, but the nature of consciousness is itself voidness. Such understanding of the five compulsive aggregates and the knowledge of them as such by means of gnosis is the entrance into nonduality."[9]

The bodhisattva Prabhāketu declared, "To say that the four main elements are one thing and the etheric space-element another is dualistic. The four main elements are themselves the nature of space. The past itself is also the nature of space. The future itself is also the nature of space. Likewise, the present itself is also the nature of space. The gnosis that penetrates the elements in such a way is the entrance into nonduality."[10]

The bodhisattva Pramati declared, "'Eye' and 'form' are dualistic. To understand the eye correctly, and not to have attachment, aversion, or confusion with regard to form—that is called 'peace.' Similarly, 'ear' and 'sound,' 'nose' and 'smell,' 'tongue' and 'taste,' 'body' and 'touch,' and 'mind' and 'phenomena'—all are dualistic. But to know the mind, and to be neither attached, averse, nor confused with regard to phenomena—that is called 'peace.' To live in such peace is to enter into nonduality."[11]

The bodhisattva Akṣayamati declared, "The dedication of generosity for the sake of attaining omniscience is dualistic. The nature of generosity is itself omniscience, and the nature of omniscience itself is total dedication. Likewise, it is dualistic to dedicate morality, tolerance, effort, meditation, and wisdom for the sake of omniscience. Omniscience is the nature of wisdom, and total dedication is the nature of omniscience. Thus, the entrance into this principle of uniqueness is the entrance into nonduality."

The bodhisattva Gambhīramati declared, "It is dualistic to say that voidness is one thing, signlessness another, and wishlessness still another. What is void has no sign. What has no sign has no wish. Where there is no wish there is no process of thought, mind, or consciousness. To see the doors of all liberations in the door of one liberation is the entrance into nonduality."

The bodhisattva Śāntendriya declared, "It is dualistic to say 'Buddha,' 'Dharma,' and 'Saṅgha.' The Dharma is itself the nature of the Buddha, the Saṅgha is itself the nature of the Dharma, and all of them are uncompounded. The uncompounded is infinite space, and the processes of all things are equivalent to infinite space. Adjustment to this is the entrance into nonduality."

The bodhisattva Apratihatanetra declared, "It is dualistic to refer to 'aggregates' and to the 'cessation of aggregates.' Aggregates themselves are cessation. Why? The egoistic views of aggregates, being unproduced themselves, do not exist ultimately. Hence such views do not really conceptualize 'These are aggregates' or 'These aggregates cease.' Ultimately, they have no such discriminative constructions and no such conceptualizations. Therefore, such views have themselves the nature of cessation. Nonoccurrence and nondestruction are the entrance into nonduality."

The bodhisattva Suvinīta declared, "Physical, verbal, and mental vows do not exist dualistically. Why? These things have the nature of inactivity. The nature of inactivity of the body is the same as the nature of inactivity of speech, whose nature of inactivity is the same as the nature of inactivity of the mind. It is necessary to know and to understand this fact of the ultimate inactivity of all things, for this knowledge is the entrance into nonduality."

The bodhisattva Puṇyakṣetra declared, "It is dualistic to consider actions meritorious, sinful, or neutral.[12] The non-undertaking of meritorious, sinful, and neutral actions is not dualistic. The intrinsic nature of all such actions is voidness, wherein ultimately there is neither merit, nor sin, nor neutrality, nor action itself. The nonaccomplishment of such actions is the entrance into nonduality."

The bodhisattva Padmavyūha declared, "Dualism is produced from obsession with self, but true understanding of self does not result in dualism. Who thus abides in nonduality is without ideation, and that absence of ideation is the entrance into nonduality."

The bodhisattva Śrīgarbha declared, "Duality is constituted by perceptual manifestation. Nonduality is objectlessness. Therefore, nongrasping and nonrejection is the entrance into nonduality."

The bodhisattva Candrottara declared, "'Darkness' and 'light' are dualistic, but the absence of both darkness and light is nonduality. Why? At the time of absorption in cessation,[13] there is neither darkness nor light, and likewise with the natures of all things. The entrance into this equanimity is the entrance into nonduality."

The bodhisattva Ratnamudrāhasta declared, "It is dualistic to detest the world and to rejoice in liberation, and neither detesting the world nor rejoicing in liberation is nonduality. Why? Liberation can be found where there is bondage, but where there is ultimately no bondage where is there need for liberation? The mendicant who is neither bound nor liberated does not experience any like or any dislike and thus he enters nonduality."

The bodhisattva Maṇikūṭarāja declared, "It is dualistic to speak of good paths and bad paths. One who is on the path is not concerned with good or bad paths. Living in such unconcern, he entertains no concepts of 'path' or 'nonpath.' Understanding the nature of concepts, his mind does not engage in duality. Such is the entrance into nonduality."

The bodhisattva Satyarata declared, "It is dualistic to speak of 'true' and 'false.' When one sees truly, one does not ever see any truth,[14] so how could one see falsehood? Why? One does not see with the physical eye, one sees with the eye of wisdom. And with the wisdom-eye one sees only insofar as there is neither sight nor nonsight. There, where there is neither sight nor nonsight, is the entrance into nonduality."

When the bodhisattvas had given their explanations, they all addressed the crown prince Mañjuśrī: "Mañjuśrī, what is the bodhisattva's entrance into nonduality?"

Mañjuśrī replied, "Good sirs, you have all spoken well. Nevertheless, all your explanations are themselves dualistic. To know no one teaching, to express nothing, to say nothing, to explain nothing, to announce nothing, to indicate nothing, and to designate nothing—that is the entrance into nonduality."

Then, the crown prince Mañjuśrī said to the Licchavi Vimalakīrti, "We have all given our own teachings, noble sir. Now, may you elucidate the teaching of the entrance into the principle of nonduality!"

Thereupon, the Licchavi Vimalakīrti kept his silence, saying nothing at all.[15]

The crown prince Mañjuśrī applauded the Licchavi Vimalakīrti: "Excellent! Excellent, noble sir! This is indeed the entrance into the nonduality of the bodhisattvas. Here there is no use for syllables, sounds, and ideas."

When these teachings had been declared, five thousand bodhisattvas entered the door of the Dharma of nonduality and attained tolerance of the birthlessness of things.

10

The Feast Brought by the Emanated Incarnation

Thereupon, the venerable Śāriputra thought to himself, "If these great bodhisattvas do not adjourn before noontime, when are they going to eat?"[1]

The Licchavi Vimalakīrti, knowing telepathically the thought of the venerable Śāriputra, spoke to him: "Reverend Śāriputra, the Tathāgata has taught the eight liberations. You should concentrate on those liberations, listening to the Dharma with a mind free of preoccupations with material things. Just wait a minute, reverend Śāriputra, and you will eat such food as you have never before tasted."

Then, the Licchavi Vimalakīrti set himself in such a concentration and performed such a miraculous feat that those bodhisattvas and those great disciples were enabled to see the universe called Sarvagandhasugandhā,[2] which is located in the direction of the zenith, beyond as many buddha-fields as there are sands in forty-two Ganges rivers. There the Tathāgata named Sugandhakūṭa[3] resides, lives, and is manifest. In that universe, the trees emit a fragrance that far surpasses all the fragrances, human and divine, of all the buddha-fields of the ten directions. In that universe, even the names "disciple" and "solitary sage" do not exist, and the Tathāgata Sugandhakūṭa teaches the Dharma to a gathering of bodhisattvas only. In that universe, all the houses, the avenues, the parks, and the palaces are made of various perfumes, and the fragrance of the food eaten by those bodhisattvas pervades immeasurable universes.

At this time, the Tathāgata Sugandhakūṭa sat down with his bodhisattvas to take his meal, and the deities called Gandhavyūhāhāra, who were all devoted to the Mahāyāna, served and attended upon the Buddha and his bodhisattvas. Everyone in the gathering at the house of Vimalakīrti was able to see distinctly this universe wherein the Tathāgata Sugandhakūṭa and his bodhisattvas were taking their meal.

The Licchavi Vimalakīrti addressed the whole gathering of bodhisattvas:

"Good sirs, is there any among you who would like to go to that buddha-field to bring back some food?"

But, restrained by the supernatural power of Mañjuśrī, none of them volunteered to go.

The Licchavi Vimalakīrti said to crown prince Mañjuśrī, "Mañjuśrī, are you not ashamed of such a gathering?"

Mañjuśrī replied, "Noble sir, did not the Tathāgata declare, 'Those who are unlearned should not be despised'?"

Then, the Licchavi Vimalakīrti, without rising from his couch, magically emanated an incarnation-bodhisattva, whose body was of golden color, adorned with the auspicious signs and marks, and of such an appearance that he outshone the whole assembly. The Licchavi Vimalakīrti addressed that incarnated bodhisattva: "Noble son, go in the direction of the zenith and when you have crossed as many buddha-fields as there are sands in forty-two Ganges rivers, you will reach a universe called Sarvagandhasugandhā, where you will find the Tathāgata Sugandhakūṭa taking his meal. Go to him and, having bowed down at his feet, make the following request of him:

" 'The Licchavi Vimalakīrti bows down one hundred thousand times at your feet, O Lord, and asks after your health—if you have but little trouble, little discomfort, little unrest; if you are strong, well, without complaint, and living in touch with supreme happiness.'

"Having thus asked after his health, you should request of him: 'Vimalakīrti asks the Lord to give me the remains of your meal, with which he will accomplish the buddha-work in the universe called Sahā. Thus, those living beings with inferior aspirations will be inspired with lofty aspirations, and the good name[4] of the Tathāgata will be celebrated far and wide."

At that, the incarnated bodhisattva said, "Very good!" to the Licchavi Vimalakīrti and obeyed his instructions. In sight of all the bodhisattvas, he turned his face upward and was gone, and they saw him no more.[5] When he reached the universe Sarvagandhasugandhā, he bowed down at the feet of the Tathāgata Sugandhakūṭa and said, "Lord, the bodhisattva Vimalakīrti, bowing down at the feet of the Lord, greets the Lord, saying: 'Do you have little trouble, little discomfort, and little unrest? Are you strong, well, without complaint, and living in touch with the supreme happiness?' He then requests, having bowed down one hundred thousand times at the feet of the Lord: 'May the Lord be gracious and give to me the remains of his meal in order to accomplish the buddha-work in the universe called Sahā. Then, those living beings who aspire to inferior ways may gain the intelligence to aspire to the great Dharma of the Buddha, and the name of the Buddha will be celebrated far and wide.' "

At that the bodhisattvas of the buddha-field of the Tathāgata Sugandhakūṭa were astonished and asked the Tathāgata Sugandhakūṭa, "Lord, where is there such a great being as this? Where is the universe Sahā? What does he mean by 'those who aspire to inferior ways'?"[6]

Having thus been questioned by those bodhisattvas, the Tathāgata Sugandhakūṭa said, "Noble sons, the universe Sahā exists beyond as many buddha-fields in the direction of the nadir as there are sands in forty-two Ganges rivers. There the Tathāgata Śākyamuni teaches the Dharma to living beings who aspire to inferior ways, in that buddha-field tainted with five corruptions. There the bodhisattva Vimalakīrti, who lives in the inconceivable liberation, teaches the Dharma to the bodhisattvas. He sends this incarnation-bodhisattva here in order to celebrate my name, in order to show the advantages of this universe, and in order to increase the roots of virtue of those bodhisattvas."

The bodhisattvas exclaimed, "How great must that bodhisattva be himself if his magical incarnation is thus endowed with supernatural power, strength, and fearlessness!"

The Tathāgata said, "The greatness of that bodhisattva is such that he sends magical incarnations to all the buddha-fields of the ten directions, and all these incarnations accomplish the buddha-work for all the living beings in all those buddha-fields."[7]

Then, the Tathāgata Sugandhakūṭa poured some of his food, impregnated with all perfumes, into a fragrant vessel and gave it to the incarnation-bodhisattva. And the ninety million bodhisattvas of that universe volunteered to go along with him: "Lord, we also would like to go to that universe Sahā, to see, honor, and serve the Buddha Śākyamuni and to see Vimalakīrti and those bodhisattvas."

The Tathāgata declared, "Noble sons, go ahead if you think it is the right time. But, lest those living beings become mad and intoxicated, go without your perfumes. And, lest those living beings of the Sahā world become jealous of you, change your bodies to hide your beauty. And do not conceive ideas of contempt and aversion for that universe. Why? Noble sons, a buddha-field is a field of pure space, but the Lord Buddhas, in order to develop living beings, do not reveal all at once the pure realm of the Buddha."

Then the incarnation-bodhisattva took the food and departed with the ninety million bodhisattvas and, by the power of the Buddha and the supernatural operation of Vimalakīrti, disappeared from that universe Sarvagandhasugandhā and stood again in the house of Vimalakīrti in a fraction of a second. The Licchavi Vimalakīrti created ninety million lion-thrones exactly like those already there, and the bodhisattvas were seated.

Then, the incarnation-bodhisattva gave the vessel full of food to Vimalakīrti, and the fragrance of that food permeated the entire great city of Vaiśālī and its sweet perfume spread throughout one hundred universes. Within the city of Vaiśālī, the brahmans, householders, and even the Licchavi chieftain Candra-cchattra, having noticed this fragrance, were amazed and filled with wonder. They were so cleansed in body and mind that they came at once to the house of Vimalakīrti, along with all eighty-four thousand of the Licchavis.

Seeing there the bodhisattvas seated on the high, wide, and beautiful lion-thrones, they were filled with admiration and great joy. They all bowed down to those great disciples and bodhisattvas and then sat down to one side. And the gods of the earth, the gods of the desire-world, and the gods of the material world, attracted by the perfume, also came to the house of Vimalakīrti.

Then, the Licchavi Vimalakīrti spoke to the elder Śāriputra and the great disciples: "Reverends, eat of the food of the Tathāgata! It is ambrosia perfumed by the great compassion. But do not fix your minds in narrow-minded attitudes,[8] lest you be unable to receive its gift."

But some of the disciples had already had the thought: "How can such a huge multitude eat such a small amount of food?"

Then the incarnation-bodhisattva said to those disciples, "Do not compare, venerable ones, your own wisdom and merits with the wisdom and the merits of the Tathāgata! Why? For example, the four great oceans might dry up, but this food would never be exhausted. If all living beings were to eat for an aeon an amount of this food equal to Mount Sumeru in size, it would not be depleted. Why? Issued from inexhaustible morality, concentration, and wisdom, the remains of the food of the Tathāgata contained in this vessel cannot be exhausted."

Indeed, the entire gathering was satisfied by that food, and the food was not at all depleted. Having eaten that food, there arose in the bodies of those bodhisattvas, disciples, Śakras, Brahmās, Lokapālas, and other living beings, a bliss just like the bliss of the bodhisattvas of the universe Sarvasukhamaṇḍitā. And from all the pores of their skin arose a perfume like that of the trees that grow in the universe Sarvagandhasugandhā.[9]

Then, the Licchavi Vimalakīrti knowingly addressed those bodhisattvas who had come from the buddha-field of the Lord Tathāgata Sugandhakūṭa: "Noble sirs, how does the Tathāgata Sugandhakūṭa teach his Dharma?"

They replied, "The Tathāgata does not teach the Dharma by means of sound and language. He disciplines the bodhisattvas only by means of perfumes. At the foot of each perfume-tree sits a bodhisattva, and the trees emit perfumes like this one. From the moment they smell that perfume, the bodhisattvas attain the concentration called 'source of all bodhisattva-virtues.' From the moment they attain that concentration, all the bodhisattvas-virtues are produced in them."

Those bodhisattvas then asked the Licchavi Vimalakīrti, "How does the Buddha Śākyamuni teach the Dharma?"

Vimalakīrti replied, "Good sirs, these living beings here are hard to discipline. Therefore, he teaches them with discourses appropriate for the disciplining of the wild and uncivilized. How does he discipline the wild and uncivilized? What discourses are appropriate? Here they are:

" 'This is hell. This is the animal world. This is the world of the lord of death. These are the adversities. These are the rebirths with crippled faculties. These are physical misdeeds, and these are the retributions for physical misdeeds. These are verbal misdeeds, and these are the retributions for verbal misdeeds. These are mental misdeeds, and these are the retributions for mental misdeeds. This is killing. This is stealing. This is sexual misconduct. This is lying. This is backbiting. This is harsh speech. This is frivolous speech. This is covetousness. This is malice. This is false view.[10] These are their retributions. This is miserliness, and this is its effect. This is immorality. This is hatred. This is sloth. This is the fruit of sloth. This is false wisdom and this is the fruit of false wisdom. These are the transgressions of the precepts. This is the vow of personal liberation. This should be done and that should not be done. This is proper and that should be abandoned. This is an obscuration and that is without obscuration. This is sin and that rises above sin. This is the path and that is the wrong path. This is virtue and that is evil. This is blameworthy and that is blameless. This is defiled and that is immaculate. This is mundane and that is transcendental. This is compounded and that is uncompounded. This is passion and that is purification. This is life and that is liberation.'[11]

"Thus, by means of these varied explanations of the Dharma, the Buddha trains the minds of those living beings who are just like wild horses. Just as wild horses or wild elephants will not be tamed unless the goad pierces them to the marrow, so living beings who are wild and hard to civilize are disciplined only by means of discourses about all kinds of miseries."

The bodhisattvas said, "Thus is established the greatness of the Buddha Śākyamuni! It is marvelous how, concealing his miraculous power, he civilizes the wild living beings who are poor and inferior. And the bodhisattvas who settle in a buddha-field of such intense hardships must have inconceivably great compassion!"[12]

The Licchavi Vimalakīrti declared, "So be it, good sirs! It is as you say. The great compassion of the bodhisattvas who reincarnate here is extremely firm. In a single lifetime in this universe, they accomplish much benefit for living beings. So much benefit for living beings could not be accomplished in the universe Sarvagandhasugandhā even in one hundred thousand aeons. Why? Good sirs, in this Sahā universe, there are ten virtuous practices which do not exist in any other buddha-field. What are these ten? Here they are: to win[13] the poor by generosity; to win the immoral by morality; to win the hateful by means of tolerance; to win the lazy by means of effort; to win the mentally troubled by means of concentration; to win the falsely wise by means of true wisdom; to show those suffering from the eight adversities how to rise above them; to teach the Mahāyāna to those of narrow-minded behavior;[14] to win those who have not produced the roots of virtue by means of the roots of virtue; and to develop living beings without interruption through the four means of unification. Those who engage in these ten virtuous practices do not exist in any other buddha-field."

Again the bodhisattvas asked, "How many qualities must a bodhisattva have, to go safe and sound to a pure buddha-field after he transmigrates at death away from this Sahā universe?"

Vimalakīrti replied, "After he transmigrates at death away from this Sahā universe, a bodhisattva must have eight qualities to reach a pure buddha-field safe and sound. What are the eight? He must resolve to himself: 'I must benefit all living beings, without seeking even the slightest benefit for myself. I must bear all the miseries of all living beings and give all my accumulated roots of virtue to all living beings. I must have no resentment toward any living being. I must rejoice in all bodhisattvas as if they were the Teacher.[15] I must not neglect any teachings, whether or not I have heard them before. I must control my mind, without coveting the gains of others, and without taking pride in gains of my own. I must examine my own faults and not blame others for their faults. I must take pleasure in being consciously aware and must truly undertake all virtues.'

"If a bodhisattva has these eight qualities, when he transmigrates at death away from the Sahā universe, he will go safe and sound to a pure buddha-field."

When the Licchavi Vimalakīrti and the crown prince Mañjuśrī had thus taught the Dharma to the multitude gathered there, one hundred thousand living beings conceived the spirit of unexcelled, perfect enlightenment, and ten thousand bodhisattvas attained the tolerance of the birthlessness of things.

11

Lesson of the Destructible and the Indestructible

Meanwhile, the area in which the Lord was teaching the Dharma in the garden of Āmrapālī expanded and grew larger, and the entire assembly appeared tinged with a golden hue. Thereupon, the venerable Ānanda asked the Buddha, "Lord, this expansion and enlargement of the garden of Āmrapālī and this golden hue of the assembly—what do these auspicious signs portend?"

The Buddha declared, "Ānanda, these auspicious signs portend that the Licchavi Vimalakīrti and the crown prince Mañjuśrī, attended by a great multitude, are coming into the presence of the Tathāgata."

At that moment the Licchavi Vimalakīrti said to the crown prince Mañjuśrī, "Mañjuśrī, let us take these many living beings into the presence of the Lord, so that they may see the Tathāgata and bow down to him!"

Mañjuśrī replied, "Noble sir, send them if you feel the time is right!"

Thereupon the Licchavi Vimalakīrti performed the miraculous feat of placing the entire assembly, replete with thrones, upon his right hand and then, having transported himself magically into the presence of the Buddha, placing it on the ground. He bowed down at the feet of the Buddha, circumambulated him to the right seven times with palms together, and withdrew to one side.

The bodhisattvas who had come from the buddha-field of the Tathāgata Sugandhakūṭa descended from their lion-thrones and, bowing down at the feet of the Buddha, placed their palms together in reverence and withdrew to one side. And the other bodhisattvas, great spiritual heroes, and the great disciples descended from their thrones likewise and, having bowed at the feet of the Buddha, withdrew to one side. Likewise all those Indras, Brahmās, Lokapālas, and gods bowed at the feet of the Buddha and withdrew to one side.

Then, the Buddha, having delighted those bodhisattvas with greetings, declared, "Noble sons, be seated upon your thrones!"

Thus commanded by the Buddha, they took their thrones.

The Buddha said to Śāriputra, "Śāriputra, did you see the miraculous performances of the bodhisattvas, those best of beings?"

"I have seen them, Lord."

"What concept did you produce toward them?"

"Lord, I produced the concept of inconceivability toward them. Their activities appeared inconceivable to me to the point that I was unable to think of them, to judge them, or even to imagine them."

Then the venerable Ānanda asked the Buddha, "Lord, what is this perfume, the likes of which I have never smelled before?"

The Buddha answered, "Ānanda, this perfume emanates from all the pores of all these bodhisattvas."

Śāriputra added, "Venerable Ānanda, this same perfume emanates from all our pores as well!"

> *Ānanda:* Where does the perfume come from?
>
> *Śāriputra:* The Licchavi Vimalakīrti obtained some food from the universe called Sarvagandhasugandhā, the buddha-field of the Tathāgata Sugandhakūṭa, and this perfume emanates from the bodies of all those who partook of that food.

Then the venerable Ānanda addressed the Licchavi Vimalakīrti: "How long will this perfume remain?"

> *Vimalakīrti:* Until it is digested.
>
> *Ānanda:* When will it be digested?
>
> *Vimalakīrti:* It will be digested in forty-nine days, and its perfume will emanate for seven days more after that, but there will be no trouble of indigestion during that time. Furthermore, reverend Ānanda, if monks who have not entered ultimate determination[1] eat this food, it will be digested when they enter that determination.[2] When those who have entered ultimate determination eat this food, it will not be digested until their minds are totally liberated. If living beings who have not conceived the spirit of unexcelled, perfect enlightenment eat this food, it will be digested when they conceive the spirit of unexcelled, perfect enlightenment.[3] If those who have conceived the spirit of perfect enlightenment eat this food, it will not be digested until they have attained tolerance.[4] And if those who have attained tolerance eat this food, it will be digested when they have become bodhisattvas one lifetime away from Buddhahood. Reverend Ānanda, it is like the medicine called "delicious," which reaches

> the stomach but is not digested until all poisons have been eliminated—only then is it digested. Thus, reverend Ānanda, this food is not digested until all the poisons of the passions have been eliminated—only then is it digested.

Then, the venerable Ānanda said to the Buddha, "Lord, it is wonderful that this food accomplishes the work of the Buddha!"

"So it is, Ānanda! It is as you say, Ānanda! There are buddha-fields that accomplish the buddha-work by means of bodhisattvas; those that do so by means of lights; those that do so by means of the tree of enlightenment; those that do so by means of the physical beauty and the marks of the Tathāgata; those that do so by means of religious robes; those that do so by means of food; those that do so by means of water; those that do so by means of gardens; those that do so by means of palaces; those that do so by means of mansions; those that do so by means of magical incarnations; those that do so by means of empty space; and those that do so by means of lights in the sky. Why is it so, Ānanda? Because by these various means, living beings become disciplined. Similarly, Ānanda, there are buddha-fields that accomplish the buddha-work by means of teaching living beings words, definitions, and examples, such as 'dreams,' 'images,' the 'reflection of the moon in water,' 'echoes,' 'illusions,' and 'mirages'; and those that accomplish the buddha-work by making words understandable. Also, Ānanda, there are utterly pure buddha-fields that accomplish the buddha-work for living beings without speech, by silence, inexpressibility, and unteachability. Ānanda, among all the activities, enjoyments, and practices of the Buddhas, there are none that do not accomplish the buddha-work, because all discipline living beings. Finally, Ānanda, the Buddhas accomplish the buddha-work by means of the four Māras and all the eighty-four thousand types of passion that afflict living beings.

"Ānanda, this is a Dharma-door called 'Introduction to all the Buddha-qualities.' The bodhisattva who enters this Dharma-door experiences neither joy nor pride when confronted by a buddha-field adorned with the splendor of all noble qualities, and experiences neither sadness nor aversion when confronted by a buddha-field apparently without that splendor, but in all cases produces a profound reverence for all the Tathāgatas. Indeed, it is wonderful how all the Lord Buddhas, who understand the equality of all things, manifest all sorts of buddha-fields in order to develop living beings!

"Ānanda, just as the buddha-fields are diverse as to their specific qualities but have no difference as to the sky that covers them, so, Ānanda, the Tathāgatas are diverse as to their physical bodies but do not differ as to their unimpeded gnosis.

"Ānanda, all the Buddhas are the same as to the perfection of their Buddha-qualities: that is, their forms, their colors, their radiance, their bodies, their marks, their nobility, their morality, their concentration, their wisdom, their liberation, their gnosis and vision of liberation, their strengths, their fearlessnesses, their special Buddha-qualities, their great love, their great compassion, their helpful intentions, their attitudes, their practices, their paths, the lengths of their lives, their teachings of the Dharma, their development and liberation of living beings, and their purification of buddha-fields. Therefore, they are all called 'Saṃyaksaṃbuddhas,' 'Tathāgatas,' and 'Buddhas.'[5]

"Ānanda, were your life to last an entire aeon, it would not be easy for you to understand thoroughly the extensive meaning and precise verbal significance of these three names. Also, Ānanda, if all the living beings of this billion-world galactic universe were like you—the foremost of the learned and the foremost of those endowed with memory and incantations[6]—and were they to devote an entire aeon, they would still be unable to understand completely the exact and extensive meaning of the three words 'Saṃyaksaṃbuddha,' 'Tathāgata,' and 'Buddha.' Thus, Ānanda, the enlightenment of the Buddhas is immeasurable, and the wisdom and the eloquence of the Tathāgatas are inconceivable."

Then, the venerable Ānanda addressed the Buddha: "Lord, from this day forth, I shall no longer declare myself to be the foremost of the learned."

The Buddha said, "Do not be discouraged, Ānanda! Why? I pronounced you, Ānanda, the foremost of the learned, with the disciples in mind, not considering the bodhisattvas. Look, Ānanda, look at the bodhisattvas. They cannot be fathomed even by the wisest of men. Ānanda, one can fathom the depths of the ocean, but one cannot fathom the depths of the wisdom, gnosis, memory, incantations, or eloquence of the bodhisattvas. Ānanda, you should remain in equanimity with regard to the deeds of the bodhisattvas. Why? Ānanda, these marvels displayed in a single morning by the Licchavi Vimalakīrti could not be performed by the disciples and solitary sages who have attained miraculous powers, were they to devote all their powers of incarnation and transformation during one hundred thousand millions of aeons."

Then, all those bodhisattvas from the buddha-field of the Tathāgata Sugandhakūṭa joined their palms in reverence and, saluting the Tathāgata Śākyamuni, addressed him as follows: "Lord, when we first arrived in this buddha-field, we conceived a negative idea, but we now abandon this wrong idea. Why? Lord, the realms of the Buddhas and their skill in liberative technique are inconceivable. In order to develop living beings, they manifest such and such a field to suit the desire of such and such a living being. Lord, please give us a teaching by which we may remember you, when we have returned to Sarvagandhasugandhā."

Thus having been requested, the Buddha declared, "Noble sons, there is a liberation of bodhisattvas called 'destructible and indestructible.' You must train yourselves in this liberation. What is it? 'Destructible' refers to compounded things. 'Indestructible' refers to the uncompounded.[7] But the bodhisattva should neither destroy the compounded nor rest in the uncompounded.[8]

"Not to destroy compounded things consists in not losing the great love; not giving up the great compassion; not forgetting the omniscient mind generated by high resolve; not tiring in the positive development of living beings; not abandoning the means of unification; giving up body and life in order to uphold the holy Dharma; never being satisfied with the roots of virtue already accumulated; taking pleasure in skillful dedication; having no laziness in seeking the Dharma; being without selfish reticence[9] in teaching the Dharma; sparing no effort in seeing and worshiping the Tathāgatas; being fearless in voluntary reincarnations; being neither proud in success nor bowed in failure; not despising the unlearned, and respecting the learned as if they were the Teacher himself; making reasonable those whose passions are excessive; taking pleasure in solitude, without being attached to it; not longing for one's own happiness but longing for the happiness of others; conceiving of trance, meditation, and equanimity as if they were the Avīci hell; conceiving of the world as a garden of liberation; considering beggars to be spiritual teachers; considering the giving away of all possessions to be the means of realizing Buddhahood; considering immoral beings to be saviors;[10] considering the transcendences to be parents; considering the aids to enlightenment to be servants; never ceasing accumulation of the roots of virtue; establishing the virtues of all buddha-fields in one's own buddha-field; offering limitless pure sacrifices to fulfill the auspicious marks and signs; adorning body, speech, and mind by refraining from all sins; continuing in reincarnations during immeasurable aeons, while purifying body, speech, and mind; avoiding discouragement, through spiritual heroism, when learning of the immeasurable virtues of the Buddha; wielding the sharp sword of wisdom to chastise the enemy passions; knowing well the aggregates, the elements, and the sense-media in order to bear the burdens of all living beings; blazing with energy to conquer the host of demons; seeking knowledge in order to avoid pride; being content with little desire in order to uphold the Dharma; not mixing with worldly things in order to delight all the people; being faultless in all activities in order to conform to all people; producing the superknowledges to actually accomplish all duties of benefit to living beings; acquiring incantations, memory, and knowledge in order to retain all learning; understanding the degrees of people's spiritual faculties to dispel the doubts of all living beings; displaying invincible miraculous feats to teach the Dharma; having irresistible speech by acquiring unimpeded eloquence;[11] tasting human and divine success by purifying the path of ten virtues; establishing the path of the pure states of Brahmā by cultivating the four immeasurables;[12] inviting the Buddhas to teach the Dharma, rejoicing in them, and applauding them, thereby obtaining the melodious voice of a Buddha; disciplining body, speech, and mind, thus maintaining constant spiritual progress; being without attachment to anything and thus acquiring the behavior of a Buddha; gathering together the order of bodhisattvas[13] to attract beings to the Mahāyāna; and being consciously aware at all times not to neglect any good quality. Noble sons, a bodhisattva who thus applies himself to the Dharma is a bodhisattva who does not destroy the compounded realm.

"What is not resting in the uncompounded? The bodhisattva practices voidness, but he does not realize voidness. He practices signlessness but does not realize signlessness. He practices wishlessness but does not realize wishlessness. He practices non-performance but does not realize non-performance. He knows impermanence but is not complacent about his roots of virtue. He considers misery, but he reincarnates voluntarily. He knows selflessness but does not waste himself. He considers peacefulness but does not seek extreme peace. He cherishes solitude but does not avoid mental and physical efforts. He considers placelessness but does not abandon the place of good actions. He considers occurrencelessness but undertakes to bear the burdens of all living beings. He considers immaculateness, yet he follows the process of the world. He considers motionlessness, yet he moves in order to develop all living beings. He considers selflessness yet does not abandon the great compassion toward all living beings. He considers birthlessness, yet he does not fall into the ultimate determination of the disciples. He considers vanity, futility, insubstantiality, dependency, and placelessness, yet he establishes himself on merits that are not vain, on knowledge that is not futile, on reflections that are substantial, on the striving for the consecration of the independent gnosis, and on the Buddha-family in its definitive meaning.[14]

"Thus, noble sons, a bodhisattva who aspires to such a Dharma neither rests in the uncompounded nor destroys the compounded.

"Furthermore, noble sons, in order to accomplish the store of merit, a bodhisattva does not rest in the uncompounded, and, in order to accomplish the store of wisdom, he does not destroy the compounded. In order to fulfill the great love, he does not rest in the uncompounded, and, in order to fulfill the great compassion, he does not destroy compounded things. In order to develop living beings, he does not rest in the uncompounded, and, in order to aspire to the Buddha-qualities, he does not destroy compounded things. To perfect the marks of Buddhahood, he does not rest in the uncompounded, and, to perfect the gnosis of omniscience, he does not destroy compounded things. Out of skill in liberative technique, he does not rest in the uncompounded, and, through thorough analysis with his wisdom, he does not destroy compounded things. To purify the buddha-field, he does not rest in the uncompounded, and, by the power of the grace of the Buddha, he does not destroy compounded things. Because he feels the needs of living beings, he does not rest in the uncompounded, and, in order to show truly the meaning of the Dharma, he does not destroy compounded things. Because of his store of roots of virtue, he does not rest in the uncompounded, and, because of his instinctive enthusiasm for these roots of virtue, he does not destroy compounded things. To fulfill his prayers, he does not rest in the uncompounded, and, because he has no wishes, he does not destroy compounded things. Because his positive thought is pure, he does not rest in the uncompounded, and, because his high resolve is pure, he does not destroy compounded things. In order to play with the five superknowledges, he does not rest in the uncompounded, and, because of the six superknowledges of the buddha-gnosis,[15] he does not destroy compounded things. To fulfill the six transcendences, he does not rest in the uncompounded, and, to fulfill the time,[16] he does not destroy compounded things. To gather the treasures of the Dharma, he does not rest in the uncompounded, and, because he does not like any narrow-minded teachings,[17] he does not destroy compounded things. Because he gathers all the medicines of the Dharma, he does not rest in the uncompounded, and, to apply the medicine of the Dharma appropriately, he does not destroy compounded things. To confirm his commitments, he does not rest in the uncompounded, and, to mend any failure of these commitments, he does not destroy compounded things. To concoct all the elixirs of the Dharma, he does not rest in the uncompounded, and, to give out the nectar of this subtle Dharma,[18] he does not destroy compounded things. Because he knows thoroughly all the sicknesses due to passions, he does not rest in the uncompounded, and, in order to cure all sicknesses of all living beings, he does not destroy compounded things.

"Thus, noble sons, the bodhisattva does not destroy compounded things and does not rest in the uncompounded, and that is the liberation of bodhisattvas called 'destructible and indestructible.' Noble sirs, you should also strive in this."

Then, those bodhisattvas, having heard this teaching, were satisfied, delighted, and reverent. They were filled with rejoicing and happiness of mind. In order to worship the Buddha Śākyamuni and the bodhisattvas of the Sahā universe, as well as this teaching, they covered the whole earth of this billion-world universe with fragrant powder, incense, perfumes, and flowers up to the height of the knees. Having thus regaled the whole retinue of the Tathāgata, bowed their heads at the feet of the Buddha, and circumambulated him to the right three times, they sang a hymn of praise to him. They then disappeared from this universe and in a split second were back in the universe Sarvagandhasugandhā.

12

Vision of the Universe Abhirati and the Tathāgata Akṣobhya

Thereupon, the Buddha said to the Licchavi Vimalakīrti, "Noble son, when you would see the Tathāgata, how do you view him?"

Thus addressed, the Licchavi Vimalakīrti said to the Buddha, "Lord, when I would see the Tathāgata, I view him by not seeing any Tathāgata. Why? I see him as not born from the past, not passing on to the future, and not abiding in the present time. Why? He is the essence which is the reality of matter,[1] but he is not matter. He is the essence which is the reality of sensation, but he is not sensation. He is the essence which is the reality of intellect, but he is not intellect. He is the essence which is the reality of motivation, yet he is not motivation. He is the essence which is the reality of consciousness, yet he is not consciousness. Like the element of space, he does not abide in any of the four elements. Transcending the scope of eye, ear, nose, tongue, body, and mind, he is not produced in the six sense-media. He is not involved in the three worlds, is free of the three defilements, is associated with the triple liberation, is endowed with the three knowledges, and has truly attained the unattainable.

"The Tathāgata has reached the extreme of detachment in regard to all things, yet he is not a reality-limit. He abides in ultimate reality, yet there is no relationship between it and him. He is not produced from causes, nor does he depend on conditions. He is not without any characteristic, nor has he any characteristic. He has no single nature nor any diversity of natures. He is not a conception, not a mental construction, nor is he a nonconception. He is neither the other shore, nor this shore, nor that between. He is neither here, nor there, nor anywhere else. He is neither this nor that. He cannot be discovered by consciousness, nor is he inherent in consciousness. He is neither darkness nor light. He is neither name nor sign. He is neither weak nor strong. He lives in no country or direction.[2] He is neither good nor evil. He is neither compounded nor uncompounded. He cannot be explained as having any meaning whatsoever.

"The Tathāgata is neither generosity nor avarice, neither morality nor immorality, neither tolerance nor malice, neither effort nor sloth, neither concentration nor distraction, neither wisdom nor foolishness. He is inexpressible. He is neither truth nor falsehood; neither escape from the world nor failure to escape from the world; neither cause of involvement in the world nor not a cause of involvement in the world; he is the cessation of all theory and all practice. He is neither a field of merit nor not a field of merit; he is neither worthy of offerings nor unworthy of offerings. He is not an object, and cannot be contacted. He is not a whole, nor a conglomeration. He surpasses all calculations. He is utterly unequaled, yet equal to the ultimate reality of things. He is matchless, especially in effort. He surpasses all measure. He does not go, does not stay, does not pass beyond. He is neither seen, heard, distinguished, nor known. He is without any complexity, having attained the equanimity of omniscient gnosis. Equal toward all things, he does not discriminate between them. He is without reproach, without excess, without corruption, without conception, and without intellectualization. He is without activity, without birth, without occurrence, without origin, without production, and without nonproduction. He is without fear and without subconsciousness;[3] without sorrow, without joy, and without strain. No verbal teaching can express him.

"Such is the body of the Tathāgata and thus should he be seen. Who sees thus, truly sees. Who sees otherwise, sees falsely."

The venerable Śāriputra then asked the Buddha, "Lord, in which buddha-field did the noble Vimalakīrti die, before reincarnating in this buddha-field?"

The Buddha said, "Śāriputra, ask this good man directly where he died to reincarnate here."

Then the venerable Śāriputra asked the Licchavi Vimalakīrti, "Noble sir, where did you die to reincarnate here?"

Vimalakīrti declared, "Is there anything among the things that you see, elder, that dies or is reborn?"

Śāriputra: There is nothing that dies or is reborn.

Vimalakīrti: Likewise, reverend Śāriputra, as all things neither die nor are reborn, why do you ask, "Where did you die to reincarnate here?" Reverend Śāriputra, if one were to ask a man or woman created by a magician where he or she had died to reincarnate there, what do you think he or she would answer?

Śāriputra: Noble sir, a magical creation does not die, nor is it reborn.

Vimalakīrti: Reverend Śāriputra, did not the Tathāgata declare that all things have the nature of a magical creation?

Śāriputra: Yes, noble sir, that is indeed so.

Vimalakīrti: Reverend Śāriputra, since all things have the nature of a magical creation, why do you ask, "Where have you died to reincarnate here?" Reverend Śāriputra, "death" is an end of performance, and "rebirth" is the continuation of performance. But, although a bodhisattva dies, he does not put an end to the performance of the roots of virtue, and although he is reborn, he does not adhere to the continuation of sin.

Then, the Buddha said to the venerable Śāriputra, "Śāriputra, this holy person came here from the presence of the Tathāgata Akṣobhya[4] in the universe Abhirati."

Śāriputra: Lord, it is wonderful that this holy person, having left a buddha-field as pure as Abhirati, should enjoy a buddha-field as full of defects as this Sahā universe!

The Licchavi Vimalakīrti said, "Śāriputra, what do you think? Does the light of the sun accompany the darkness?"

Śāriputra: Certainly not, noble sir!

Vimalakīrti: Then the two do not go together?

Śāriputra: Noble sir, those two do not go together. As soon as the sun rises, all darkness is destroyed.

Vimalakīrti: Then why does the sun rise over the world?

Śāriputra: It rises to illuminate the world, and to eliminate the darkness.

Vimalakīrti: Just in the same way, reverend Śāriputra, the bodhisattva reincarnates voluntarily in the impure buddha-fields in order to purify the living beings, in order to make the light of wisdom shine, and in order to clear away the darkness. Since they do not associate with the passions, they dispel the darkness of the passions of all living beings.

Thereupon, the entire multitude experienced the desire to behold the universe Abhirati, the Tathāgata Akṣobhya, his bodhisattvas, and his great disciples. The Buddha, knowing the thoughts of the entire multitude, said to the Licchavi Vimalakīrti, "Noble son, this multitude wishes to behold the universe Abhirati and the Tathāgata Akṣobhya—show them!"

Then the Licchavi Vimalakīrti thought, "Without rising from my couch, I shall pick up in my right hand the universe Abhirati and all it contains: its hundreds of thousands of bodhisattvas; its abodes of devas, nāgas, yakṣas, gandharvas, and asuras, bounded by its Cakravāḍa mountains; its rivers, lakes, fountains, streams, oceans, and other bodies of water; its Mount Sumeru and other hills and mountain ranges; its moon, its sun, and its stars; its devas, nāgas, yakṣas, gandharvas, and asuras themselves; its Brahmā and his retinues; its villages, cities, towns, provinces, kingdoms, men, women, and houses; its bodhisattvas; its disciples; the tree of enlightenment of the Tathāgata Akṣobhya; and the Tathāgata Akṣobhya himself, seated in the middle of an assembly vast as an ocean, teaching the Dharma. Also the lotuses that accomplish the buddha-work among the living beings; the three jeweled ladders that rise from its earth to its Trāyastriṃśa heaven, on which ladders the gods of that heaven descend to the world to see, honor, and serve the Tathāgata Akṣobhya and to hear the Dharma, and on which the men of the earth climb to the Trāyastriṃśa heaven to visit those gods. Like a potter with his wheel, I will reduce that universe Abhirati, with its store of innumerable virtues, from its watery base up to its Akaniṣṭha heaven, to a minute size and, carrying it gently like a garland of flowers, will bring it to this Sahā universe and will show it to the multitudes."

Then, the Licchavi Vimalakīrti entered into a concentration, and performed a miraculous feat such that he reduced the universe Abhirati to a minute size, and took it with his right hand, and brought it into this Sahā universe.

In that universe Abhirati, the disciples, bodhisattvas, and those among gods and men who possessed the superknowledge of the divine eye all cried out, "Lord, we are being carried away! Sugata, we are being carried off! Protect us, O Tathāgata!"

But, to discipline them, the Tathāgata Akṣobhya said to them, "You are being carried off by the bodhisattva Vimalakīrti. It is not my affair."

As for the other men and gods, they had no awareness at all that they were being carried anywhere.

Although the universe Abhirati had been brought into the universe Sahā, the Sahā universe was not increased or diminished; it was neither compressed nor obstructed. Nor was the universe Abhirati reduced internally, and both universes appeared to be the same as they had ever been.

Thereupon, the Buddha Śākyamuni asked all the multitudes, "Friends, behold the splendors of the universe Abhirati, the Tathāgata Akṣobhya, the array of his buddha-field, and the splendors of these disciples and bodhisattvas!"

They replied, "We see them, Lord!"

The Buddha said, "Those bodhisattvas who wish to embrace such a buddha-field should train themselves in all the bodhisattva-practices of the Tathāgata Akṣobhya."

While Vimalakīrti, with his miraculous power, showed them thus the universe Abhirati and the Tathāgata Akṣobhya, one hundred and forty thousand living beings among the men and gods of the Sahā universe conceived the spirit of unexcelled, perfect enlightenment, and all of them formed a prayer to be reborn in the universe Abhirati. And the Buddha prophesied that in the future all would be reborn in the universe Abhirati. And the Licchavi Vimalakīrti, having thus developed all the living beings who could thereby be developed, returned the universe Abhirati exactly to its former place.

The Lord then said to the venerable Śāriputra, "Śāriputra, did you see that universe Abhirati, and the Tathāgata Akṣobhya?"

Śāriputra replied, "I saw it, Lord! May all living beings come to live in a buddha-field as splendid as that! May all living beings come to have miraculous powers just like those of the noble Licchavi Vimalakīrti!

"We have gained great benefit from having seen a holy man such as he. We have gained a great benefit from having heard such teaching of the Dharma, whether the Tathāgata himself still actually exists or whether he has already attained ultimate liberation. Hence, there is no need to mention the great benefit for those who, having heard it, believe it, rely on it, embrace it, remember it, read it, and penetrate to its depth; and, having found faith in it, teach, recite, and show it to others and apply themselves to the yoga of meditation upon its teaching.

"Those living beings who understand correctly this teaching of the Dharma will obtain the treasury of the jewels of the Dharma.

"Those who study correctly this teaching of the Dharma will become the companions of the Tathāgata. Those who honor and serve the adepts of this doctrine will be the true protectors of the Dharma. Those who write, teach, and worship this teaching of the Dharma will be visited by the Tathāgata in their homes. Those who take pleasure in this teaching of the Dharma will embrace all merits. Those who teach it to others, whether it be no more than a single stanza of four lines, or a single summary phrase from this teaching of the Dharma, will be performing the great Dharma-sacrifice. And those who devote to this teaching of the Dharma their tolerance, their zeal, their intelligence, their discernment, their vision, and their aspirations, thereby become subject to the prophesy of future Buddhahood!"

Epilogue

Antecedents and Transmission of the Holy Dharma[1]

Then Śakra, the prince of the gods, said to the Buddha, "Lord, formerly I have heard from the Tathāgata and from Mañjuśrī, the crown prince of wisdom, many hundreds of thousands of teachings of the Dharma, but I have never before heard a teaching of the Dharma as remarkable as this instruction in the entrance into the method of inconceivable transformations.[2] Lord, those living beings who, having heard this teaching of the Dharma, accept it, remember it, read it, and understand it deeply will be, without a doubt, true vessels of the Dharma; there is no need to mention those who apply themselves to the yoga of meditation upon it. They will cut off all possibility of unhappy lives, will open their way to all fortunate lives, will always be looked after by all Buddhas, will always overcome all adversaries, and will always conquer all devils. They will practice the path of the bodhisattvas, will take their places upon the seat of enlightenment, and will have truly entered the domain of the Tathāgatas. Lord, the noble sons and daughters who will teach and practice this exposition of the Dharma will be honored and served by me and my followers. To the villages, towns, cities, states, kingdoms, and capitals wherein this teaching of the Dharma will be applied, taught, and demonstrated, I and my followers will come to hear the Dharma. I will inspire the unbelieving with faith, and I will guarantee my help and protection to those who believe and uphold the Dharma."

At these words, the Buddha said to Śakra, the prince of the gods, "Excellent! Excellent, prince of gods! The Tathāgata rejoices in your good words. Prince of gods, the enlightenment of the Buddhas of the past, present, and future is expressed in this discourse of Dharma. Therefore, prince of gods, when noble sons and daughters accept it, repeat it, understand it deeply, write it completely, and, making it into a book, honor it, those sons and daughters thereby pay homage to the Buddhas of the past, present, and future.

"Let us suppose, prince of gods, that this billion-world-galactic universe were as full of Tathāgatas as it is covered with groves of sugarcane, with rosebushes, with bamboo thickets, with herbs, and with flowers, and that a noble son or daughter were to honor them, revere them, respect and adore them, offering them all sorts of comforts and offerings for an aeon or more than an aeon. And let us suppose that, these Tathāgatas having entered ultimate liberation, he or she honored each of them by enshrining their preserved bodies in a memorial *stūpa*[3] made of precious stones, each as large as a world with four great continents, rising as high as the world of Brahmā, adorned with parasols, banners, standards, and lamps. And let us suppose finally that, having erected all these *stūpas* for the Tathāgatas, he or she were to devote an aeon or more to offering them flowers, perfumes, banners, and standards, while playing drums and music. That being done, what do you think, prince of gods? Would that noble son or daughter receive much merit as a consequence of such activities?"

Śakra, the prince of gods, replied, "Many merits, Lord! Many merits, O Sugata! Were one to spend hundreds of thousands of millions of aeons, it would be impossible to measure the limit of the mass of merits that that noble son or daughter would thereby gather!"

The Buddha said, "Have faith, prince of gods, and understand this: Whoever accepts this exposition of the Dharma called 'Instruction in the Inconceivable Liberation,'[4] recites it, and understands it deeply, he or she will gather merits even greater than those who perform the above acts. Why so? Because, prince of gods, the enlightenment of the Buddhas arises from the Dharma, and one honors them by the Dharma worship,[5] and not by material worship. Thus it is taught, prince of gods, and thus you must understand it."

The Buddha then further said to Śakra, the prince of gods, "Once, prince of gods, long ago, long before aeons more numerous than the innumerable, immense, immeasurable, inconceivable, and even before then, the Tathāgata called Bhaiṣajyarāja[6] appeared in the world: a saint, perfectly and fully enlightened, endowed with knowledge and conduct, a blissful one, knower of the world, incomparable knower of men who need to be civilized, teacher of gods and men, a Lord, a Buddha.[7] He appeared in the aeon called Vicaraṇa in the universe called Mahāvyūha.

"The length of life of this Tathāgata Bhaiṣajyarāja, perfectly and fully enlightened one, was twenty short aeons. His retinue of disciples numbered thirty-six million billion, and his retinue of bodhisattvas numbered twelve million billion. In that same era, prince of gods, there was a universal monarch called King Ratnacchattra, who reigned over the four continents and possessed seven precious jewels. He had one thousand heroic sons, powerful, strong, and able to conquer enemy armies. This King Ratnacchattra honored the Tathāgata

Bhaiṣajyarāja and his retinue with many excellent offerings during five short aeons. At the end of this time, the King Ratnacchattra said to his sons, 'Recognizing that during my reign I have worshiped the Tathāgata, in your turn you also should worship him.'

"The thousand princes gave their consent, obeying their father the king, and all together, during another five short aeons, they honored the Tathāgata Bhaiṣajyarāja with all sorts of excellent offerings.

"Among them, there was a prince by the name of Candracchattra, who retired into solitude and thought to himself, 'Is there not another mode of worship, even better and more noble than this?'

"Then, by the supernatural power of the Buddha Bhaiṣajyarāja, the gods spoke to him from the heavens: 'Good man, the supreme worship is the Dharma-worship.'

"Candracchattra asked them, 'What is this "Dharma-worship"?'

"The gods replied, 'Good man, go to the Tathāgata Bhaiṣajyarāja, ask him about the "Dharma-worship," and he will explain it to you fully.'

"Then, the prince Candracchattra went to the Lord Bhaiṣajyarāja, the saint, the Tathāgata, the insuperably, perfectly enlightened one, and having approached him, bowed down at his feet, circumambulated him to the right three times, and withdrew to one side. He then asked, 'Lord, I have heard of a "Dharma-worship," which surpasses all other worship. What is this "Dharma-worship"?'

"The Tathāgata Bhaiṣajyarāja said, 'Noble son, the Dharma-worship is that worship rendered to the discourses taught by the Tathāgata. These discourses are deep and profound in illumination. They do not conform to the mundane and are difficult to understand and difficult to see and difficult to realize. They are subtle, precise, and ultimately incomprehensible. As Scriptures, they are collected in the canon of the bodhisattvas,[8] stamped with the insignia of the king of incantations and teachings.[9] They reveal the irreversible wheel of Dharma, arising from the six transcendences, cleansed of any false notions. They are endowed with all the aids to enlightenment and embody the seven factors of enlightenment. They introduce living beings to the great compassion and teach them the great love. They eliminate all the convictions of the Māras, and they manifest relativity.

"'They contain the message of selflessness, living-beinglessness, lifelessness, personlessness, voidness, signlessness, wishlessness, nonperformance, nonproduction, and nonoccurrence.

"'They make possible the attainment of the seat of enlightenment and set in motion the wheel of the Dharma. They are approved and praised by the chiefs of the gods, nāgas, yakṣas, gandharvas, asuras, garuḍas, kiṃnaras, and mahoragas.

They preserve unbroken the heritage of the holy Dharma, contain the treasury of the Dharma, and represent the summit of the Dharma-worship. They are upheld by all holy beings and teach all the bodhisattva practices. They induce the unmistaken understanding of the Dharma in its ultimate sense. They certify that all things are impermanent, miserable, selfless, and peaceful, thus epitomizing the Dharma.[10] They cause the abandonment of avarice, immorality, malice, laziness, forgetfulness, foolishness, and jealousy, as well as bad convictions, adherence to objects, and all opposition. They are praised by all the Buddhas. They are the medicines for the tendencies of mundane life, and they authentically manifest the great happiness of liberation. To teach correctly, to uphold, to investigate, and to understand such Scriptures, thus incorporating into one's own life the holy Dharma—that is the "Dharma-worship."

"'Furthermore, noble son, the Dharma-worship consists of determining the Dharma according to the Dharma; applying the Dharma according to the Dharma; being in harmony with relativity; being free of extremist convictions; attaining the tolerance of ultimate birthlessness and nonoccurrence of all things; realizing selflessness and living-beinglessness; refraining from struggle about causes and conditions, without quarreling, or disputing; not being possessive; being free of egoism; relying on the meaning and not on the literal expression; relying on gnosis and not on consciousness; relying on the ultimate teachings definitive in meaning and not insisting on the superficial teachings interpretable in meaning; relying on reality and not insisting on opinions derived from personal authorities;[11] realizing correctly the reality of the Buddha; realizing the ultimate absence of any fundamental consciousness; and overcoming the habit of clinging to an ultimate ground. Finally, attaining peace by stopping everything from ignorance to old age, death, sorrow, lamentation, misery, anxiety, and trouble, and realizing that living beings know no end to their views concerning these twelve links of dependent origination; then, noble son, when you do not hold to any view at all, it is called the unexcelled Dharma-worship.'[12]

"Prince of gods, when the prince Candracchattra had heard this definition of Dharma-worship from the Tathāgata Bhaiṣajyarāja, he attained the conformative tolerance of ultimate birthlessness; and, taking his robes and ornaments, he offered them to the Buddha Bhaiṣajyarāja, saying, 'When the Tathāgata will be in ultimate liberation, I wish to defend his holy Dharma, to protect it, and to worship it. May the Tathāgata grant me his supernatural blessing, that I may be able to conquer Māra and all adversaries and to incorporate in all my lives the holy Dharma of the Buddha!'

"The Tathāgata Bhaiṣajyarāja, knowing the high resolve of Candracchattra, prophesied to him that he would be, at a later time, in the future, the protector, guardian, and defender of the city of the holy Dharma. Then, prince of gods, the prince Candracchattra, out of his great faith in the Tathāgata, left the household life in order to enter the homeless life of a monk and, having done so, lived making great efforts toward the attainment of virtue. Having made great effort and being well established in virtue, he soon produced the five superknowledges, understood the incantations, and obtained the invincible eloquence. When the Tathāgata Bhaiṣajyarāja attained ultimate liberation, Candracchattra, on the strength of his superknowledges and by the power of his incantations, made the wheel of the Dharma turn just as the Tathāgata Bhaiṣajyarāja had done and continued to do so for ten short aeons.

"Prince of gods, while the monk Candracchattra was exerting himself thus to protect the holy Dharma, thousands of millions of living beings reached the stage of irreversibility on the path to unexcelled, perfect enlightenment, fourteen billion living beings were disciplined in the vehicles of the disciples and solitary sages, and innumerable living beings took rebirth in the human and heavenly realms.

"Perhaps, prince of gods, you are wondering or experiencing some doubt about whether or not, at that former time, the King Ratnacchattra was not some other than the actual Tathāgata Ratnārcis.[13] You must not imagine that, for the present Tathāgata Ratnārcis was at that time, in that epoch, the universal monarch Ratnacchattra. As for the thousand sons of the King Ratnacchattra, they are now the thousand bodhisattvas of the present blessed aeon, during the course of which one thousand Buddhas will appear in the world. Among them, Krakucchanda and others are already born, and those remaining will still be born, from Kakutsunda up to the Tathāgata Roca, who will be the last to be born.[14]

"Perhaps, prince of gods, you are asking yourself if, in that life, in that time, the Prince Candracchattra who upheld the Holy Dharma of Lord Tathāgata Bhaiṣajyarāja was not someone other than myself. But you must not imagine that, for I was, in that life, in that time, the Prince Candracchattra. Thus, it is necessary to know, prince of gods, that among all the worships rendered to the Tathāgata, the Dharma-worship is the very best. Yes, it is good, eminent, excellent, perfect, supreme, and unexcelled. And therefore, prince of gods, do not worship me with material objects but worship me with the Dharma-worship! Do not honor me with material objects but honor me by honor to the Dharma!"

Then the Lord Śākyamuni said to the bodhisattva Maitreya, the great spiritual hero, "I transmit to you, Maitreya, this unexcelled, perfect enlightenment which I attained only after innumerable millions of billions of aeons, in order that, at a later time, during a later life, a similar teaching of the Dharma, protected by your supernatural power, will spread in the world and will not disappear. Why?

Maitreya, in the future there will be noble sons and daughters, devas, nāgas, yakṣas, gandharvas, and asuras, who, having planted the roots of virtue, will produce the spirit of unexcelled, perfect enlightenment. If they do not hear this teaching of the Dharma, they will certainly lose boundless advantages and even perish. But if they hear such a teaching, they will rejoice, will believe, and will accept it upon the crowns of their heads. Hence, in order to protect those future noble sons and daughters, you must spread a teaching such as this!

"Maitreya, there are two gestures of the bodhisattvas.[15] What are they? The first gesture is to believe in all sorts of phrases and words, and the second gesture is to penetrate exactly the profound principle of the Dharma without being afraid. Such are the two gestures of the bodhisattvas. Maitreya, it must be known that the bodhisattvas who believe in all sorts of words and phrases, and apply themselves accordingly, are beginners and not experienced in religious practice. But the bodhisattvas who read, hear, believe, and teach this profound teaching with its impeccable expressions reconciling dichotomies and its analyses of stages of development—these are veterans in the religious practice.

"Maitreya, there are two reasons the beginner bodhisattvas hurt themselves and do not concentrate on the profound Dharma. What are they? Hearing this profound teaching never before heard, they are terrified and doubtful, do not rejoice, and reject it, thinking, 'Whence comes this teaching never before heard?' They then behold other noble sons accepting, becoming vessels for, and teaching this profound teaching, and they do not attend upon them, do not befriend them, do not respect them, and do not honor them, and eventually they go so far as to criticize them. These are the two reasons the beginner bodhisattvas hurt themselves and do not penetrate the profound Dharma.

"There are two reasons the bodhisattvas who do aspire to the profound Dharma hurt themselves and do not attain the tolerance of the ultimate birthlessness of things. What are these two? These bodhisattvas despise and reproach the beginner bodhisattvas, who have not been practicing for a long time, and they do not initiate them or instruct them in the profound teaching. Having no great respect for this profound teaching, they are not careful about its rules. They help living beings by means of material gifts and do not help them by means of the gift of the Dharma. Such, Maitreya, are the two reasons the bodhisattvas who aspire to the profound Dharma hurt themselves and will not quickly attain the tolerance of the ultimate birthlessness of all things."

Thus having been taught, the bodhisattva Maitreya said to the Buddha, "Lord, the beautiful teachings of the Tathāgata are wonderful and truly excellent. Lord, from this time forth, I will avoid all such errors and will defend and uphold this attainment of unexcelled, perfect enlightenment by the Tathāgata during innumerable hundreds of thousands of millions of billions of aeons! In the future, I will place in the hands of noble sons and noble daughters who are worthy vessels of the holy Dharma this profound teaching. I will instill in them the power of memory with which they may, having believed in this teaching, retain it, recite it, penetrate its depths, teach it, propagate it, write it down, and proclaim it extensively to others.

"Thus I will instruct them, Lord, and thus it may be known that in that future time those who believe in this teaching and who enter deeply into it will be sustained by the supernatural blessing of the bodhisattva Maitreya."

Thereupon the Buddha gave his approval to the bodhisattva Maitreya: "Excellent! Excellent! Your word is well given! The Tathāgata rejoices and commends your good promise."

Then all the bodhisattvas said together in one voice, "Lord, we also, after the ultimate liberation of the Tathāgata, will come from our various buddha-fields to spread far and wide this enlightenment of the perfect Buddha, the Tathāgata. May all noble sons and daughters believe in that!"

Then the four Mahārājas, the great kings of the quarters,[16] said to the Buddha, "Lord, in all the towns, villages, cities, kingdoms, and palaces, wherever this discourse of the Dharma will be practised, upheld, and correctly taught, we, the four great kings, will go there with our armies, our young warriors, and our retinues, to hear the Dharma. And we will protect the teachers of this Dharma for a radius of one league so that no one who plots injury or disruption against these teachers will have any opportunity to do them harm."

Then the Buddha said to the venerable Ānanda, "Receive then, Ānanda, this expression of the teaching of the Dharma. Remember it, and teach it widely and correctly to others!"

Ānanda replied, "I have memorized, Lord, this expression of the teaching of the Dharma. But what is the name of this teaching, and how should I remember it?"

The Buddha said, "Ānanda, this exposition of the Dharma is called 'The Teaching of Vimalakīrti,'[17] or 'The Reconciliation of Dichotomies,'[18] or even 'Section of the Inconceivable Liberation.'[19] Remember it thus!"

Thus spoke the Buddha. And the Licchavi Vimalakīrti, the crown prince Mañjuśrī, the venerable Ānanda, the bodhisattvas, the great disciples, the entire multitude, and the whole universe with its gods, men, asuras and gandharvas, rejoiced exceedingly. All heartily praised these declarations by the Lord.

List of Abbreviations

Ch.	Chinese language.
Chap.	Chapter.
H	Chinese version of VKN by Hsüan Tsang.
k.	Kārikā (verse in Skt. work).
K	Chinese version of VKN by Kumārajīva.
l.	line (plural, ll.).
Lamotte	Étienne Lamotte, *L'Enseignement de Vimalakīrti* (Louvain, 1962).
lit.	Literally.
Lotus	H. Kern, *Saddharma-Puṇḍarīka, or Lotus of the True Law*, Sacred Books of the East, Vol. XXI (London, 1884).
Luk	Charles Luk, *The Vimalakīrti Nirdeśa Sūtra* (Berkeley, Calif., 1972).
MMK	Nāgārjuna, *Prajñā nāma mūlamadhyamakakārikā* (see K. Inada, *Nāgārjuna* [Buffalo, N.Y., 1970], for Skt. and translation).
Mvy	*Mahāvyutpatti*, Skt.-Tib. lexicon, ed. Sakaki (Kyoto, 1916).
n.	footnote (plural, ns.).
no.	number (plural, nos.).
p.	page (plural, pp.).
Pañcaviṃśati	*Pañcaviṃśatisāhasrikāprajñāpāramitāsūtra*, ed. N. Dutt (London, 1934).
Prasannapadā	Candrakīrti, *Prasannapadā nāma mūla madhyamakavṛtti*, Skt. ed. L. de la Vallée Poussin, Bibliotheca Buddhica IV (St. Petersburg, 1903–1913).

SN	*Samdhinirmocana sūtra*, Lamotte, Tib. text and French translation (Louvain, 1935).
Śatasāhasrikā	*Śatasāhasrikāprajñāpāramitāsūtra*, ed. P. Ghosa, Bibliotheca Indica (Calcutta, 1914).
Śikṣāsamuccaya	Śāntideva, *Śikṣāsamuccaya*, ed. P. L. Vaidya, Buddhist Skt. texts, No. 11 (Darbhanga, 1961).
Skt.	Sanskrit language.
T	Tib. translation of VKN by Dharmatāśila (Tib. Chos Ñid Tshul Khrims).
Tib.	Tibetan language.
TKSB	*Tsoṅ Khapai gSuṅ 'Bum* (collected works of Tsoṅ Khapa).
VKN	*The Vimalakīrti Nirdeśa Sūtra.*
Vol.	Volume.
VV	Nāgārjuna, *Vigrahavyāvartanī*, Skt. ed., P. L. Vaidya, Buddhist Skt. texts, No. 10, pp. 277–295 (Darbhanga, 1960).

Notes

Introduction

1. *Pañcaviṃśati*, p. 38. *Śatasāhasrikā*, p. 118, p. 812, p. 930. Lamotte, p. 309. *na śūnyatayā rūpaṃ śūnyaṃ / nānyatra rūpācchūnyatā / rūpaṃ eva śūnyatā / sūnyataiva rūpaṃ*. See below, p. 74.

2. VV, k. 72; *yaḥ śūnyatām pratītya samutpādaṃ madhyamāṃ pratipadaṃ ca / ekārthaṃ nijagāda praṇamāmi tam apratimasaṃbuddham*.

3. See K. Inada, *The Mūlamadhyamakakārikās of Nāgārjuna* (Buffalo, 1970).

4. MMK, XXIV ks. 1, 29. *yadi śūnyamidaṃ sarvaṃ* . . . and *yadyaśūnyamidaṃ sarvaṃ* . . . .

5. Tsoṅ Khapa poses the dilemma and its resolution as follows: "Who sees the inexorable causality of all things in saṃsāra and nirvāṇa and destroys any sort of conviction of objectivity, thus enters the path that pleases the Buddha. The apparent is inevitably relative and the void is bereft of any conviction—as long as these two understandings arise separately, one still has not realized the Buddha's intended meaning. But, when they are simultaneously together, at the mere sight of the inevitable relativity certain knowledge completely destroys the objective mental habit, and the analysis of right view is accomplished" (TKSB, Vol. *pha*, f. 250).

6. *Ratnāvalī*, IV, ks. 94–96. *yathaiva vaiyākaraṇo mātṛkamapi pāṭhayet / buddho avadat tathā dharmaṃ vineyānāṃ yathākṣamam // keṣāṃcidavadad dharmaṃ pāpebhyoviniviṛttaye / keṣāṃcitpuṇyasiddhyarthaṃ keṣāṃcid dvayaniśritam // dvayāniśritam ekeṣāṃ gambhīraṃ bhīrubhiṣanaṃ / śūnyatākaruṇāgarbham ekeṣāṃ bodhisādhanam //*.

7. Skt. *acintyavimokṣa*. See Epilogue.

8. See Lamotte, *Appendice*, Note III, pp. 407–413.

9. Skt. *upāyakauśalya*. My translation is partially derived from Lamotte's "*habilité en moyens salvifique*."

10. See p. 91.

11. See Lamotte's discussion of this concept (Lamotte, *Introduction*, pp. 33–37), even though he emphasizes the rhetorical meaning more than the behavioral meaning.

12. Tsoṅ Khapa formulates the mode in which to proceed after the "accomplishment of analysis of right view": "Furthermore, while appearance eliminates absolutism and voidness eliminates nihilism, when one knows how voidness is manifest as cause and effect, one will not be deprived by extremist conviction." (TKSB, Vol. *pha*, f. 250.)

13. See n. 6 (*śūnyatā karuṇā garbhaṃ*).

14. See p. 46.

15. See p. 64.

16. See p. 54.

17. *Guhyasamājatantra* (Skt. S. Bagchi [editor], Buddhist Sanskrit Texts, No. 9, Darbhanga, 1965). Generally recognized as one of the earliest systematic Tantric texts, it expounds a philosophically pure Middle Way nondualism, combined with an explicit teaching of the reconciliation of dichotomies (i.e., how even evil can be transmuted to enlightenment, etc.) and an elaborate meditational methodology, employing sacred formulae (*mantra*), rituals, and visualizations.

18. Tantric practice begins with the yogin's visualization of the universe as a pure realm arranged around himself as the supreme Buddha Vajradhara, filled with deified forms of Buddhas and bodhisattvas magically emanated by himself as witnesses of the esoteric teaching, etc. See *Guhyasamāja*, Chap. 1.

19. The meditation of jewels, Buddhas, sacred universes (*maṇḍala*), etc., as existing in full detail inside a mustardseed on the tip of the yogin's nose is a characteristic exercise in the *Guhyasamāja*, as in Chap. 3.

20. See p. 21. It is especially appropriate, in the light of the early Tantric tradition, for Vimalakīrti, as a layman, to be an adept.

21. See pages 64–66, where Vimalakīrti states that the "wrong way" leads to Buddhahood, Mañjusrī states that all passions constitute the "Tathāgata-family" (itself an important Tantric concept), and Mahākaśyapa states that only those guilty of the five deadly sins can conceive the spirit of enlightenment. *Guhyasamāja*, Chap. 5, k. 4, states: "Even those who have committed great sins, such as the five deadly sins, will succeed on the Buddha-vehicle, there in the great ocean of the Mahāyāna" (*ānantaryaprabhṛtayaḥ mahāpāpakṛto 'pi ca/siddhyante buddhayāne 'smin mahāyānamahodadhau//*). It then goes on to list in VKN fashion all sorts of terrible crimes of lust and hatred, ending with the phrase that such "a mentally nondualistic, intelligent person's Buddhahood is attained" (*siddhyate tasya buddhatvaṃ nirvikalpasya dhīmataḥ//*).

22. See p. 67. In the Tantric male-female symbolism of the *Guhyasamāja* and other Tantras, the female consort is called the "Wisdom" (*prajña*) and the male the "Liberative Technique" (*upāya*), and the bell (*ghaṇṭa*) and diamond-scepter (*vajra*) also symbolize female and male, respectively.

23. See p. 53. This type of yogic power is classified as a lesser attainment (*siddhi*), the superior attainment being Buddhahood, in all Tantric methodologies.

24. See p. 61. The *Guhyasamāja* elaborates the symbolism of the "Five Tathāgatas," the leaders of the Tathāgata-families, who are usually called Vairocana, Amitābha, Akṣobhya, Ratnasaṃbhava, and Amoghasiddhi, and thus correspond to the Tathāgatas listed by the goddess too closely to be merely coincidentally related. *Tathāgataguhyaka*, further, is a subtitle of the *Guhyasamāja* itself.

25. Vimalakīrti's special relation to the Tathāgata Akṣobhya (see p. 93) is highly significant in this context, as Akṣobhya is central among the "Five Tathāgatas," as he occupies the heart in the esoteric methodology which locates the five in the five important spots in the human body.

26. These connections, and others which the informed reader may pick out for himself, between the *Vimalakīrti* and the esoteric Tantric methodology are of great interest in that they reveal the wholeness of the Mahāyāna practice, which has innumerable different facets and methods for persons with different aptitudes and inclinations to practice. They may also give some pause to those scholars who, while admiring the Mahāyāna Scriptures, tend to point to Tantric methodology as something decadent, not in tune with the Middle Way (how much less the so-called pristine "original Buddhism"). From the hints in the *Vimalakīrti*, it is clear that Tantra is nothing more than the systematization of the practice of "reconciliation of dichotomies," providing the methodology with which to realize the visionary glories of interlocking buddha-fields, such as are witnessed at dramatic moments in all Mahāyāna Scriptures, and leading the heroic practitioner to the unique goal of all Mahāyāna teachings, namely Buddhahood. Conversely, it is no less obvious, and those enamored of the esoteric might take note, that these Tantric methodologies are inseparably based on the profound and subtle Middle Way, which must be clearly understood before they can be usefully employed. We cannot truly love Wisdom until we have beheld her!

Chapter 1

1. Skt. *buddhakṣetra.* Roughly, a synonym for "universe," although Buddhist cosmology contains many universes of different types and dimensions. "Buddha-field" indicates, in regard to whatever type of world-sphere, that it is the field of influence of a particular Buddha. For a detailed discussion of these concepts, see Lamotte, *Appendice*, Note I.

2. Skt. *bhagavān buddha.* "Lord" is chosen as the term of greatest respect in English, thus corresponding to *bhagavān* (see Glossary 3, under "lord").

3. This was an important city of the Buddha's time, the capital of the Licchavi Republic. (See Lamotte, pp. 80–83; p. 97, n. 1.).

4. Skt. *arhat.* "Saint," derived from the Latin *sanus*, "clean," aptly describes the Buddhist arhat, who has reached this stage by cleansing himself of all defiling passions and ignorance.

5. This list of qualities of the holy disciples (*āryaśrāvaka*) is absent in the Chinese of K and H. It is, however, frequently found in Mahāyāna scriptures (see Lamotte, p. 98, n. 2).

6. Skt. *mahāsattva.* This translation follows the Tib. *sems dpa chen po* (lit. "great mind-hero"), whose translation from Skt. derives from the *lo tsva ba*'s analysis of *sattva* as meaning "hero," rather than simply "being."

7. Skt. *mahābhijñā.* These are either five or six in number (see Glossary 2).

8. Skt. *buddhādhiṣṭhāna* (lit. "support of the Buddha"). This concept refers to the miraculous energy of the Buddha, which sustains all bodhisattvas in their myriad endeavors.

9. This phrase is absent in T but is included in K and H.

10. Skt. *kalyāṇamitra* (lit. "virtuous friend"). A Mahāyāna teacher is termed "friend," or "benefactor," which indicates that a bodhisattva-career depends on one's own effort and that all a teacher can do is inspire, exemplify, and point the way.

11. Skt. *dhāraṇī.* These incantations, or spells, are mnemonic formulas, possessed by advanced bodhisattvas, that contain a quintessence of their attainments, not simply magical charms—although the latter are included (see Glossary 3, under "incantation)."

12. The ten transcendences (*daśapāramitāḥ*), which correspond to the ten stages (*daśabhūmayaḥ*) of the bodhisattva (see Glossary 2).

13. Skt. *anupalabdhidharmakṣānti*. See Glossary 3, under "incomprehensibility" and "tolerance."

14. Skt. *avaivartikadharmacakra*. The fact that the Dharma is not a single dogma, law, or fixed system, but instead an adaptable body of techniques available for any living being to aid in his development and liberation is emphasized by this metaphor. This wheel is said to turn by the current of energy from the needs and wishes of living beings, and its turning automatically converts negative energies (e.g., desire, hatred, and ignorance) to positive ones (e.g., detachment, love, and wisdom).

15. Skt. *puṇyajñānasaṃbhāra*. The two great stores to be accumulated by the bodhisattva: the store of merit, arising from his practice of the first three transcendences, and the store of wisdom, arising from his practice of the last two transcendences (see Glossary 2, under "two stores").

16. Skt. *lakṣaṇānuvyañjana*. The thirty-two signs and the eighty marks of a superior being (see Glossary 2).

17. Skt. *pratītyasamutpāda*. In most contexts, this term is properly translated by "dependent origination." But in the Mādhyamika context, wherein the concept of the ultimate nonorigination of all things is emphasized, "relativity" better serves to convey the message that things exist only in relation to verbal designation and that nothing exists as an independent, self-sufficient entity, even on the superficial level (see Glossary 3, under "relativity").

18. Tib. *mtha dañ mtha med par lta bai bag chags kyi mtshams sbyor ba kun bcod pa*; Skt. *antānantadṛṣṭivāsanābhisaṃdhisamucchedaka*. "Convictions concerning finitude" refers to two sorts of extremism, absolutism and nihilism, and "convictions concerning infinitude" refers to convictions that hypostatize voidness (i.e., infinity, etc.) as a self-existent entity. Thus the bodhisattvas are said here to have realized, even on the subconscious level, both the voidness of things and the voidness of voidness.

19. Skt. *daśabalāni*, *catvārivaiśāradyāni*, and *aṣṭādaśāveṇikabuddhadharmāḥ*. For the list of these, see Glossary 2.

20. Skt. *durgati*. The three bad migrations are those of (1) denizens of hells, (2) inhabitants of the "limbo" of the *pretaloka*, where one wanders as an insatiably hungry and thirsty wretch, and (3) animals, who are trapped in the pattern of mutual devouring (Tib. *gcig la gcig za*). See Glossary 2.

21. For exhaustive references concerning the presence of some of these bodhisattvas in other Mahāyāna sūtras, see Lamotte, pp. 100–102, ns. 12–33. The Chinese lists in K and H vary somewhat; see Luk, pp. 3–4, for K; and Lamotte, p. 102, for H. For information about the more well-known bodhisattvas, see Glossary 1.

22. In the Buddhist popular cosmology, a *Brahmā* is the supreme creator-god of a particular universe, which thus conforms nominally to the Indian belief of the day. The particular Mahāyāna vision of a multiplicity of universes is evidenced by the presence of ten thousand of these gods, each one from his own universe, and their leader, Śikhin, coming from the *Aśoka* ("sorrowless") universe.

23. A Śakra, alias Indra, is a king of gods of the desire-realm (*kāmadhātu*) of a particular universe; hence a Śakra is lower in status than a Brahmā, who resides at the summit of the realm of pure matter (*rūpadhātu*).

24. The Lokapālas are the World-Protectors, alias the Mahārājas, who act as guardians of the four quarters, namely, Vaiśravana, Dhṛtarāṣṭra, Virūḍhaka, and Virūpākṣa. They are particularly prominent in the *Suvarṇābhāsa-sūtra,* wherein they come forth and vow to uphold the Dharma and protect its teachers and practitioners. Again, each universe has its own set of four, so quite a few may be assumed to be present in this assembly.

25. The list from "devas" to "mahoragas" are names for the eight kinds of supernatural beings always present in the Buddha's audience: gods, benevolent dragonlike beings, forest-demons, fairies, titans, eaglelike magical birds, mountain creatures like horse-headed humans, and serpentlike creatures (*devanāgayakṣagandharvāsuragaruḍakiṃnaramahoraga*).

26. Bhikṣus are full-fledged monks who live by begging, and bhikṣuṇīs are their female counterparts. Laymen and laywomen (*upāsaka* and *upāsikā*) are householders with definite vows that set them off from the ordinary householder.

27. Tib. *dkon mchog 'byun gnas* (lit. "Jewel-Mine"). The Chinese versions give his name as "Jewel-Ray" (*Ratnarāśi*), although the Skt. *Ratnākara* is supported by his appearance in a number of other Mahāyāna sūtras, where he is also identified as a Licchavi, a merchant's son, and a great bodhisattva of the tenth stage. For full references, see Lamotte, p. 103, n. 38.

28. The jewels were gold, silver, pearl, sapphire, ruby, emerald, and diamond, although various sources alter this list slightly.

29. Skt. *trisahasramahāsahasralokadhātu* (lit. "three-thousand-great-thousand-world realm"). Each of these is composed of one thousand realms, each of which contains one thousand realms, each of which contains one thousand realms = one thousand to the third power = one billion worlds. The term "galaxy" was chosen to evoke the sense of inconceivable scope intended by the original Skt. term, as such cosmological terms were never aimed at material precision, but rather at triggering an imaginative vision of inconceivable cosmic immensity. I have modified the following catalogue of objects and places to conform to a more modern cosmology.

30. This list of mountains, according to Lamotte (p. 104, n. 41), occurs in other Mahāyāna sūtras but does not correspond to usual Buddhist cosmology, except for the fact that Sumeru, mentioned first, is in the center (of each world) and Mount Cakravāḍa, actually a mountain range, is mentioned and surrounds each world of four continents. This list is first in the order of T.

31. Tib. *źi gnas pha rol phyin mchog brñes*; Skt. *śamathāpāramitāprāpta. Śamathā* can be adequately rendered "mental quiescence" when it refers in general to one of the two main types of Mahāyāna meditation; the other is "transcendental analysis" or "analytic insight" (*vipaśyana*). In this verse, however, Ratnākara refers to it in its aspect of final attainment; hence "trance" best conveys the sense of extreme one-pointed fixation of mind.

32. Tib. *skyes bui khyu mchog*; Skt. *puruṣarṣabha*. This common epithet of the Buddha contains the simile comparing him to the chief bull of a herd of cattle because of his power and majesty.

33. Tib. *'chi med 'gro*; Skt. *amṛtaga* (lit. "goes to deathlessness"). The Buddhas' teachings lead to nirvāṇa; in nirvāṇa there is no birth, and where there is no birth there is no death.

34. The subtle difference here between T and Ch. of K and H is noteworthy. T causally relates "deep analysis of things" (Skt. *dharma-pravicaya*) to the teaching of their ultimate meaning, which accords with the Indo-Tibetan emphasis on "transcendental analysis" (*vipaśyana*) as indispensable for realization of the ultimate nature of things. Ch. (both K and H) puts the two (analysis and the ultimate) in opposition, saying, " (You are) expert in analysis of the nature of all things, (*yet* are) unmoved with respect to the ultimate meaning, (as you have) already attained sovereignty with respect to all things."

35. The fact about Buddhist doctrine that most baffled ancient critics is that the cause and effect of karma operates without any ego principle to link the doer of an action and the experiencer of that action's karmic effects.

36. Skt. *tīrthika*. Although "heterodox" may be less familiar than the familiar "heretic," it is less fraught with the connotations of fanaticism; such connotations do not apply in Buddhism because it is not simply a "faith" to be believed or disbelieved. The Tibetan grammar leaves it ambiguous as to whether the absence of feeling, etc., refers to enlightenment or to the heterodox. K and H indicate the former, but we have chosen the latter to avoid characterizing supreme enlightenment as a mere "nonthought," etc., since it obviously transcends all polarities. Further, it is in keeping with the tenor of the Scripture to distinguish between enlightenment and the mere attainment of even the most advanced samādhi.

37. Tib. *lan gsum bzlas pa chos kyi 'khor lo rnam maṅ po*. Although T does not mention the aspects as "twelve," Lamotte supplies this from the occurrence of the formula in other Scriptures, where the three revolutions correspond respectively to the paths of Insight (*darśanamārga*), Meditation (*bhāvanāmārga*), and Mastery (*aśaikṣamārga*), each revolution having four aspects corresponding to the Four Holy Truths. The first revolution involves recognition of each truth, the second thorough knowledge of each, and the third complete realization of each. See Lamotte, p. 107, n. 49; Mvy, nos. 1309–1324. However, since T does not mention the "twelve aspects" (nor do K and H), but rather "many aspects," it is possible that what is referred to is the three doctrines of the Buddha elaborated in the *Saṃdhinirmocanasūtra*, also known as the "Three Turnings of the Wheel of Dharma"; namely, the Hinayāna teaching of the Four Holy Truths, the Mādhyamika teaching of the Transcendent Wisdom, and the Vijñānavāda teaching of "Fine Discrimination Between Existence and Nonexistence" (see SN, VII, no. 30, pp. 85, 206).

38. After this verse, there are two verses in K and H, not in T. For verses in K, see Luk, p. 7, ll. 3–10; for H see Lamotte, p. 108. Since H tends to be more consistent with T, I will translate H: "The billion-world galaxy, with its realms of gods and dragons, appears in the little parasols offered to the Lord; thus we bow to his vision, knowledge, and mass of virtues. The Lord displays the worlds to us with this miracle—they all are like a play of lights, as all bear witness in astonishment. Obeisance to the Lord of ten powers, endowed with knowledge and vision."

39. Skt. *āveṇikabuddhadharma*. This and the subsequent two verses (Chap. 3) illustrate some of the special buddha-qualities, which total eighteen (see Glossary 2 for a complete list).

40. This verse in T appears to be a contraction of two verses in K and H: "The Lord speaks with but one voice, but all beings, each according to his kind, gain understanding, each thinking that the Lord speaks his own language. This is a special quality of the Buddha. The Lord speaks with but one voice, but all beings, each according to his own ability, act upon it, and each derives his appropriate benefit. This is a special quality of the Buddha." For K see Luk, p. 7. For an interesting discussion of the speech of the Buddha, see Lamotte, pp. 109–110, n. 52.

41. This and the preceding two lines ascribe to the Buddha the attainment of the three doors of liberation (see Glossary 2).

42. Tib. *byaṅ chub sems dpa rnams kyi saṅs rgyas kyi źiṅ yoṅs su dag pa*; Skt. *bodhisattvānāṃ buddhakṣetrapariśodhana* (or *pariśuddhi*). Although the explanations given by the Buddha obviate the need for discussion of the meaning of this term, it is worthwhile to note that this concept is the logical corollary of the bodhisattva's conception of enlightenment: that it be attained for the sake of all sentient beings as well as for his own sake. Thus, the bodhisattva's quest for enlightenment does not involve merely his own development, although that is of course primary; it must also involve his cultivation of a whole "field" of living beings, those who, through karmic interconnection, have destinies intertwined with his, occupying the same worlds as he, etc. Hence, his purification of a buddha-field is a mode of expressing his ambition to cultivate a whole world or universe while he cultivates himself, so that he and his field of living beings may reach enlightenment simultaneously.

43. Tib. *'phags pa lta bui dbaṅ po*; Skt. *āryendriyāni* or *pañcendriyāni*. The five spiritual faculties (see Glossary 2).

44. K and H differ here quite radically. H: "For example, sons, if one should wish to construct a palace in an unoccupied place and then adorn it, he could do so freely and without hindrance, but if he wished to build it in empty space itself, he could never succeed. In the same way, the bodhisattva, although he knows that all things are like empty space, produces pure qualities, for the development and benefit of living beings. That is the buddha-field which he embraces. To embrace a buddha-field in this way is not like building in empty space." K: "It is as if a man wished to build a building in a vacant place—he could do so without difficulty. But (if he wished to do it) in empty space, he could not succeed. Likewise, the bodhisattva, in order to cultivate all living beings, wants to embrace a buddha-field. One who thus wishes to embrace a buddha-field (does not do so) in the void."

The first impulse of the translator is to resort to the Ch. versions in the interest of simplicity and ease, since the simile there is much more clearly drawn: vacant lot = living beings, empty space = any sort of materialistic notion about a buddha-field; *ergo* building on solid needs of living beings succeeds, and any other way fails. However, upon reflection, what does the Buddha wish to convey in this example? Are not living beings and their needs and purposes just as ultimately empty as "all things"? Would not the concretization of the benefit of living beings violate the definition of liberative technique integrated with wisdom given by Vimalakīrti himself (see Chap. 5, p. 47)? Is it not more fitting to understand the Buddha here as telling us not to concretize any mundane aims, however beneficial, but that the bodhisattva's great compassion must always adhere to the wisdom that sees the ephemerality of all purposive notions, constructed or constructive? When we undertake something we know to be essentially impossible, through the sheer intensity of compassion, do we not enter the realm of inconceivability? Finally, may not the Buddha be speaking in tune with his own subsequent miraculous display, as he demonstrates the actual possibility for him, no less than for space-age technology, of building a pure buddha-field in the empty space of ultimate voidness?

45. Tib. *bsam pa*; Skt. *āśaya*. Positive thought aids in the conception of the spirit of enlightenment and in the cultivation of the transcendences; in general, it is a joyous attitude to help living beings and accomplish virtue. For further discussion see Glossary 3 and Lamotte, *Appendice*, Note II.

46. H changes the order of these four to conception, positive thought, virtuous application, and high resolve. Either order is quite acceptable, since the four work together throughout the bodhisattva's career.

47. Tib. *yaṅ dag pa ñid du ṅes pa*; Skt. *samyaktvaniyata*. This generally describes one who has reached the holy path, either in Hinayāna or Mahāyāna practice (see Glossary 3, and Lamotte, p. 115, n. 65).

48. Skt. *catvāryapramāṇāni*. Immeasurable states, otherwise known as "pure abodes" (*brahmāvihāra*). A common Tibetan prayer formulates them as follows: Immeasurable love arises from the wish for all living beings to have happiness and the cause of happiness. Immeasurable compassion arises from the wish for all living beings to be free from suffering and its cause. Immeasurable joy arises from the wish that living beings not be sundered from the supreme happiness of liberation. And immeasurable impartiality arises from the wish that the preceding—love, compassion, and joy—should apply equally to all living beings, without attachment to friend or hatred for enemy. See Glossary 2.

49. These basic precepts are five in number for the laity: (1) not killing, (2) not stealing, (3) chastity, (4) not lying, and (5) avoiding intoxicants. For monks, there are three or five more; avoidance of such things as perfumes, makeup, ointments, garlands, high beds, and afternoon meals.

50. This phrase is taken from K (it is absent in T and H) because it rounds out the list of ten virtues, being the counterpart of the sin known as "frivolous speech." "Free of divisive intrigues and adroit in reconciling factions" basically describes one virtue, the opposite of "backbiting" (see Glossary 2) under "ten sins" and "ten virtues."

51. This step of "development..." is included in the progression by both K and H, and, since it makes more explicit the transition from liberative technique to the buddha-field itself, we have included it (although it is absent in T).

52. Tib. *ye śes sgrub pa*; Skt. *jñānasādhana* (lit. "practice through knowledge," taking it as *jñānena sādhanaṃ*). Transcendental practice, as opposed to practice at an earlier stage.

53. Śāriputra was one of the foremost disciples of the Buddha, especially renowned in Hinayāna texts for his wisdom; he was called "foremost of the wise" (*prajñāvatām agrya*). In this sūtra, as well as in other Mahāyāna scriptures, he becomes the "fall guy" par excellence, as he is often inclined to express the Hinayāna point of view, which is then roundly rejected by the Buddha, by Vimalakīrti, or by one of the bodhisattvas. In fairness to him, it is often noted that the petty thoughts that arise in his mind, for which he is severely criticized, are caused to arise there by the magical influence of the Buddha or of Vimalakīrti, so that a thought that may be entertained by numerous members of the assembly may be brought into the open and rejected. He serves therefore as an archetype of the disciple-personality and need not be condemned as exceptionally obtuse personally.

54. Skt. *paranīrmitavaśavartin*. The deities of this, the sixth level of the gods of the desire-realm, appropriate and enjoy the magical creations of others; hence their name, literally, "who assume control of the emanations of others." Their abode contains all the wonders created elsewhere and is referred to as a standard of splendor.

55. Lit. the Buddha "Jewel-Array," his universe, lit. "infinite array of jewel-qualities."

56. The heaven of the "Thirty-Three," second level of the desire-realm, located on top of Mount Sumeru in the Buddhist cosmology.

57. Tib. *rjes su 'thun pai bzod pa*; Skt. *anulomikī kṣāntiḥ*. This is the stage of tolerance attained on the sixth bodhisattva-stage, that of "Confrontation" (*abhimukhī*).

58. Skt. *Śrāvakayāna*. Teaching of the disciples.

59. Skt. *dharmacakṣu*. One of the "five eyes," representing superior insights of the Buddhas and bodhisattvas (see Glossary 2).

60. Skt. *bodhicittotpāda*. This refers to an extremely important moment in the lives of a living being: It marks his entrance into the Mahāyāna, i.e., the "Great Vehicle" of the bodhisattva. It is a turning point of psychic development, a point where a being realizes simultaneously that (1) his "normal" consciousness is ignorance, like sleep compared to awakened consciousness, (2) it is possible, desirable, and essential that he awake from this wretched sleep of ignorance, and (3) other living beings are caught in the same trap and must be awakened by him as he becomes awakened. In short, one conceives of the possibility of Buddhahood and becomes inspired to attain it. Thus, it is more than "an arising of thought," or "production of mind" of enlightenment. It is a conception, as life begins in a conception, of a higher spirit that inspires and spiritualizes mind and life, that aims at enlightenment and, in so aiming, is itself a manifestation of enlightenment. All treatises on the Mahāyāna begin with detailed descriptions of this event, the methods of its cultivation, and its virtues and benefits.

Chapter 2

1. Tib. *mi 'jigspa*; Skt. *vaiśāradya*. See Glossary 2, under "four fearlessnesses."

2. Thus, his conduct and knowledge conformed to the six transcendences.

3. The three realms of all universes (*tridhātavaḥ*) (see Glossary 2, under "three worlds").

4. Tib. *slas*; Skt. *sahacāri*. Female attendants who normally assisted the wife of a wealthy householder.

5. Tib. *'jig rten daṅ 'jig rten las 'das pai gsaṅ sṅags daṅ bstan bcos*; Skt. *laukikalokottara-mantraśāstra*. This is a possible reference to Tantric practices, but it is missing in both K and H, who mention only "mundane practices."

6. Vimalakīrti is here shown as the embodiment of the practice of "reconciliation of dichotomies."

7. This sentence is absent in K and H.

8. Both K and H have, instead of this phrase, ". . . because he taught them loyalty and filial devotion."

8a. Tib. *mi rtag par* is missing, but supplied from K, H, and Lamotte, p. 130.

9. These similes are famous in Hinayāna as well as Mahāyāna. The fact of their presence in Hinayāna teachings was used by Prāsaṅgika philosophers such as Buddhapālita and Candrakīrti, to prove that insubstantiality or selflessness of phenomena (*dharmanairātmyā*) was taught in Hinayāna. For further references, see Lamotte, p. 132, n. 23.

10. According to Lamotte, the four hundred and four diseases are classified with one hundred and one arising from each of four primary elements. But according to the "eight branches" (*aṣṭāṇga*) of Indian and Tibetan medicine, they arise from the three humors, *vāyu*, *pīta*, and *praseka* (vital airs, bile, and phlegm, Tib. *rluṅ mkhris bad kan gsum*), when their balance becomes disturbed: i.e., one hundred and one from airs, one hundred and one from bile, one hundred and one from phlegm, and one hundred and one from unhealthy combinations of all three.

11. Skt. *skandhadhātvāyatanāni*. These classifications of the psychophysical elements of persons are fundamental in Buddhist doctrine, as they explain the workings of an egoless being. For a discussion of these important concepts, see Glossary 2, "five aggregates," "twelve media," and "eighteen elements." Comparison of these three categorizations of the elements of existence to murderers, snakes, and an empty town is traditional. See Chap. 4, n. 24, and Lamotte, p. 136, n. 28.

12. *Dharmakāya*. Ultimate Body.

13. Tib. has simply "born from merit and charity." I followed K. The store of merit culminates in the Sambhogakāya, Body of Beatitude, and the store of wisdom culminates in the Dharmakāya, Ultimate Body.

14. Skt. *śīla*, *samādhi*, *prajñā*, *vimukti*, and *vimuktijñānadarśana* are the five Dharma-aggregates, or pure aggregates, or members of the Dharma-body of the Buddha (see Lamotte, p. 139, n. 30, and Glossary 2, under "five pure aggregates").

15. These are the two main types of Mahāyāna meditation. The former corresponds to the fifth transcendence and includes all practices that cultivate one-pointedness of mind; the latter corresponds to the sixth transcendence, especially the analytic penetration to the realization of personal selflessness (*pudgalanairātmya*) and phenomenal selflessness (*dharmanairātmya*), or voidness. The latter is not so well known as the former, which is commonly considered to be the main type of meditation: nondiscursive, one-pointed, etc. Nevertheless, it is said frequently in both Scriptures and commentaries that without integrated practice of both, the higher stages of enlightenment will not be attained. For more details, see Glossary 3 (under "mental quiescence" and "transcendental analysis").

16. Tib. *bag yod*; Skt. *apramāda*. This special type of conscious awareness is born, in relation to the most minute details of the relative world, of the realization of voidness, a fact that gives further corroboration of the apparent paradox that knowledge of the apparently trivial is born of knowledge of ultimate reality. "Who realizes voidness, he is conscious" (*yaḥ śūnyatāṃ jānati so 'pramattaḥ. Anavataptahradāpasaṃkramaṇasūtra*, quoted in *Prasannapadā*, Ch. 13).

Chapter 3

1. T has Chaps. 3 and 4 as one chapter, but I followed K and H in dividing them into two.

2. Skt. *utsāhate*. This has been translated most frequently in its meaning of "fitness, capacity," as each of the monks and bodhisattvas asked by the Buddha to visit Vimalakīrti replies with the same phrase: "I am not fit..." or "I am not able...." However, from the Tibetan use of the word *spro ba*, which means to be enthusiastic, inspired, gladdened, I chose to interpret this in its meaning of enthusiasm, which in the negative gives "I am not enthusiastic..." or "I am reluctant...." That is, none of those asked by the Buddha are actually pretending to be unable to visit Vimalakīrti; they only plead their unwillingness, timidity, etc., in order to be excused by the Buddha from carrying out his command.

3. Skt. *tridhātavaḥ*. World of three realms: of desire, pure matter, and immateriality (see Glossary 2, under "three worlds").

4. Skt. *nirodha*. The third Holy Truth, equivalent to nirvāṇa (see Glossary 2, under "Four Holy Truths").

5. Vimalakīrti confounds Śāriputra by demanding of him the ability to reconcile dichotomies in actual practice, i.e., by rejecting Śāriputra's Hinayāna position and expecting him to follow the way of the bodhisattva. Śāriputra reacts in the same way as the other monks and bodhisattvas in this and the following chapter: He is overwhelmed and speechless, yet intuitively recognizes the rightness of Vimalakīrti's statements. He can neither accept them and put them into practice nor reject them outright (see Lamotte, p. 142, n. 3).

6. Maudgalyāyana was known as the "foremost of those endowed with miraculous powers" (*ṛddhimatāṃ agrya*) and was paired with Śāriputra as one of the two leading disciples of the Buddha. Vimalakīrti chastises him basically for failing to use his "wisdom eye," his superknowledge of telepathy (*paracittajñāna*), to determine that his listeners were willing and able to learn and understand the Mahāyāna teaching of the profound nature of reality, and for teaching them instead the Hinayāna teaching, with its one-sided emphasis on world-rejection, etc.

7. Tib. *rlabs thams cad daṅ bral ba*; Skt. *sarvataraṅgavirahita.* Lit. "free of all waves" (of thought).

8. Skt. *dharmadhātu.* This is not the *dharmadhātu* (phenomenal element) included among the eighteen elements (see Glossary 2). It is one of the five synonyms of voidness included in Maitreya's *Madhyāntavibhāga,* I, 15—*tathatā bhūtakoṭiśca 'nimittaṃ paramārthatā / dharmadhātuśca paryāyāḥ śūnyatāyāḥ samāsataḥ //*—where it is analyzed in a rather unusual way as "the element of Dharma, from which arise the holy qualities of the saints. . . ." However, Tib. *dbyiṅs* definitely indicates interpretation of *dhātu* as space, realm, etc., rather than element; so, with the proviso that it is a synonym of voidness, I have translated it "ultimate realm" (i.e., no relative realm at all). See Glossary 3, under "ultimate realm."

9. Skt. *bhūtakoṭi.* Also included among the synonyms discussed in n. 8. See Glossary 3, under "reality-limit."

10. This passage follows H quite closely, but K is somewhat different in details (see Luk, pp. 21–22).

11. This refers to those teachings (of *śūnyatā,* etc.) the Buddha reserves for disciples of greatest ability, definitive teachings (*nītārthavacana*) as opposed to teaching meant to develop disciples (to the point when they can understand the definitive teachings), which are known as interpretable teachings (*neyārthavacana*). See Glossary 3, under "definitive meaning."

12. Mahākāśyapa was known as "the foremost among the upholders of the ascetic practices" (*dhūtaguṇavādinām agraḥ*) and was the Buddha's successor as leader of the Saṅgha after the Parinirvāṇa. Here he is engaged in one of the twelve ascetic practices (see Glossary 2), that of living on food begged as alms (*paiṇḍapātika*). Thus, in the very execution of his specialty he is scolded by Vimalakīrti, who points out to him that such practices are intrinsically worthless and are useful only if combined with the true equanimity reached through the wisdom that realizes voidness.

13. Skt. *ekadeśamaitrī.* Kāśyapa is favoring the poor here by depriving the rich of the chance to give food to him and thus benefit themselves.

14. Tib. *ril por 'dzin pa*; Skt. *piṇḍagrāha* (lit. "notion of mass"). The sense, which ordinarily binds us, of the "objective" solidity and physical reality of things.

15. Skt. *buddhagotra.* All living beings belong to this exalted family because all have the capacity to wake up to enlightenment, conceiving its spirit within themselves and thenceforward seeking its realization (see Chap. VIII and Glossary 1).

16. Skt. *Yasya na svabhāvaparabhāvau tad na jvalati, yad na jvalati tad na śāmyate.* This seemingly irrelevant statement, which occurs again in Vimalakīrti's speech to Kātyāyana (p. 29), is, in fact, highly relevant to the main Hinayāna concern: the burning of the misery of the world, in which, they believe, man's condition is like that of one whose head is ablaze. Hence their major preoccupation is to extinguish that fire, just as a burning man will seek water with a frantic intensity to save himself. Thus Vimalakīrti is telling Mahākāśyapa and Kātyāyana that since they do not have intrinsic substance, self, or any imparted substance (i.e., self constituted by relationship with other things), they do not really exist and, therefore, they cannot burn with the misery of the world and there is nothing to extinguish in liberation (*nirvāṇa* literally meaning "extinguishment").

17. See Glossary 2, under "eight branches of the holy path" and "eight false paths of perversion."

18. Among Subhūti's other strong points, he was known as the "foremost among those worthy of offerings," *dakṣiṇeyānāṃ agraḥ*" (see Lamotte, p. 154, n. 27). Thus Vimalakīrti challenges him precisely about his worthiness, defining it by testing Subhūti's equanimity in the face of all the most unworthy things he can think of and causing Subhūti to feel frightened and confused by his own adherence to dualities such as good and evil.

19. Tib. *'jig lta* or *'jig tshogs la lta ba*; Skt. *kāyadṛṣṭi* or *satkāyadṛṣṭi*. See Glossary 3, under "egoistic views."

20. Tib. *mtshams med lṅa*—lit. "the five (sins) (whose retribution is) immediate (after death)." See Glossary 3.

21. These truths are considered valid in the Mahāyāna as well as in the Hinayāna, but their interpretation differs (see Glossary 2).

22. By "fruit," Vimalakīrti means any of the culminating stages of realization attained by those who practice the teachings, such as the four holy truths, the twofold selflessness, etc.

23. These six were well-known opponents of the Buddha, teachers of nihilism, sophism, determinism, asceticism, etc. They were allowed to proclaim their doctrines unchallenged until a famous assembly at Śrāvastī, where the Buddha eclipsed them with a display of miracles and teachings. For details of their doctrines and further references, see Glossary 2, under "six heterodox teachers."

24. Tib. *ñon moṅs pa med pa* (lit. "absence of passions," or afflictions). However,K and H use "nondisputation," equivalent to Skt. *araṇa*, which is actually equivalent to dispassion, since the "struggle," or "disputation," referred to is internal, the turbulence of inner struggle of one prey to passions. This is perhaps more appropriate here, since Subhūti was renowned for his attainment of this state (see Lamotte, p. 154, n. 27; *araṇavihārīnām agro*, etc.).

25. K and H: "if those who make offerings to you do not find in you a field of merit."

26. According to the Mahāyānistic understanding of the miraculous nature of the Three Bodies of the Buddha, especially the "Incarnation-Body" (*Nirmāṇakāya*), Vimalakīrti himself is an extremely likely candidate to be one of its operatives. Thus, one steeped in the Mahāyāna faith would see him here as being subtly playful with Subhūti. See Glossary 3, "incarnation-body."

27. Tib. *yi ge de dag thams cad ni yi ge med pa ste / rnam par grol ba ni ma gtogs so / chos thams cad ni rnam par grol bai mtshan ñid do.* K and H differ slightly, but essentially have the same meaning: "Language does not have an independent nature. When it is no more, there is liberation." In other words, no independent nature = ultimately nonexistent; it is no more = when the ultimate is realized; then liberation = when even words are realized to be liberation, there is no more duality, and there is realization. Ch. stresses the experiential moment of pure gnosis of voidness. Tib. expresses this gnosis along with its nondual, postattainment wisdom (*pṛṣṭhalabdhajñāna*). It is Vimalakīrti's last word on nonduality to instruct Subhūti.

28. Pūrṇa, "son of Maitrāyaṇī," was known as "the foremost of expounders of the Dharma" (*dharmakathikānām agraḥ*; see Lamotte, p. 160, n. 42). According to the Pāli sources (as cited by Lamotte), this very incident, or one similar to it, resulted in five hundred young monks' attainment of sainthood. In any case, it can be assumed that Pūrṇa was often entrusted with the instruction of young monks, and it was just such an occasion on which Vimalakīrti apprehended him. His reproaches are along the same line as those given to Maudgalyāyana, only more explicit, i.e., that the great disciples should not teach the Dharma because they cannot recognize the affinity for the Mahāyāna in their pupils.

29. This means they attained the eighth bodhisattva stage, called "The Immovable," where the bodhisattva becomes irreversible (*avaivartika*) and previous to which he is liable to regression, even to forgetting the spirit of enlightenment already conceived in former lifetimes, as in the case of these monks.

30. Kātyāyana was renowned as the founder of the Abhidharma tradition of analysis of the meaning of the Buddha's discourses. He was pronounced by the Buddha, according to the Pāli sources, to be the "foremost expounder of the detailed meaning of the concise declarations (of the Buddha)" (*aggo saṅkhittena bhāsitassa vitthārena attham vibhajantānam*). True to form, Vimalakīrti finds him when he is engaged in the execution of his special expertise (see Lamotte, p. 162, n. 49 and Glossary 1.

31. These four are called the "four insignia of the Dharma" (*dharmamudra*) or "four epitomes" (see Glossary 2).

32. K and H insert: "That all things do not exist ultimately is the meaning of voidness."

33. See n. 16.

34. Aniruddha was said to be "foremost among possessors of the divine eye" (*agro divyacakṣukānām*). See Lamotte, p. 167, n. 56, and Glossary 1.

35. Skt. *dīvyacakṣu*. This is the name for the supernormal ability to see to an unlimited distance, observe events on other worlds, see through mountains, etc. See n. 36 below.

36. Skt. *pañcābhijñāḥ*. The divine eye is one of these (see Glossary 2, under "five superknowledges"), and it can be attained by heterodox yogis as well as Buddhist saints and bodhisattvas.

37. This dilemma was more embarrassing to Aniruddha than confounding, since logically he could have answered that of course his divine eye was compounded, just like that of heterodox adepts. Vimalakīrti touched his pride in this critique; hence the dilemma he poses here bears only superficial resemblance to the Mādhyamika dialectic.

38. Upāli was especially well known as expert in Vināya, the code of monastic discipline, and was its chief compiler after the Parinirvāṇa (*vināyadharāṇām agraḥ*).

39. Tib. *the tsom sol te bdag cag gñis ltuṅ ba las phyuṅ śig* (lit. "remove our doubts and take us both out from the infraction!"). The "absolution" consists in the senior monk's listening to their confession and encouraging their resolution not to repeat the infraction. Thus he grants no dispensations in regard to the retributive effects and only gives them the opportunity to come to a new understanding and decision in their own minds. This is traditional in Buddhist discipline.

40. The "nature of the mind" referred to is its voidness, or selflessness.

41. "Purity" is inserted according to K and H, as making more explicit the "intrinsic nature."

42. Skt. *Vināyadhara.* As usual, Vimalakīrti makes his point on the disciple's home ground: Upāli was known as *vināyadharāṇāṃ agraḥ*, "foremost upholder of the discipline," as the two monks mention in the next paragraph.

43. Rāhula was the actual son of the Buddha and was admired in the Saṅgha as a renunciant and devotee because he forsook the throne to join the Saṅgha under his father. The Pāli sources show him dubbed "foremost among those eager for training" (*śikṣhākāmānam agro*). See Lamotte, p. 177, n. 70, and Glossary I.

44. Tib. *thog mai daṅ tha mai mthar lta ba daṅ bral bao.* K and H have instead: "Renunciation is beyond this, that, and in between, being above the sixty-two false views."

45. Some verses of Tsoṅ Khapa summarize the Mahāyāna "mind of renunciation" very aptly: "Reverse the interest in this life by thinking over again and again that leisure and opportunity (to practice the Dharma) are hard to find and that there is no (fixed) duration of life. Reverse interest in the life hereafter by constantly meditating upon the inexorability of karma and the sufferings of the world. Through such concentration, when there is not the slightest ambition, even for a split second, for even the greatest successes in the world, the mind of renunciation has arisen." See G. Wangyal, *Door of Liberation* (New York, Girodias, 1973), Chap. V.

46. Even after his explanation, the young men still confuse renunciation, a mental concentration, with the mundane act of entering the monkhood. So Vimalakīrti has to remind them that the conception of the spirit of enlightenment is the true renunciation, not just a mere change of clothes and habits.

47. T has thirty-two hundred, but K and H have thirty-two, which seems more reasonable.

48. Ānanda was renowned for many things: learning, mindfulness, steadfastness, etc., and was the second leader of the Saṅgha, after Mahākāśyapa. Vimalakīrti finds fault with him when he is being "foremost of attendants" (*aggo upaṭṭhākānām*), caring for the Buddha's apparent needs as he did faithfully for twenty-five years.

49. See Lamotte, p. 183, n. 77, for learned references to this incident in other sources, notably *Vatsasūtra.*

50. Tib. *gźan mu stegs can spyod pa pa daṅ kun tu rgyu daṅ gcer bu pa daṅ tsho ba pa dag*; equivalent to Skt. *anyatīrthika caraka parivrajaka nirgrantha jīvika.* I have simply rendered this "heterodox sectarians" so as not to burden the reader with irrelevant names, as this expression is a cliché for all the heterodox groups occurring in other Mahāyāna Scriptures (see Lamotte, p. 186, n. 81).

51. Voices from sky-gods are common in Mahāyāna Scriptures.

52. See Lamotte, p. 186, n. 82, for another version of this episode translated by Kumārajīva in *Prajñāpāramitopadeśa.*

Chapter 4

1. Maitreya (lit. "Loving One") was predicted by Śākyamuni to be the next Buddha on earth; he was designated to reign in the Tuṣita heaven, whence all Buddhas descend to earth, until his incarnation, which, according to Buddhist belief, will occur in 4456 A.D. His characterization in Mahāyāna scriptures is that of having a certain naiveté. Mañjuśrī often chides him, and Vimalakīrti does not let him rest on his laurels.

2. Tuṣita is the fourth level of the heavens of the desire-realm (see n. 1).

3. Skt. *niyāmāvakrānti*. See Chap. 1, n. 47, and Glossary 3, under "ultimate determination."

4. K and H give a different reading: "How then, Maitreya, did you receive the prophecy of your attainment of Buddhahood after only one more birth? Did you receive it as the reality of birth or as the reality of death? In the former case, this reality is uncreated, and in the latter case, it does not die." As always, Ch. is less abstract than Tib., but both agree on the general tenor of Vimalakīrti's refutation of Maitreya's acceptance of the prophecy as being valid on the ultimate level of reality (*paramārthasatyatā*). On the question of the validity of prophecies on the superficial and ultimate levels, see Lamotte, p. 189, n. 89.

5. The thrust of Vimalakīrti's instruction here is that "being enlightened" and "being unenlightened" are valid designations only on the superficial, designative, relative level of truth. "Discriminative construction" is that mental process that seeks to "absolutize" a relative thing, taking "ignorance" and "enlightenment" as ultimately real things. Thus in all the subsequent negational descriptions of enlightenment, the phrase "on the ultimate level" may be understood to avert a nihilistic interpretation. See Introduction, pp. 1 ff.

6. Skt. *dharmadhātu*. See Chap. 3, n. 8.

7. Skt. *bhūtakoṭi*. See Chap. 3, n. 9.

8. Skt. *ṣaḍāyatanāni*. Visual, auditory, olfactory, gustatory, tactile, and mental (see Glossary 2, under "six sense-media").

9. Tib. *rnam par rig pa med pa*; Skt. *avijñapti* (lit. "without means of cognition"). Again, it may be stressed that all these statements imply the qualification "ultimately" (*paramārthena*).

10. Lit. "Light-Array." He was mentioned among the bodhisattvas in the assembly on p. 11.

11. Tib. *byaṅ chub kyi sñiṅ po* (lit. "essence of enlightenment"); Skt. *bodhimaṇḍa*. Haribhadra defines it as "a place used as a seat, where the *maṇḍa*, here 'essence,' of enlightenment is present." See Lamotte, p. 198, n. 105. The main "seat of enlightenment" is the spot under the bo tree at Buddhagaya, where the Buddha sat and attained unexcelled, perfect enlightenment. It is not to be confused with *bodhimaṇḍala*, "circle of enlightenment."

12. This paragraph correlates the seat of enlightenment with the six transcendences.

13. This paragraph correlates the seat of enlightenment with the four immeasurables.

14. Skt. *abhijñā*.

15. Skt. *saṃgrahavastu*. See Glossary 2, under "four means of unification."

16. Tib. *ṅes par sems pa*. Analytic concentration that gains insight into the nature of reality, synonymous with "transcendental analysis" (*vipaśyana*); see Glossary 3.

17. Skt. *bodhipakṣikadharma*. See Glossary 2, under "thirty-seven aids to enlightenment."

18. K and H: "It is the seat of interdependent origination, because it is like infinite space." Ch. thus takes pratītyasamutpāda (see Glossary 1) as equivalent to śūnyatā, which is correct as regards its ultimate nature. Vimalakīrti refers to the "cessation-order" of the twelve links of origination: that is, stopping ignorance stops synthetic activity; stopping synthetic activity stops consciousness; stopping consciousness stops name-and-form; stopping name-and-form stops the six sense-media; stopping the sense-media stops contact; stopping contact stops sensation; stopping sensation stops craving; stopping craving stops grasping; stopping grasping stops existence; stopping existence stops birth; and stopping birth stops old age and death. This is the sequence of realization of the twelvefold chain during the attainment of enlightenment on the seat of enlightenment.

19. Skt. *saddharmasaṃgraha*. Here taken as "incorporation" in the sense of the bodhisattva's incorporation of the holy Dharma in all phases of his daily life.

20. Tib. *'gro kar 'dzin pa*. This bodhisattva is mentioned in Mvy, No. 728, and in the *Rāṣṭrapālaparipṛccha* section of the *Ratnakūṭa Sūtra*. See Lamotte, p. 204, n. 120.

21. Kauśikā, Śakra, and Indra all refer to the same god, centrally prominent in the Vedas, who in Buddhist cosmogony is regarded as the king of gods in the desire-realm.

22. Skt. *Śākyaputrīya*. This implies that Jagatīṃdhara, although a layman, has religious vows of celibacy in the bodhisattva order of Śākyamuni.

23. Here Vimalakīrti is shown as an emanation of the Buddha, who encountered these same goddesses as temptresses during his night under the bodhi tree, where he subdued them. Here, Vimalakīrti not only subdues them but goes a step further and causes them to conceive the spirit of enlightenment.

24. See Chap. 2, n. 11. The aggregates murder the spirit of enlightenment when falsely considered as "I" and "mine" through egoistic views. The elements, when egoistically misapprehended as constituting an experiencing subject, its objects, and its perceptions, poison the health of liberation. And the sense-media are like an empty town, as there is no personality living within them.

25. It is commonly observed by the Buddha and all the great Buddhist philosophers, such as Nāgārjuna, that many feel frightened when taught the profound teaching of voidness because of misapprehensions about that most healing of concepts.

26. Skt. *dharmamukha*. Certain teachings are called "Dharma-doors," as they provide access to the practice of the Dharma.

27. Tib. *drin gzo ba*, or *byas pa gzo ba*; Skt. *kṛtajñaḥ*. This is one of the important themes of the meditation of the spirit of enlightenment, of love and compassion. The kind deeds of the Tathāgata consist in his appearance in the world in order to save living beings, as a kind mother will even sacrifice her life for her beloved child. This kindness is repaid by generating the same compassion for all other living beings and conceiving the spirit of enlightenment.

28. Sudatta is more commonly called Anāthapiṇḍada; he was a great philanthropist of Śrāvastī, known as "the foremost of donors" (Pāli; *aggo dāyakānaṃ*). For numerous references see Lamotte, p. 211, n. 135.

29. Skt. *mahāyajña*. The great sacrifice was an ancient Indian custom which, in Vedic times, was the central ritual of the Brahmanic religion. It usually consisted of sacrifices to the gods of various material things. By the Buddha's time, it was not uncommon for such an occasion to become rather a formalized period of donation to priests, ascetics, and beggars. However, the Buddha commonly declared that sacrifice and the giving of material things was infinitely less meritorious than sacrifice of egoism and the giving of the Dharma. This is the tenor of Vimalakīrti's critique.

30. Last phrase incorporated from K and H.

31. Last phrase incorporated from K and H.

32. This accords with the "Joy Immeasurable, which realizes the ultimate liberation of all beings from the beginningless," the standard description of the third of the "four immeasurables." See Glossary 2.

33. Skt. *jīvitendriya.* One of the nonmental motivations, defined as the force of life-duration, being a concept of the Abhidharma. See T. Stcherbatski, *Central Conception of Buddhism* (London, 1923), p. 105.

34. H follows T, but K has "of realizing firmness of body, life, and wealth, consummated in the three indestructibles." The three indestructibles are infinite body, endless life, and boundless wealth (see Luk, p. 46, n. 3), but this concept is apparently not found in Skt. or in Tib. Nevertheless, Tib. has the same meaning because the "body, health, and wealth" here referred to are not mundane in nature, but refer to the true body, etc., of the Buddha. See pp. 22–23.

35. In a later work, this would be taken as an obvious reference to Tantric yoga, but here, this yoga might also be interpreted as a reference to the highest yoga of the bodhisattva, the yoga of the inconceivable liberation. See Chap. 6.

36. Sudatta here misses the point, apparently, and, instead of awakening to the transvaluation of the notion of sacrifice, he again resorts to a material sacrifice. Thus, Vimalakīrti has to go beyond his previous statements and stage the following miracle to make his point.

Chapter 5

1. Mañjuśrī Kumārabhūta is traditionally regarded as the wisest of bodhisattvas. In Tibetan tradition he is known as *rgyal bai yab gcig,* the "Sole Father of Buddhas," as he inspires them in their realization of the profound. He is represented as bearing the sword of wisdom in his right hand and a volume of the *Prajñāpāramitāsūtra* in his left. He is always youthful in appearance, like a boy sixteen.

2. Skt. *yamakavyatyastāhārakuśala.* The twelfth of the eighteen special qualities of the bodhisattva (Mvy, nos. 787–804). See Glossary 2, under "eighteen special qualities of bodhisattva."

3. This enigmatic exchange signals the Mādhyamika tenor of the conversation. I have combined elements from K and T, their differences being insignificant in the light of their agreement on the deeper meaning. Vimalakīrti alludes to the simultaneity of the two levels of truth: On the ultimate level, no one comes, is seen, is heard; but on the superficial level, there he is, is seen, and is heard. There is no conflict between the two, since the seer does not see the voidness of the seer, the seeing, and the seen—all three *are* themselves voidness. Mañjuśrī agrees, emphasizing the impossibility of certain knowledge, in the ultimate sense, of superficial realities and thus the ephemeral, dreamlike nature of their conventional reality of coming, going, and seeing.

4. This extremely terse and subtle dialogue must be translated with the greatest grammatical precision to avoid confusion in meaning. It is all too tempting to translate the instrumental case (Ch. *yii*, Tib. *kyis*) as genitive, rendering the phrase "empty *by means of* emptiness" (*stoṅ pa ñid kyis stoṅ pa*) as "empty *of* emptiness," which then can be identified as the well-known voidness of voidness (*śūnyatāśūnyatā*), Vimalakīrti says here only that the buddha-fields are empty because that is their ultimate nature, not that they are equivalent to the emptiness of emptiness.

5. Mañjuśrī implies that Vimalakīrti is negating the validity of the superficial reality (*saṃvṛtisatya*), since, granted that the ultimate nature is emptiness, does that mean that any particular superficial thing, such as a buddha-field, is empty, even as a relative thing?

6. Vimalakīrti ignores the implication and repeats his statement of the ultimate reality of all things, mentioning specifically mental constructions (*parikalpa*) in place of buddha-fields.

7. Then Mañjuśrī challenges Vimalakīrti's use of the ultimate nature of emptiness, probing to see if Vimalakīrti might be hypostatizing emptiness as something, which could be constructed mentally or conceptualized.

8. Vimalakīrti rejects that possibility, finally introducing the concept of "emptiness *of* emptiness," i.e., that emptiness is itself but a conceptual construction and, as such, is itself empty of substantial, ultimate reality.

9. Skt. *dṛṣṭigata*. See Glossary 2, under "sixty-two convictions."

10. K: "Sickness is neither of the element earth, nor separate from it; and the same pertains to the other elements. Sicknesses of living beings arise from the four primary elements, and I am sick because of their sicknesses."

11. T: *ñes bar spyod pa thams cad bstan pa ste / 'pho bas ni ma yin no.* K and H: ". . . But not to consider that they have entered into the past." Tib. *'pho ba* can mean either "transmigration at death," or "transference," such as the transference of sin to another, who absolves the sinner with his blessing. This is not practiced in Buddhism, as no absolution is effective: Karmic effects cannot be avoided in any case, and the important thing is to cultivate the states of mind that refrain from wrongdoing.

12. Skt. *pūrvāntābhūta*. This refers to the Buddhist reasoning that there can have been no beginning of time because something cannot come from nothing; therefore there was no time when there was nothing, as opposed to the something that appears to be here now. Hence to indicate their sense of an eternal past, this phrase is used, rendered "from beginningless time."

13. The two thought processes here outlined follow the pattern of the meditation of the two selflessnesses: personal selflessness and phenomenal selflessness, or selflessness of things (*pudgalanairātmya* and *dharmanairātmya*). In short Vimalakīrti is equating sickness with the bodhisattva's very existence in the world, and the cure he prescribes is the cure for all misery in the world.

14. The concluding phrase on the voidness of voidness is incorporated from K. Note the central Mādhyamika thesis that all things exist conventionally as "mere designations" (*prajñaptimātra*).

15. This phrase is incorporated from K and H. Other slight differences between Ch. and Tib. in these passages do not alter the essential meaning.

16. In perceiving objects, we unconsciously assent to their apparent, self-sufficient, ultimate existence and thereby are confirmed in our innate phenomenal egoism. The only antidote for this deepest root of saṃsāric life is the subtle awareness of voidness.

17. Skt. *anupalabdhi*, or *anālambana*. About this important method, Bhāvaviveka has this to say (*Tarkajvāla*, IV, ad. k. 23): "In order to abandon adherence to materialism, one should condition oneself to the cultivation of nonperception. So doing, even a single instant of the undistorted, spontaneous realization of the reality of all things will eliminate the stream of passions with their instinctual drives, these instincts being the cohesive force in objective appearance. Thus, when no objects are perceived, there is no occasion for the arising of instinct. This is the method of the Mahāyāna."

18. This example explaining the word "*bodhisattva*" is strong evidence for the fact that "*sattva*" here has its meaning of "hero" or "warrior," rather than merely its meaning of "living being." This puts the Tib. *byaṅ chub sems dpa*, "enlightenment-mind-hero," in a favorable light.

19. Skt. *anunayadṛṣṭikaruṇā* (lit. "compassion of emotional conviction"). This is false compassion, according to the Mahāyāna, as it is not integrated with wisdom, hence not effective in actually alleviating the sufferings of living beings. See Glossary 3, under "great compassion."

20. "Reincarnation" is here used in the sense of "voluntary rebirth" to distinguish the coming into the world of a bodhisattva as opposed to the birth of a normal being.

21. The phrase concerning motivation is incorporated from K, as it renders more explicit the exact difference between the two practices.

22. This phrase is also incorporated from K. See n. 21.

23. Tib. *bag la ñal ba*; Skt. *anuśaya*. This is equivalent to *vāsanā*, "instinctual predilection," and refers in Buddhist psychology to the subconscious habit patterns that underlie emotional responses such as desire and hatred.

24. Wisdom–liberative technique integration (*prajñopāyādvaya*) is the fundamental formulation of the Mahāyāna path. It is the main dichotomy reconciliation the bodhisattva must incorporate in his practice. It is carried over into the symbolism of the Tantra, where wisdom = bell = female and technique = vajra = male. Thus this integration finds its most exalted symbol in the Tantric representation of the Buddha as male and female in union.

25. K and H have one more domain here, "wherein practice is neither pure nor impure."

26. K has "transcendent knowledge"; but that would not be paradoxical, in keeping with the general pattern of this description, whereas "transcendence" conveys the idea of the bodhisattva accomplishing the transcendences for other living beings as well as for himself.

27. See Glossary 2, under "five superknowledges." The "Knowledge of exhaustion of defilements" is one of the five or six; hence the paradox.

28. K supplies the location here.

29. The preceding statements concerning the four foci, the four right efforts, the four bases of magical powers, the five spiritual faculties, the five powers, the seven factors of enlightenment, and the eightfold path (from K) are the practices known as the thirty-seven aids to enlightenment, which are all discussed in Glossary 2.

30. Original Skt. quoted in Śāntideva's *Śikṣāsamuccaya*, p. 145, l. 22: *saddharmacakra-pravartana-mahāparinirvāṇa-saṃdarśanagocaraś ca bodhisattvacaryāparityāgagocaraś cāyam api bodhisattvasya gocaraḥ.*

Chapter 6

1. The five aggregates that constitute all beings of the desire-realm (see Glossary 2).

2. Skt. *skandhadhātvāyatana.* The "three dharmas" that are basic in the Abhidharmic analysis of reality, as being inclusive of everything in saṃsāra and nirvāṇa. See Glossary 2, under "five (functional) aggregates," "eighteen elements," and "twelve sense-media."

3. These are the Four Holy Truths, which, along with the directives relating to each, are basic in Hinayāna teaching.

4. A direct attack on the followers of the Hinayāna.

5. That is, production of nirvāṇa and destruction of defilements.

6. This concludes Vimalakīrti's definition of the "religion" of Buddhism in its true sense. Any personal interest (i.e., selfish interest) in anything, even "Dharma," "nirvāṇa," etc., is nonetheless a selfish interest, and the Dharma obtains only in the absence of selfish interest.

7. That is, through his miraculous power of teleportation.

8. Approximately India, although the cosmology does not correspond precisely to modern geography.

9. This enthronement of the audience for a religious discourse is most remarkable in the light of Buddhist tradition, where there is an explicit interdiction against teaching the Dharma to anyone who is seated even a few inches higher than the teacher. It is another instance of a Tantric tinge, as the initiate is symbolically enthroned by the preceptor to receive the consecrations.

10. The "inconceivable liberation" is said later (p. 54) to be only a fragment of an inconceivably great teaching. As Lamotte points out (p. 250, n. 11), this probably refers to the teaching of the *Avataṃsakasūtra*, known as *Acintyavimokṣasūtra.* This highlights the uniqueness of Vimalakīrti, who encompasses quintessentially the major doctrines of both *Prajñāpāramitā* and *Avataṃsaka*, the former emphasizing wisdom and the latter, liberative technique.

11. These deities abide, respectively, on the four sides of Sumeru and on the summit.

12. A reminder that all these miraculous feats are only for the purpose of disciplining living beings. Similarly, only those hearers who are imaginatively sensitive to the extraordinary warp of dimensional distortion set up by Vimalakīrti will understand the inconceivable weave of his instruction in the inconceivable liberation.

13. K is more brief here, giving essentially the second of the three sentences in this paragraph. He is as explicit as T.

14. Skt. *vātamaṇḍala.* The ancient cosmology maintained that the cosmos was encircled by an atmosphere of fierce winds of impenetrable intensity (see Lamotte, p. 255, n. 15).

15. There is little doubt that this refers to the same teaching given in the *Avataṃsaka.* It is, however, highly questionable whether it mentions any particular text, as Tib. *bstan pa* (Skt. *nirdeśa*) is "teaching" rather than a "text," as in *Vimalakīrtinirdeśa* (teaching of Vimalakīrti).

16. Kāśyapa brings up an interesting point: From the Mahāyāna viewpoint the saints (arhats) of the Hināyana are less fortunate than even the beginner bodhisattvas because, having eliminated their personal suffering, they cannot easily empathize with other living beings and hence find it hard to be inspired with great compassion. This makes their progress from sainthood to full Buddhahood much slower than that of the bodhisattva. This loss of opportunity occasions the "cry of regret."

17. Although Vimalakīrti might seem to be relentless in thus demolishing Mahākāśyapa's notion of evil (his rigid dualism that holds Māra as the opposite of liberation and virtue), just as the great disciple was filled with despair at his own sense of inadequacy before the teaching of inconceivability, Vimalakīrti actually is encouraging him. Things, even Māras, are not what they seem, and if Māra can be a bodhisattva, then possibly a great disciple might attain to the Mahāyāna more easily than his habitual notions might allow him to think.

Chapter 7

1. Twenty views of the aggregates as "I" or "mine" (see Glossary 3, under "egoistic views").

2. This is the definition of the highest type of compassion: "nonperceiving great compassion" (*anupalambhamahākaruṇā*). Thus such compassion is pure sensitivity, with no cognitive grasp on any person or thing as the identifiable object of its powerful feeling (see Glossary 3, under "great compassion").

3. Skt. *mahāmaitrī.* In an effort to maintain distinctions between Buddhism and Christianity, translators have used all sorts of euphemisms for this basic term. Granted, it is not the everyday "love" that means "to like"; it is still the altruistic love that is the finest inspiration of Christ's teaching, as well as of the Mahāyāna.

4. Mañjuśrī voices the pressing question about the great love and compassion of the bodhisattva: Seeing living beings as nonexistent, how can he feel love and compassion for them? As Vimalakīrti indicates, the bodhisattva's love is not merely commiseration but a spontaneous overflow of his great joy and relief in realizing the radiant nature of reality. Although he grasps no living being, he, being empty of himself, is utterly sensitive to the oppressive gravity of the "living being" feeling of others, and his love is an outpouring of his awareness of their true nature.

5. The folk etymology of *arhat* is *arīṇāṃ hantṛ*—"killer of enemies" (passions and ignorance).

6. K: ". . . because it is causeless."

7. K and H: ". . . because it is always opportune."

8. K and H: "It is the rendering of blessings without expectation of return."

9. Skt. *saṃsāra* = life = the cycle of births and deaths (see Glossary 3, under "life").

10. That is, the protection of the Buddha is found, not in mere dependence on him, but in self-reliant cultivation of one's own positive mind.

11. The Skt. original of this famous dialogue has been preserved in the *Śikṣāsamuccaya*, pp. 80, 81: *saṃsārabhayabhītena kiṃ pratisartavyam / āha saṃsārabhayabhītena mañjuśrī bodhisattvena buddhamāhātmyāṃ pratisartavyam / āha buddhamāhātmyāsthātukāmena kutra sthātavyam / āha buddhamāhātmye· sthātukāmena sarvasattvasamatāyāṃ sthātavyam / āha sarvasattvasamatāyāṃ sthātukāmena kutra sthātavyam / āha sarvasattvasamatāyāṃ sthātukāmena sarvasattvapramokṣāya sthātavyam.*

12. Tib. *'jig tshogs*; Skt. *satkāya*. Object of egoistic or materialist interest (*satkāyadṛṣṭi*).

13. Original Skt., *Śikṣāsamuccaya*, p. 140, 1. 20: *abhūtaparikalpasya kiṃ mūlam / āha viparyastā saṃjñā mūlam / āha viparyastāyāḥ saṃjñāyāḥ kiṃ mūlam / āha apratiṣṭhānaṃ mūlam / āha apratiṣṭhāyāḥ kiṃ mūlam / āha yan mañjuśrīr apratiṣṭhānaṃ na tasya kiṃcinmūlam iti hyapratiṣṭhānamūlapratiṣṭhitāḥ sarvadharmāḥ*. Śāntideva introduces the quote by the following remark: "If the superficial reality is baseless, how can it be either valid or invalid? (Its validity is comparable to) the illusion of a man (which can arise) even without a post being there (to be misperceived). And furthermore, where is the advocate of voidness who admits the ultimate existence of a post that would serve as basis of the false perception of a man? Thus, all things are rootless, their root not being established in reality."

14. Monks are not allowed to wear garlands or perfumes, etc.

15. Since the bodhisattvas have purged their subconsciousnesses of the instinctual roots of emotional habit-patterns, they do not fear the surface manifestations of passions inevitable in worldly life because these cannot affect them deeply.

16. K: "Liberation is neither within nor without, nor in between."

17. Here Śāriputra's silence fails where Vimalakīrti's famous silence on the subject of nonduality succeeds (see Chap. 9, n. 15). Thus silence per se is not necessarily reflective of highest wisdom.

18. The Hinayanists, from the bodhisattva point of view.

19. Skt. *Śrāvakayāna, pratyekabuddhayāna, mahāyāna*. See Glossary 2, under "three vehicles."

20. For numerous references concerning the Mahāyāna doctrine of the "unique vehicle" (*ekayāna*), most explicitly stated in the *Lotus Sūtra*, see Lamotte, p. 275, n. 32.

21. Original Skt., *Śikṣāsamuccaya*, p. 143, ll. 30–31: *Punaraparaṃ bhadanta śāriputra ye praviśantīdaṃ gṛhaṃ teṣāṃ samanantarapraviṣṭānāṃ sarvakleśā na bādhante 'yaṃ dvitīya āścaryādbhuto dharmaḥ*. Śāntideva introduces the quote by saying that "the purity of the bodhisattva's enjoyments is for the benefit of others, like the purity of his own being."

22. According to Lamotte (p. 278, n. 34), this refers to four famous treasures, each guarded by a great nāga-king; by Piṅgala at Kaliṅga, Pāṇḍuka at Mithila, Elapātra at Gandhāra, and Śankho at Kāśi (Benares).

23. Lamotte (p. 220, n. 3; p. 280, n. 36) follows K and his commentators in identifying this "Dharma-door" with a sūtra called *Tathāgātācintyaguhyanirdeśa*. However, it does not seem quite certain that so many Tathāgatas would be required to expound the same text. Rather, it seems that this assembly of Tathāgatas refers to the formation of a cosmic *maṇḍala*, such as is formed in the first chapter of *Guhyasamājatantra*, and the "Secrets of the Tathāgata" would then be the general name for any sort of Tantric teaching. This would bear out the description of Vimalakīrti as understanding "the mundane and transcendental sciences and esoteric practices" (p. 21) and (by Mañjuśrī) as penetrating "all the esoteric mysteries of the bodhisattvas and the Buddhas" (p. 42). This evidence can have been overlooked by scholars of great erudition only because of their firm conviction that Tantrism did not exist in India at the time of Vimalakīrti, or even of that Scripture. Scholars native to the Buddhist tradition would disagree.

24. Śāriputra evidences his belief that enlightenment can be obtained only by men and that women must first reincarnate in male form to reach the highest goal. Thus he cannot understand why the goddess would not use her power to become a man.

25. This whole incident is quite similar to an exchange that takes place between Śāriputra and the daughter of Sāgara, the nāga-king, in the *Lotus Sūtra* (pp. 250–254). For an interesting discussion of the prejudice against females in Buddhism in general and of the Mādhyamika negation of this prejudice as executed, for example, by the goddess, see Lamotte, p. 280, n. 37.

Chapter 8

1. Tib. *de bzin gśegs pai rigs*. This term arises from a classification of beings into different groups (families) according to their destinies: disciple-family, solitary-family, Buddha-family, etc. The Mādhyamika school, and the sūtras that are its foundation, maintains that all living beings belong to the Buddha-family, that Hinayāna nirvāṇa is not a final destiny, and that the saints must eventually enter the Mahāyāna path. Mañjuśrī carries this idea to the extreme, finding the Tathāgata-family everywhere, in all mundane things. See p. 65, and Lamotte, *Appendice*, Note VII.

2. That is, the miraculous Mahāyāna.

3. That is, the jewel of the spirit of enlightenment.

4. Following K and H, as T: "He follows the ways of the elements and the sense-media, but . . ." is obscure.

5. All these enumerations, all being the opposite of Buddha-qualities and most of them evil, are listed in Glossary 2.

6. Original Skt. of last phrase from *Śikṣāsamuccaya*, p. 7, 1. 9.: *sumerusamāṃ satkāyadṛṣṭim utpādya bodhicittam utpādyate / tataśca buddhadharmā virohanti*.

7. Skt. *pañcakāmagunaḥ*. Visibles, sound, scent, taste, and tangibles.

8. The disciples are bereft of the emotional patterns related to inspiration, aspiration, etc., which are necessary to form an intense high resolve to attain anything. The bodhisattva does not catch up to them in wisdom until he reaches the eighth stage (*acalā*), the "immovable"; hence he retains the emotional structure necessary for cultivation of great compassion until that high stage.

9. This corresponds to the symbolism of the "Father-Mother Buddha" (Tib. *saṅs rgyas yab yum*) central in the Tantras, in the form of the tutelary deity (Skt. *idaṃ devatā*; Tib. *yi dam*). The mother is wisdom (*prajñā*) and the father, liberative technique (*upāya*).

10. See Glossary 2, under "thirty-seven aids to enlightenment."

11. See Glossary 2, under "four means of unification."

12. K: "With the undefiled qualities as trees."

13. T has only "Covered with pure lotuses." K gives "seven purities": purity of (1) body and voice, or morality, (2) mind, (3) self-control, or vision, (4) resolution of doubts, (5) discernment of paths, (6) knowledge and insight into bondage, and (7) nirvāṇa. See Lamotte, p. 294, n. 26.

14. Following K and H.

15. Following K and H.

16. Following K and H.

17. K and H: "Although he knows that the buddha-fields are void like living beings, he practices purification of buddha-fields to teach and civilize those living beings."

18. Original Skt. from *Śikṣāsamuccaya*, p. 172: *sarvasattvāna ye rūpā rutaghoṣāśca īritāḥ / ekakṣaṇena darśenti bodhisattvā viśāradāḥ*. See p. 54.

19. Skt. *te jīrṇavyādhitā bhonti mṛtamātmāna darśayī / sattvānām paripākāya māyādharmavikrīḍitāḥ*.

20. Skt. *kalpoddāhaṃ ca darśenti uddahitvā vasuṃdharāṃ / nityasaṁjñina sattvānām anityamiti darśayī*.

21. Skt. *sattvaiḥ śatasahasrebhirekarāṣtre nimantritāḥ / sarveṣāṃ gṛha bhuñjanti sarvānnāmanti bodhaye*.

22. Skt. *ye kecin mantravidyā vā śilpasthānā bahūvidhāḥ / sarvatra pāramiprāptāḥ sarvasattvasukhāvahāḥ*.

23. Skt. *yāvanto loka pāṣaṇḍāḥ sarvatra pravrajanti te / nānādṛṣṭigataṃ prāptāṃs te sattvāṇ paripācati*.

24. Skt. *candrā vā bhonti sūryā vā śakrabrahma prajeśvarāḥ / bhavanti āpas tejaśca pṛthivī mārutas tathā*.

25. Skt. *rogāntarakalpeṣu bhaiṣajyaṃ bhonti uttamāḥ / yena te sattva mucyante sukhī bhonti anāmayāḥ*.

26. Skt. *durbhikṣāntarakalpeṣu bhavantī pāṇabhojanam / kṣudhāpipāsām apanīya dharmaṃ deśenti prāṇināṃ*.

27. Skt. *śastrāntarakalpeṣu maitrīdhyāyī bhavanti te / avyāpāde niyojenti sattvakoṭiśatāṇ bahūṇ*. These three periods of time are part of the Buddhist scheme of the evolution and devolution of the world. A great aeon (*mahākalpa*) contains four aeons (*kalpa*). Each of the four aeons contains twenty intermediate aeons (*antarakalpa*). Our world lasts for twenty of these intermediate aeons. At the end of each intermediate aeon, except for the first and the twentieth, three periods of time occur during which various disasters befall the human beings of that period. The first, the time of swords, lasts seven days, and men go crazy and murder each other. The second, the time of sickness, lasts seven months and seven days, and human beings are stricken with plagues. The third lasts seven years, seven months, and seven days; there is drought and extreme misery of starvation. (See *Abidharmakośa* III, p. 207; Lamotte, p. 296, n. 37.)

28. Skt. *mahāsaṃgrāmamadhye ca samapakṣā bhavanti te / saṅdhisāmagri rocenti bodhisattvā mahābalāḥ.*

29. Skt. *ye cāpi nirayāḥ kecid buddhakṣetreṣvacintiṣu / saṃcintya tatra gacchanti sattvānāṃ hitakāraṇāt.*

30. Skt. *yāvantyo gatayah kāścit tiryagyonau prakāśitāḥ / sarvatra dharmaṃ deśenti tena ucyanti nāyakāḥ.*

31. Skt. *kāmabhogāṃś ca darśenti dhyānaṃ ca dhyāyināṃ tathā / vidhvastamāraṃ kurvanti avatāraṃ na denti te.*

32. Skt. *agnimadhye yathā padmaṃ abhūtaṃ taṃ vinirdiśet / evaṃ kāmāṃś ca dhyānaṃ ca abhūtaṃ te vidarśayī.* Ch. variant here unsupported by Skt.

33. Skt. *saṃcintya gaṇikāṃ bhonti puṃsāṃ ākarṣaṇāya te / rāgāṅkuram ca saṃlobhya buddhajñāne sthāpayanti te.*

34. Skt. *grāmikāś ca sadā bhonti sārthavāhāḥ purohitāḥ / agrāmātyātha cāmātyaḥ sattvānāṃ hitakāraṇāt.*

35. Skt. *daridrāṇāṃ ca sattvānāṃ nidhānā bhonti aksayāḥ / teṣāṃ dānāni datvā ca bodhicittaṃ janenti te.*

36. Skt. *mānastabdheṣu sattveṣu mahānagnā bhavanti te / sarvamānasamudghātaṃ bodhiṃ prārthenti uttamāṃ.*

37. Skt. *bhayārditānāṃ sattvānāṃ saṁtiṣṭhante 'grataḥ sadā / abhayaṃ tesu datvā ca paripācenti bodhaye.*

38. Skt. *pañcābhijñāś ca te bhūtvā ṛṣayo brahmacāriṇaḥ / śīle sattvāṇ niyojenti kṣāntisauratyasaṃyame.*

39. Skt. *upasthānagurūṇ sattvāṇ paśyantīha viśāradāḥ / ceṭā bhavanti dāsā vā śiṣyatvam upayānti ca.*

40. Skt. *yena yenaiva cāṅgena sattvo dharmarato bhavet / darśenti hi kriyāḥ sarvā mahopāyasuśikṣitāḥ.*

41. Skt. *yeṣām anantā śikṣā hi anantaś cāpi gocaraḥ / anantajñānasampannā anantaprāṇimocakāḥ.*

42. Skt. *na teṣāṃ kalpakoṭībhiḥ kalpakoṭiśatair api / buddhair api vadadbhis tu guṇāntaḥ suvaco bhavet.*

Chapter 9

1. "Nonduality" (*advayatva*) = "Middle Path" (*madhyamapratipat*) = freedom from extremes of being and nothingness (*antadvayavivarjita*). For numerous references, see Lamotte, pp. 301–302, n. 1.

2. The bodhisattvas named in this chapter are not well known in other contexts, with the exception of Priyadarśana (p. 74) and Akṣayamati (p. 75), who is the Buddha's interlocutor in the important *Akṣayamatinirdeśasūtra*.

3. See Introduction, p. 5.

4. Skt. *samāropa* and *apavāda*. These two correspond to "realism" and "nihilism," respectively, in the system of the *Saṃdhinirmocana*, elaborated by Āryāsaṅga in the "mind-only" philosophy. It terms of the "three-nature" (*trilakṣana*) theory, realism involves confusion of the conceptually constructed with the relative, and nihilism involves repudiation of all three natures through repudiation of the relative along with the conceptually constructed.

5. Small differences in K and H do not affect the meaning. "Uniqueness" corresponds to realism, the idea that each thing has its special character as a fixed essence. "Characterlessness" corresponds to nihilism.

6. K and H differ: "'Creation' (Skt. *saṃskṛta*; Ch. 有爲) and 'noncreation' (Skt. *asaṃskṛta*; Ch. 無爲) are dualistic. . . ," etc. (The rest is parallel.) Actually, what is *saṃskṛta* is miserable, and what is *asaṃskṛta* is nirvāṇa, i.e., happiness. Thus this difference is not significant.

7. That is, saṃsāra and nirvāṇa.

8. H: "'Destructible' and 'indestructible' are dualistic. Knowing there to be nothing destroyed or undestroyed, the bodhisattva calls 'destructible' what is utterly destroyed. Utterly destroyed, it is not to be destroyed. The destruction is instantaneous, yet there is no production or destruction in an instant, so it is actually indestructible. There being no 'destruction' in reality, there is no 'indestructibility.' To realize their voidness by nature is the entrance. . . ." K is more brief, but essentially in agreement. It should be remembered here that "destructible" = the relative, and "indestructible" = the absolute. Thus, Pratyakṣadarśana is affirming that the superficial *is* the ultimate, etc. See pp. 88–90.

9. See Introduction, pp. 1–4.

10. K: "The four elements and the void are twain. But the nature of the four elements is the nature of the void. The past and the future are void, thus the present is also void. To know the nature of the elements in this way is to enter. . . ."

11. Nonduality is applied to the twelve sense-media, i.e., the six faculties (eye, ear, nose, tongue, body, and mind) and their six objects (form, sound, smell, taste, texture, and phenomena). See Glossary 2, under "six sense-faculties," "six sense-objects," and "twelve sense-media."

12. Skt. *āniñjya*. Actions that, being neither good nor evil, produce neither good nor bad karmic effects, hence are "neutral" in result.

13. Skt. *nirodhasamāpatti*. The absorption in ultimate cessation or nirvāṇa.

14. One of the synonyms of voidness is "truthlessness," (Tib. *bden par med pa*), truth being a relative validity and the ultimate being beyond truth and falsehood. Last two sentences follow H.

15. This is the most famous moment of the Scripture: Vimalakīrti's moment of silence on the subject of nonduality, i.e., the ultimate. It is noteworthy, however, that Vimalakīrti does talk a great deal about the ultimate on many other occasions; his silence here is given its special impact by the series of profound statements preceding it, which culminate in the statement of Mañjuśrī to the effect that silence is itself the best explanation of nonduality. Hence all silence is not to be exaggeratedly taken as the profoundest teaching, but only such a silence in the special context of profound thought on the ultimate. For example, the silences of the disciples in Chap. III, as they became speechless when confronted by the eloquent criticism of Vimalakīrti, are not taken to be profound; nor is the silence of Śāriputra when questioned by the goddess in Chap. 8 accepted as anything extraordinary.

Candrakīrti, in his *Prasannapadā* (p. 57, 1. 7–8), has this to say in regard to the question as to whether the Enlightened Ones employ logical arguments or not: "Who can say if the Holy Ones (employ logical arguments) or not? The ultimate is inherent (even) in the 'Keeping Silent of the Holy Ones.' What then would cause us to imagine whether they employ logical arguments or do not employ logical arguments?" It is important to note that equating the ultimate with the "Keeping Silent of the Holy Ones" in no way precludes the ultimacy of their speech. As the Goddess says to Śāriputra (p. 59): "...do not point to liberation by abandoning speech! Why? The holy liberation is the equality of all things!"

Thus, to imitate the Scripture's pattern of expression: "Silence" and "speech" are dualistic. Just as speech is ultimately meaningless, so silence exists only in contrast with speech. Penetration into the equality of silence and speech is the entrance...(see Lamotte, pp. 317–318, n. 43.

Chapter 10

1. Those of the bodhisattvas who are monks, or who maintain ascetic practices, are allowed to eat only before noon; otherwise they must wait until dawn of the next day.

2. According to Lamotte, p. 319, n. 2, this universe is mentioned in *Śikṣāsamuccaya*, *Laṅkāvatāra*, and *Prasannapadā*.

3. In *Prasannapadā*, this universe is said to be ruled by Samantabhadra, not Sugandhakūṭa (see Lamotte, p. 320, n. 3).

4. Tib. *de bźin gśegs pai mtshan*; Skt. *tathāgatanāma*. Tib. *mtshan* can be interpreted as *mtshan ñid* (Skt. *lakṣaṇa*), i.e., "the marks of the Tathāgata." But this has a rather obscure meaning, whereas Tib. *mtshan* is also the honorific for Tib. *miṅ* ("name"), and this is readily understandable because it is frequently mentioned in Mahāyāna texts that the mere name of the Buddha confers great benefit when heard or pronounced.

5. According to K and H, he was seen rising in the air; but T has it that his speed was invisibly swift.

6. As there is no Hinayāna, much less ordinary individuals, in that exalted universe (see p. 78), they do not even know what might be meant by "aspire to inferior ways."

7. Thus Vimalakīrti is praised as having the full mastery of the operations of the *nirmāṇakāya* (incarnation-body of the Buddha), i.e., as indistinguishable from the Buddhas.

8. Tib. *ñi tshe bai spyod pa*; Skt. *pradeśakārin* (Mvy, 1610). This term refers to the restricted, biased, narrow-minded attitudes and practices of the Hinayāna, which itself is called Skt. *prādeśikayāna* ("limited, or narrow-minded, vehicle") (Mvy, 1254). It is narrow-minded because it posits the reality of the elements of existence as apparently perceived and because it aspires only to personal liberation, not to the exaltation of Buddhahood. Thus Vimalakīrti is telling the disciples to set aside their prejudices while eating this blessed food.

9. Original Skt., from *Śikṣāsamuccaya*, p. 144, ll. 1–4: *atha tato bhojanāt sarvāvatī sā parṣat tṛptā bhūtā / na ca tad bhojanaṃ kṣīyate / yaiś ca bodhisattvaiḥ śrāvakaiś ca śakrabrahmalokapālais tadanyaiś ca sattvais tad bhojanaṃ bhuktaṃ teśāṃ tādṛśaṃ sukhaṃ kāye 'vakrāntaṃ yādṛśaṃ sarvasukhamaṇḍitāyāṃ lokadhātau bodhisattvānāṃ sukham / sarvaromakūpebhyaś ca teśāṃ tādṛśo gandhaḥ pravāti tad yathāpi nāma tasyām eva sarvagandhasugandhāyāṃ lokadhātau vṛkṣāṇāṃ gandhaḥ.*

10. That is, the ten paths of evil karmic action (see Glossary 2, under "ten sins").

11. Vimalakīrti epitomizes for the guest-bodhisattvas the teachings of the First Wheel of Dharma, that of the Four Holy Truths, the basis of the Hinayāna practice, and the Abhidharma philosophy.

12. This paragraph is modified in style with the help of H.

13. Tib. *sdud pa*; Skt. *samgraha*. Lit. "collect," i.e., gather together into the Mahāyāna.

14. See n. 8.

15. Skt. *Śāstṛ*, i.e., Buddha.

Chapter 11

1. Skt. *niyāma*. Destiny for the ultimate element, reached at the stage of āryá (see Chap. 1, n. 47).

2. Original Skt., from *Śikṣāsamuccaya*, p. 144, 1. 5: *yaiś ca bhadanta ānanda bhikṣubhiranavakrāntaniyāmair etad bhojanaṃ bhuktaṃ teśāṃ evāvakrāntaniyāmānāṃ pariṇaṃsyati.*

3. Original Skt., from *Śikṣāsamuccaya*, p. 140, 1. 6: *yair anutpāditabodhicittaiḥ sattvaiḥ paribhuktaṃ teśāṃ utpāditabodhicittānāṃ pariṇaṃsyati.*

4. Original Skt., from *Śikṣāsamuccaya*, p. 140, 1. 7: *yair utpāditabodhicittair bhuktaṃ teśāṃ pratilabdhakṣāntikānāṃ pariṇaṃsyati.*

5. Lit., "Perfectly Accomplished Enlightened One," "Thus(-ness)-Gone One," and "Awakened One."

6. Ānanda, as well as being "foremost of attendants" (see Chap. 3, n. 48), was also styled by the Buddha as the "foremost of the learned" (Skt. *bahuśrutānām agryaḥ*) and as the "foremost of those endowed with memory and incantations" (Skt. *smṛtidhāraṇīprāptānām agryaḥ*). Thus he was the one who remembered the vast body of the Scriptures and recited them from memory during the first collection of the Sūtra Piṭaka, after the Buddha's passing into final liberation.

7. That is, destructible (Skt. *kṣaya*) = compounded (Skt. *saṃskṛta*) = the superficial (Skt. *saṃvṛtti*) = *saṃsāra*. Indestructible (*akṣaya*) = uncompounded (Skt. *asaṃskṛta*) = the ultimate (Skt. *paramārtha*) = *nirvāṇa*.

8. That is, the bodhisattva does not put an end to saṃsāra for himself alone, nor does he seek ultimate repose in the Hinayāna nirvāṇa. The following instruction represents the Buddha's own summation of the bodhisattva's reconciliation of dichotomies that Vimalakīrti has been expounding throughout the Scripture.

9. Skt. *ācāryamuṣṭi* (lit. "The tight fist of the [bad] teacher").

10. Immoral persons, along with other living beings who suffer their immoral acts, provide the bodhisattva the opportunity to expiate through suffering any traces of bad karma, as well as to practice generosity, tolerance, etc., and eventually to gather into the discipline those same immoral persons.

11. Skt. *apratihatapratibhāṇa*. This is another synonym for Buddhahood because only at that stage does the turning of the Wheel of Dharma become automatic, effortless, and irresistible.

12. See Chap. 1, n. 48, and Glossary 2.

13. Skt. *bodhisattvasaṅgha*. The third Jewel, the Saṅgha, is defined in two ways: as the Disciple-Order (śrāvakasaṅgha) and as the Bodhisattva-Order (bodhisattvasaṅgha). Thus, from the Mahāyāna viewpoint, not only Hinayāna monks but also bodhisattvas constitute the Saṅgha.

14. Skt. *nītārtha*. Meaning that is exact concerning the ultimate and not to be otherwise interpreted.

15. The sixth superknowledge (*āsravakṣayajñāna*) is attained only by saints, of whom the Buddha is foremost.

16. That is, he does not wish his own ultimate liberation until it is time for the ultimate liberation of all living beings.

17. Hinayāna teachings.

18. Tib. *chos kyi rtsi ba thams cad sgrub pai phyir 'dus ma byas la mi gnas so / 'di tar chos chuṅ ṅui sman sbyor bai phyir 'dus byas zad par mi byed do*. This sentence is absent in K and H. The phrase *chos chuṅ ṅui sman* is problematic, but I have translated "subtle" rather than "slight," as better conveying the subtlety of effect of such an elixir, in keeping with the metaphor.

Chapter 12

1. Skt. *rūpatathatāsvabhāva*, i.e., voidness, as "essence which is reality" is a euphemism for "essencelessness" (*niḥsvabāvatā*). Thus the Tathāgata is the voidness of matter, i.e., matter in the ultimate sense, not mere relative matter—and so on for the remaining four aggregates. For interesting references on the ultimate nonexistence of the Tathāgata, see Lamotte, p. 354, n. 1. The reference given there is worth repeating here (from *Prasannapadā*, p. 435, quoting a *Vaipūlyasūtra*): "Those who see me by means of form, or who follow me by means of sound—they are involved with false and ruinous views and will never see me at all. The Buddhas are to be seen by means of ultimate reality, since those leaders are Dharma-bodies, and ultimate reality is impossible to know, as it is not an object of discernment."

2. K and H: "He lives neither in any place, nor in no place."

3. Tib. *kun gźi*; Skt. *ālaya*, identifiable with *ālayavijñāna*. However, as reference to the elaborate Vijñānavādin psychology of the "store-consciousness" is out of place in this sūtra, I have simply termed it "subconsciousness." K and H have "worry."

4. The Buddha of Abhirati, presiding over the eastern direction. In Tantra, one of the five *Tathāgatas* (see Lamotte, pp. 360–362, n. 9).

Epilogue

1. T numbers this as the twelfth chapter (my Chaps. 3 and 4 are one chapter in T). I took the liberty of calling this final section "Epilogue" to preserve the count of chapters as twelve.

2. Skt. *Acintyavikurvaṇanayapraveśanirdeśa*. This is a description, not a title of the sūtra, as it is not mentioned on p. 102, where the Buddha gives the titles to Ānanda.

3. Tib. *mchod rten*. A monument shaped like a mound or cone, which is erected as a memorial to the mind of the Buddha, with sacred scriptures representing his speech and traditional images representing his body.

4. Skt. *Acintyavimokṣanirdeśa*.

5. Skt. *Dharmapūja*. See pp. 98–99.

6. Lit. "King of Healers," normally considered the patron Buddha of medicine. This "former life" (jātaka) story gives the "antecedents" referred to in the title of this chapter, revealing events of past lives of Sākyamuni, etc.

7. These names of the Buddha form part of a traditional litany consisting of eighty names. See Mvy, nos. 1–80.

8. The *bodhisattvapiṭaka* refers to the collection of the Vast (*vaipūlya*) Sūtras of the Mahāyāna, supposed to have been collected supernaturally by a great assembly of bodhisattvas led by Maitreya, Mañjuśrī, and Vajrapāṇi.

9. Vajrapāṇi.

10. These four are called the "epitomes of the Dharma (*dharmoddana*) or "insignia of the Dharma" (*dharmamudrā*). See Glossary 2.

11. These are called the "four reliances" and are usually given in a different order: see Glossary 2.

12. See Chap. 5, n. 17.

13. Ratnārcis was one of the twelve Tathāgatas who came often to Vimalakīrti's house (p. 61) and is, according to the *Prajñāpāramitā* the Buddha of the universe Upaśānta, in the western direction (see Lamotte, p. 384, n. 27).

14. According to this belief in the blessed aeon of one thousand Buddhas, Śākyamuni is the fourth, Maitreya will be the fifth, and Kakutsunda the sixth to incarnate in this Sahā universe. Maitreya is not mentioned here because he is considered to be already present in a sense, as Sākyamuni proceeds to transmit the authority for the teaching to him.

15. Gesture (*mudrā*) in the sense of characteristic attitude, or behavior.

16. That is, the Lokapālas.

17. Skt. *Vimalakīrtinirdeśa.*

18. Skt. *Yamakavyatyastābhinirhāra.*

19. Skt. *Acintyavimokṣaparivarta.* In regard to these titles, see Introduction, pp. 4 and 6.

Glossary

Sanskrit

Abhidharma. Conventionally, the general name for the Buddhist teachings presented in a scientific manner, as a fully elaborated transcendental psychology. As one of the branches of the Canon, it corresponds to the discipline of wisdom (the *Sūtras* corresponding to meditation, and the *Vinaya* to morality). Ultimately the Abhidharma *is* "pure wisdom, with its coordinate mental functions" (*prajñāmalā sānucārā*), according to Vasubandhu.

Abhidharmakośa. An important work written by Vasubandhu, probably in the fourth century, as a critical compendium of the Abhidharmic science.

Abhirati (lit. "Intense Delight"). The universe, or buddha-field of the Tathāgata Akṣobhya, lying in the east beyond innumerable galaxies, whence Vimalakīrti came to reincarnate in our Sahā universe.

Acintyavimokṣa. Inconceivable liberation of the bodhisattvas, a name of the *Avataṃsaka-sūtra*, and a subtitle of the VKN.

Ajita Keśakambala. One of the six heterodox teachers defeated by the Buddha at Śrāvastī.

Akaniṣṭha. The highest heaven of the form-world, where a Buddha always receives the anointment of the ultimate wisdom, reaching there mentally from his seat of enlightenment under the Bodhi-tree.

Akṣayamati. A bodhisattva in the assembly at Vimalakīrti's house, often figuring in other Mahāyana sūtras, especially *Akṣayamatinirdeśasūtra.*

Akṣobhya. Buddha of the universe Abhirati; also prominent in Tantric works as one of the five Dhyāni Buddhas, or Tathāgatas.

Amitābha. The Buddha of boundless light; one of the five Tathāgatas in Tantrism; a visitor in Vimalakīrti's house, according to the goddess's report.

Āmrapālī. A courtesan of Vaiśālī who gave her garden to the Buddha and his retinue, where they stay during the events of the sūtra.

Ānanda. A major disciple of the Buddha; his personal attendant.

Anantaguṇaratnavyūha. A universe of Buddha Ratnavyūha, also mentioned in the *Lalitavistarasūtra.*

Aniruddha. A disciple and cousin of the Buddha who was famed for his meditative prowess and superknowledges.

arhat. According to Buddhist tradition, one who has conquered his enemy passions (*kleśa-ari-hata*) and reached the supreme purity. See Glossary 3, "saint."

ārya. "Holy" in Buddhism; correctly "noble" only in normal Indian ethnic context.

Āryadeva. One of the great masters of Indian Buddhism. The main disciple of Nāgārjuna, he lived in the early A.D. centuries and wrote numerous important works of Mādhyamika philosophy.

Āryāsaṅga. This great Indian philosopher lived in the fourth century and was the founder of the Vijñānavāda, or "Consciousness-Only," school of Mahāyāna Buddhism.

āryaśrāvaka. A holy disciple; practitioner of Hinayāna teaching.

Aśoka. Universe whence comes the Brahmā Śikhin.

asura. Titan (see Glossary 2, under "five states of existence").

Atiśa (982–1055). Perhaps the last of the universally acclaimed masters of Indian Buddhism, he was extremely influential in Tibetan Buddhism, as he spent the last seventeen years of his life in Tibet, bringing many important teachings and aiding in the work of correction of teachings translated earlier.

Avalokiteśvara. A bodhisattva emblematic of the great compassion; of great importance in Tibet as special protector of the religious life of the country and in China, in female form, as Kwanyin, protectress of women, children, and animals.

Avataṁsakasūtra. This vast Mahāyāna Scripture deals with the miraculous side of the Mahāyāna. It is important in relation to the VKN, since the latter's fifth chapter, "The Inconceivable Liberation," is a highly abbreviated version of the essential teaching of the former.

Avīci hell. The lowest hell.

Bhaiṣajyarāja (lit. "King of Medicine"). Tathāgata of the universe Mahavyūha, during the aeon called Vicaraṇa, who taught the Prince Chandracchattra, a former life of Buddha Śākyamuni, about the Dharma-worship (see VKN, Epilogue, above). In later Buddhism, this Buddha is believed to be the supernatural patron of healing and medicine.

Bhāvaviveka (c. A.D. 400). A major Indian philosopher, a master of the Mādhyamika school of Buddhism, who founded a sub-school known as Svātantrika.

bhikṣu (lit. "beggar"). Buddhist mendicant monk; *bhikṣuṇī* is the female counterpart.

bodhimaṇḍa. The seat of enlightenment, wherein is concentrated the essence of enlightenment, as fully described by Vimalakīrti to Prabhavyūha, in Chap. 4 above.

bodhisattva. A living being who has produced the spirit of enlightenment in himself and whose constant dedication, lifetime after lifetime, is to attain the unexcelled, perfect enlightenment of Buddhahood.

Bodhisattvapiṭaka. There is a Mahāyāna Scripture of this name, but the word more usually refers to the whole collection (*piṭaka*) of Mahāyāna Scriptures, to distinguish them from the Three Collections (*Tripiṭaka*) of the Hinayāna.

Brahmā. Creator-lord of a universe, there being as many as there are universes, whose number is incalculable. Hence, in Buddhist belief, a title of a deity who has attained supremacy in a particular universe, rather than a personal name. For example, the

Brahmā of the Aśoka universe is personally called Śikhin, to distinguish him from other Brahmās.

Buddha (lit. "awakened one"). Title of one who has attained the highest attainment possible for a living being. "The Buddha" often designates Śākyamuni because he is the Buddha mainly in charge of the buddha-field of our Sahā universe.

Buddha Gaya. Ancient name for the town in Bihar province, where the Buddha attained his highest enlightenment under the Bodhi-tree. Modern name, Bodh Gaya.

buddhagotra (lit. "family" or "lineage of the Buddha"). One becomes a member on the first bodhisattva stage.

Buddhapālita (c. fourth century). A great Mādhyamika master, who was later regarded as the founder of the Prāsaṅgika sub-school.

Cakravāḍa. A mountain in this sūtra and many others; but, in systematized Buddhist cosmology, the name of the ring of mountains that surrounds the world.

Candracchattra. Son of the king Ratnacchattra, mentioned in the former-life story told by the Buddha to Śakra in the Epilogue.

Candracchattra. Chief of the Licchavi.

Candrakīrti (c. sixth century). The most important Mādhyamika philosopher after Nāgārjuna and Āryadeva, he refined the philosophical methods of the school to such a degree that later members of the tradition considered him one of the highest authorities on the subject of the profound nature of reality.

Ch'an. Chinese word for *dhyāna*, which was adopted as the name of the school of Mahāyāna practice founded by Bodhidharma, and later to become famous in the west as Zen.

Chos Ñid Tshul Khrims. Tibetan translator of the VKN in the ninth century, also well known for his collaboration in compiling the *Mahāvyutpatti* (Skt.-Tib. dictionary).

Cittamātra. A name of the Vijñānavāda school of Mahāyāna Buddhist philosophy.

deva. General term for all sorts of gods and deities.

Dharma. The second of the Three Jewels, that is, the teaching of the Buddha.

Duṣprasāha. Buddha of the universe Marīci, located sixty-one universes away; mentioned also in other Mahāyāna Scriptures, with the interesting coincidence that his teaching ceased at the moment Śākyamuni began teaching at Benares.

Gandhamādana. A mountain known for its incense trees.

gandharva (lit. "scent-eater"). A heavenly musician.

Gandhavyūhāhāra. Deities who attend on the Buddha Sugandhakūta in the universe Sarvagandhasugandhā.

garuḍa. Magical bird, which protects from snakes.

Guhyasamājatantra. Perhaps the earliest Scripture of Indian Buddhist Tantrism (c. third century), some of whose doctrines are strikingly similar to the "reconciliation of dichotomies" of the VKN.

Himadri. A mountain.

Hinayāna. The "Lesser Vehicle" of Buddhism, taught by the Buddha for those unable immediately to conceive the spirit of enlightenment, as a means for them to attain personal liberation. It is used of course in the Mahāyāna Scriptures, as a contrast to their own "Great Vehicle," which is taught as a means for living beings of the loftiest aspiration to attain the liberation of self and others through simultaneous perfection of wisdom and compassion, that is called Buddhahood.

Hsüan Tsang (seventh century). One of the greatest translators in world history, he traveled to India, where he lived for many years, studying Sanskrit and all the sciences of the day. On his return to China he translated many volumes of important philosophical and religious works. He translated the VKN in 650.

Indra. A major god in the Vedic pantheon, he dwindled in importance after Vedism was transformed into Hinduism in the early A.D. centuries. However, he was reinstated in Buddhist Scriptures as the king of the gods and as a disciple of the Buddha and protector of the Dharma and its practicers.

Jagatīṃdhara. A bodhisattva layman of Vaiśālī, who is saved by Vimalakīrti from being fooled by Māra posing as Indra.

Jambudvīpa. The "Rose-apple continent," a name for the human world in the ancient Indian cosmology, it can be translated perhaps as "this earth," or even as "India."

Jina (lit. "Conqueror"). A name of the Buddha.

Kakuda Kātyāyana. One of the six heterodox teachers.

Kakutsunda. The sixth Buddha of the "Good Aeon" (*bhadrakalpa*) of one thousand Buddhas, our own Śākyamuni having been the fourth, and Maitreya expected to come as the fifth.

Kālaparvata. A mountain.

karma. Generally meaning "work," or "action," it is an important concept in Buddhist philosophy as the cumulative force of previous actions, which determines present experience and will determine future existences.

Kauśikā. Another name for Indra.

kiṃnara. A mythical being with a horse's head and human body.

Krakucchanda. First of the thousand Buddhas of this good aeon of our universe.

Kumārajīva. Translator of the VKN into Chinese (344–409).

Lalitavistarasūtra. The "Scripture of the Great Play," in which the life of the Buddha is recorded.

Laṅkāvatārasūtra. The "Scripture of the Visit to Ceylon," it records the Buddha's teachings to Rāvaṇa, the king of that country, and is an important scriptural source for the Vijñānavāda school.

Licchavi. Name of the tribe and republican city-state whose capital was Vaiśālī, where Vimalakīrti lived, and the main events of the VKN take place.

Lokapālas (lit. "World-Protectors"). They are the same as the four Mahārājas, the great kings of the quarters, whose mission is to report on the activities of mankind to the gods of the Trayastriṃśa heaven and who have pledged to protect the practitioners of the Dharma.

Lotsvaba. Tibetan word for a translator, derived from the Skt. *lokacakṣuḥ*, which means "Eye of the People," or "Eye of the World" (like Greek *cosmos*, Skt. *loka* means both "world" and "people"). In Tibet, the translators were honored with this title of "Cosmic Eye," because their study and work enabled the people to see the higher teachings brought from the Holy Land of India.

Madhyamaka. Teaching of the Middle Way.

Mādhyamika. School based on Madhyamaka, and followers of that school.

Madhyāntavibhāga. The "Analysis of the Middle and the Extremes," it is an important work of Vijñānavāda philosophy, said to have been received as a revelation from the future Buddha Maitreya by the great scholar and saint, Āryāsaṅga, after twelve years of meditation.

Mahācakravāḍa. A mountain, or sometimes a range of mountains.

Mahākāśyapa. Foremost disciple of the Buddha; he inherited the leadership of the Saṅgha after the Parinirvāṇa.

Mahākātyāyana. Disciple of the Buddha noted for his skill in analysis of the Buddha's discourses and, traditionally, the founder of the Abhidharma.

Mahāmucilinda. A mountain.

Mahāsiddha. A "Great Sorcerer," a master of the esoteric teachings and practices of Mahāyāna Buddhism.

Mahāvyūha. The name of one of the bodhisattvas in the assembly in Chap. 1. Also the name of the universe in the distant past where the Buddha Bhaiṣajyarāja presided, and taught the prince Chandracchattra about the Dharma-worship (in the Epilogue).

Mahāyāna. The "Great Vehicle" of Buddhism, called "great" because it carries all living beings to enlightenment of Buddhahood. It is distinguished from the Hinayāna, including the Śrāvakayāna (Disciple Vehicle) and Pratyekabuddhayāna (Solitary Sage Vehicle), which only carries each person who rides on it to their own personal liberation.

mahoraga. A mythical serpent race.

Maitreya. A bodhisattva present throughout the sūtra, prophesied as one birth away from Buddhahood and designated by Śākyamuni as the next Buddha in the succession of one thousand Buddhas of our era. According to tradition, he resides in the Tuṣita heaven preparing for his descent to earth at the appropriate time.

maṇḍala. A mystic diagram, usually consisting of a square within a circle, used to define a sacred space in the context of esoteric rituals of initiation and consecration preliminary to certain advanced meditational practices.

Mañjuśrī. The eternally youthful crown-prince (*kumārabhūta*), so called because of his special identification with the *Prajñāpāramitā*, or Transcendence of wisdom. As Prince of Wisdom, he is the only member of the Buddha's retinue who volunteers to visit Vimalakīrti, and he serves as Vimalakīrti's principal interlocutor throughout the Scripture.

Māra. The devil, or evil one, who leads the forces of the gods of the desire-world in seeking to tempt and seduce the Buddha and his disciples. But according to Vimalakīrti he is actually a bodhisattva who dwells in the inconceivable liberation and displays evil activities in order to strengthen and consolidate the high resolve of all bodhisattvas.

Marīci. Universe of the Buddha Duṣprasāha.

Māskārin Gośāliputra. One of the six heterodox teachers.

Maudgalyāyana (*Mahā-*). One of the chief disciples, paired with Śāriputra.

Merudhvaja. Buddha-field beyond buddha-fields as numerous as the sands of thirty-six Ganges rivers, administered by the Buddha Merupradīparāja, whence Vimalakīrti obtains the lion-thrones on which he seats his visitors.

Merupradīparāja. Buddha of the universe Merudhvaja.

Mucilinda. A mountain.

nāga. One of the lords of the ocean, appearing as a great, many headed, sea dragon.

Nāgārjuna. Saint, scholar, and mystic of Buddhist India from about four hundred years after the Buddha; discoverer of the Mahāyāna Scriptures and author of the fundamental Madhyamaka treatise.

Nārāyana. In Indian lore, incarnation of Viṣṇu, whose strength was legendary (see *Abhidharmakośa* VII, pp. 72–74).

Nirgrantha Jñātiputra. One of the six heterodox teachers.

nirvāṇa. Final liberation from suffering. In the Hinayāna it is believed attainable by turning away from the world of living beings and transcending all afflictions and selfishnesses through meditative trances. In the Mahāyāna, it is believed attainable only by the attainment of Buddhahood, the nondual realization of the indivisibility of life and liberation, and the all-powerful compassion that establishes all living beings simultaneously in their own liberations.

Pāli. The canonical language of Ceylonese Buddhists, believed to be very similar to the colloquial language spoken by Śākyamuni Buddha.

parinirvāṇa. A more emphatic term for *nirvāṇa*, when it is used in reference to the apparent passing away of a physical body of a Buddha.

Prabhāvyūha. A bodhisattva present in the opening assembly, who later tells the story of his encounter with Vimalakīrti, who discourses to him about the seat of enlightenment.

Prajñāpāramitā. Transcendental wisdom, being the profound nondual understanding of the ultimate reality, or voidness, or relativity, of all things; personified as a goddess, she is worshiped as the "Mother of all Buddhas" (*Sarvajinamātā*).

Prajñāpāramitāsūtra. The Scripture in which the transcendental wisdom is taught. There are nineteen versions of different lengths, ranging from the *Heart Scripture* of a few pages to the *Hundred-Thousand.* A great deal of information about these Scriptures can be found in the works of Dr. Edward Conze.

Prajñāpāramitopadeśa. A commentary on the *Prajñāpāramitāsūtras*, composed by Kumārajīva from oral traditions derived from Nāgārjuna, and partially translated from Chinese into French by Dr. Etienne Lamotte, as *Traité de la Grande Vertu de la Sagesse*, Louvain, 1944–1949 (Bibliotheque du Muséon, 18).

Prāsaṅgika. The sub-school of the Mādhyamika philosophical school founded by Buddhapalita and further developed by Candrakīrti.

Prasannapadā. Candrakīrti's major commentary on Nāgārjuna's *Fundamental Stanzas on Wisdom.*

pratītyasamutpāda. Relativity, or dependent origination.

pratyekabuddha. A solitary sage, practitioner of Hinayāna teaching.

Priyadarśana. A young Licchavi, believed by Tibetan tradition to have been a former life of Nāgārjuna, as based on the *Suvarnaprabhāsasūtra.*

Purāṇa Kāśyapa. One of the six heterodox teachers.

Pūrṇamaitrāyaṇīputra. Disciple of the Buddha noted for his ability as a preacher of the Hinayāna teaching, especially skillful in the conversion and training of young monks.

Rāhula. Śākyamuni Buddha's own son, who became a distinguished disciple.

Ratnabahula. One of the Buddhas who assembled at Vimalakīrti's house to teach esoteric practices, according to the goddess (Chap. 7).

Ratnacandra. One of the Buddhas who assembled at Vimalakīrti's house to teach the *Tathāgataguhyaka*, according to the goddess.

Ratnacchattra. Wheel-turning king said by the Buddha to be a former incarnation of the Buddha Ratnārcis.

Ratnākara. Wealthy young Licchavi noble who leads the delegation that brings the precious parasols to the Buddha.

Ratnaparvata. A mountain.

Ratnārcis. One of the Buddhas who appear in the house of Vimalakīrti on esoteric occasions.

Ratnaśrī. One of the Buddhas who appear in the house of Vimalakīrti on esoteric occasions.

Ratnāvalī. An important work of Nāgārjuna's, in which he concisely summarizes the ethical, psychological, and philosophical teachings of the Mahāyāna.

Ratnavyūha. Name of one of the bodhisattvas in the original assembly; also the name of a Buddha who presides in the universe called Anantaguṇaratnavyūha, yet who comes to Vimalakīrti's house at the latter's supplication, to participate in the esoteric teachings. He can be identified with the Tathāgata Ratnasaṃbhava, one of the five major Buddhas of the *Guhyasamājatantra.*

Roca. Mentioned by the Buddha as the last of the thousand Buddhas of this aeon.

Sahā. Universe and buddha-field of Śākyamuni; our world.

Śakra. In Buddhist texts, usual name for Indra, king of gods. As in the case of Brahmā, a title, or status, rather than a personal name. Each universe has its Śakra; hence "twelve thousand Śakras" (p. 12), etc., assembled from different universes.

Śakya. Name of the tribe dwelling in Northern India in which Gotama, or Śākyamuni, Buddha was born as prince Siddhārtha.

Śākyamuni. The "Sage of the Śakyas," name of the Buddha of our era, who lived c. 563–483 B.C.

samādhi. Concentration of total mental equanimity which is such a powerful mental state it can be turned to accomplish amazing results.

Saṃdhinirmocanasūtra. The "Scripture of the Revelation of the Inner Intention," it was the most important Mahāyāna Scripture for Āryāsaṅga and the Vijñānavāda school.

Saṃjāyin Vairaṭiputra. One of the six heterodox teachers.

saṃsāra. The cycle of birth and death; that is, life as experienced by living beings under the influence of ignorance, not any sort of objective world external to the persons experiencing it.

Saṃtuṣita. King of the gods of the Tuṣita heaven.

Saṃyaksaṃbuddha (lit. "perfectly accomplished Buddha"). Name of the Buddha.

Saṇgha. The third of the Three Jewels (Triratna) of Buddhism, the Buddha, the Teaching, and the Community. Sometimes narrowly defined as the community of mendicants, it can be understood as including lay practitioners.

Śāntideva (eighth century). A great master of the Mādhyamika, famous for his remarkable work, "Introduction to the Practice of Enlightenment" (*Bodhicaryāvatāra*).

Śāriputra. One of the major disciples, paired with Maudgalyāyana, and noted for having been praised by the Buddha as foremost of the wise; hence, the most frequent target for Vimalakīrti's attacks on the disciples and on the Hinayāna in general.

Sarvagandhasugandhā. Universe of the Buddha Sugandhakūṭa; a universe wherein the Dharma is taught through the medium of scent.

Sarvārthasiddha. One of the Buddhas who appear in Vimalakīrti's house to teach the *Tathāgataguhyaka*, according to the goddess.

Sarvarūpasaṃdarśanā. This bodhisattva asks Vimalakīrti the whereabouts of his family, etc., thus prompting the latter's extraordinary verses on the family and accoutrements of all bodhisattvas (Chap. 8).

Sarvasukhamaṇḍita. A universe, or buddha-field, where the bodhisattvas live in a constant state of bliss.

śāstra. A type of Indian religious, philosophical, or scientific work whose importance lies not in its scriptural authority but in its systematic study of particular problems or techniques.

Śikṣāsamuccaya. The "Compendium of Precepts," in which Śāntideva collects pertinent quotes from the Mahāyāna Scriptures and presents them according to a pattern suited for systematic practice. The quotations he included from the VKN are the only extant remnants of the original Skt. text of the VKN.

Siṃhakīrti. One of the Buddhas who teach the *Tathāgataguhyaka* on certain occasions in Vimalakīrti's house.

Siṃhasvara. One of the Buddhas who appear at Vimalakīrti's house.

śrāvaka (lit. "listener"). Disciple of the Buddha and follower of the Hīnayāna teaching.

Śrāvastī. Capital city of the kingdom of Kosala, ruled by one of the Buddha's royal patrons, king Prasenajit, where the Buddha often dwelt in the Jetavana grove, site of many Mahāyāna Scriptures.

Sthiramati (c. fourth century). One of the important masters of the Vijñānavāda school, he wrote important commentaries on the works of Vasubandhu and Āryāsaṅga.

Śubhavyūha. A supreme god, or Brahmā, of another universe, who visits our universe to converse with Aniruddha about the divine eye, and is taught instead by Vimalakīrti in Chap. 3.

Subhūti. Disciple noted for his profound concentration on voidness; as interlocutor of the Buddha, a major figure in the *Prajñāpāramitāsūtras*.

Sudatta. (Anāthapiṇḍada); a lay follower of the Buddha, noted for his generosity as a patron.

Sugandhakūṭa. Buddha of the universe Sarvagandhasugandhā, from whom Vimalakīrti's emanation-bodhisattva obtains the vessel of ambrosial food that magically feeds the entire assembly without diminishing in the slightest.

Sugata (lit. "who goes to bliss," a contraction of the Sanskrit *sukhaṃ gataḥ*). A name of the Buddha.

Sumeru. The king of mountains; the axial mountain of the flat world in the exoteric cosmology.

śūnyatā. Voidness, emptiness; specifically, the emptiness of absolute substance, truth, identity, intrinsic reality, or self of all persons and things in the relative world, being quite opposed to any sort of absolute nothingness (see Glossary 3, under "emptiness").

śūnyatāśūnyatā. The voidness of voidness, an important concept that indicates the ultimate conceptuality of all terms, even those for the ultimate, to avoid the major error of absolutising the ultimate.

sūtra. In general Indian usage, the word for a highly condensed arrangement of verses that lends itself to memorization, serving as a basic text for a particular school of thought. In Buddhism, a Scripture, inasmuch as it records either the direct speech of the Buddha, or the speech of someone manifestly inspired by him.

Suvarṇābhāsasūtra. The "Scripture of the Golden Light," particularly famous for its discussion of law, kingship, and other topics important to the political life of nations. Alternate name, *Suvarṇaprabhāsasūtra*.

Tantra. Meaning "method" in general, in Buddhism it refers to an important body of literature dealing with a great variety of techniques of advanced meditations, incorporating rituals, incantations, and visualisations, that are stamped as esoteric until a practitioner has already attained a certain stage of ethical and philosophical development.

Tarkajvāla. The "Blaze of Reason," an important treatise of Bhāvaviveka's, in which he critically discusses all the major philosophical views of his day.

Tathāgata (lit. "Thus-gone" or "Thus-come," one who proceeds always in consciousness of the ultimate reality, or thatness of all things). A name of the Buddha.

Trāyastriṃśa. The Heaven of the Thirty-Three, one of the many heavens in Buddhist cosmology.

Tsoṅ Khapa (1357–1419). One of the greatest of all Tibetan Lamas, his saintliness was evidenced in his altruistic deeds that caused a renaissance in Tibet, his enlightenment in the extraordinary subtlety and profundity of his thought, and his scholarship in the breadth and clarity of his voluminous writings.

Tuṣita. A heaven, the last stopping place of a Buddha before his descent and reincarnation on earth; at present the abode of the future Buddha Maitreya.

Upāli. Disciple; originally the barber of the Śakya princes, ordained together with them, and noted as an expert on the Vinaya.

Vaiśālī. Great city during the Buddha's time, capital of the Licchavi republic; at present the town of Basarh, Muzaffarpur district, in Tirhut, Bihar province of India.

Vajrapāṇi. An important bodhisattva, "Wielder of the Thunderbolt," whose compassion is to manifest in a terrific form to protect the practicers of the Dharma from harmful influences.

Vasubandhu (fourth century). The younger brother of Āryāsaṅga, he was one of the greatest scholars in Buddhist history, author of the *Abhidharmakośa*, the most definitive work on the Abhidharma, and later of numerous important works on the Vijñānavāda philosophy.

Veda. Name of the ancient sacred Scriptures of Brahmanism, most famous of which is the *Ṛg Veda.*

Vicaraṇa. The name of the long-past aeon during which the Buddha Bhaiṣajyarāja presided in the buddha-field Mahāvyūha.

Vigrahavyāvartanī. An important work of Nāgārjuna's, in which he refuted the idea that logic was useless in attaining the correct view of ultimate reality.

Vijñānavāda. The school of "Consciousness-Only" founded by Maitreya and Āryāsaṅga, which shares with the Mādhyamika most of the philosophical techniques of the Mahāyāna, while differing on the interpretation of the profound meaning of voidness, or the ultimate reality.

Vinaya. One of the three *Piṭakas*, or "Baskets," of the Buddhist canon; the one dealing specifically with the code of the monastic disipline.

yakṣa. A forest demon.

yamakavyatyastāhāra. Reconciliation of dichotomies.

Zen. Japanese pronunciation of Ch. Ch'an, meaning contemplation (*dhyāna*), and name of the school of practice that emphasizes direct realization of enlightenment through meditation.

Numerical Categories

one way, path of. Equivalent to "path of the unique vehicle" (*ekanayamārga, ekayānamārga*), referring to the Mahāyāna doctrine that the vehicles of the disciples and the solitary sages are only provisional and do not lead to the ultimate goal. Eventually, everyone on the path must enter the Great Vehicle of the bodhisattva to reach the single goal of all of the Buddha's teachings: the unexcelled, perfect enlightenment of Buddhahood.

two obscurations (*āvaraṇadvaya*). Passionate obscuration (*kleśāvaraṇa*) and objective obscuration (*jñeyāvaraṇa*); the former may be eliminated by arhats and bodhisattvas of a certain stage, while the latter is eliminated only at Buddhahood.

two selves (*ātmadvaya*). Personal self (*pudgalātma*) and phenomenal self (*dharmātma*), which are the ultimately non-existent objects we presume we perceive as the essential cores of persons and things.

two selflessnesses (*nairātmyadvaya*). Personal selflessness (*pudgalanairātmya*) and phenomenal selflessness (*dharmanairātmya*), both being descriptions of the ultimate reality, which is the absence of the "two selves," the realization of which is called "transcendental wisdom" (*prajñāpāramitā*).

two stores (*puṇyajñānasaṃbhāra*). The stores of merit and of wisdom; all deeds of bodhisattvas contribute to their accumulation of these two stores, which ultimately culminate in the two bodies of the Buddha, the body of form and the ultimate body.

two truths (*satyadvaya*). The superficial truth (*samvṛttisatya*) and the ultimate truth (*paramārthasatya*), or the relative truth and the absolute truth, or the conventional truth and the supreme truth.

three bad migrations (*durgati*). The migrations in hell, in the limbo of hungry ghosts, or in the animal kingdom.

three bodies of the Buddha (*trikāya*). The "Ultimate Body" (*dharmakāya*), the "Beatific Body" (*saṃbhogakāya*), and the "Incarnational Body" (*nirmāṇakāya*).

three defilements (*mala*). There is no conclusive evidence as to whether this refers to the taints of the three poisons (see entry) or to the three contaminations (*āsrava*)—by desire, by existence, and by ignorance. "Free of the three defilements" (*trimalavigata*) is often used as an epithet of the Buddha.

three doors (of action) (*karmamukha*). Body (*kāya*), speech (*vāk*), and mind (*citta*).

three doors of liberation (*vimokṣamukha*). Voidness (*śūnyatā*), signlessness (*animittatā*), and wishlessness (*apraṇihitatā*).

Three Jewels (*Triratna*). The "Holy Trinity," or three precious things in Buddhism: the Buddha, the Dharma (his teaching), and the Saṅgha (the community of practitioners of that teaching).

three knowledges (*vidya*). Three of the six superknowledges (see entry): knowledge of former (and future) lives (*purvanivāsānusmṛtijñāna*), knowledge of magical operations (*ṛddhividhijñāna*), and knowledge of termination of birth and defilement (*utpādāsravakṣayajñāna*).

three liberations, or triple liberation. See "three doors of liberation."

three meditations (*samādhi*). The heroic meditation (*śuraṃgama*), the illusory meditation (*māyopama*), and the adamantine meditation (*vajropama*).

three poisons (*viṣa*). Desire (*kāma-rāga*), hatred (*dveṣa*), and folly (*moha*), the three basic passions that cause the suffering of the world.

three realms. See "three worlds."

three revolutions of the wheel of Dharma (*dharmacakratriparivartam*). All three revolutions concern the Four Holy Truths (see entry) because they are taught from the point of view of the Path of Insight (*darśanamārga*), the Path of Meditation (*bhāvanāmārga*), and the Path of Mastery (*aśaikṣamārga*). See Chap. 1, n. 37.

three vehicles (*yāna*). The vehicles of the disciples (*śrāvakayāna*), of the solitary sages (*pratyekabuddhayāna*), and of the bodhisattvas (*Mahāyāna*).

three worlds (*tridhātu*). The desire-world (*kāmadhātu*), the material or form-world, (*rūpadhātu*), and the immaterial or formless world (*ārūpyadhātu*).

four absorptions (*samāpatti*). Absorption in the spheres of infinite space (*ākāśānantyāyatana*), infinite consciousness (*vijñānānantyāyatana*), nothingness (*akiṃcanyāyatana*), and neither consciousness nor unconsciousness (*naivasaṃjñānaivāsaṃjñāyatana*).

four bases of magical power (*ṛddhipāda*). The first basis of magical power consists of the energy from the conscious cultivation of concentration of will (*chandasamādhiprahāṇasaṃskārasamanvāgataḥ*). The second consists of the energy from the conscious cultivation of concentration of mind (*citta-*). The third consists of concentration of effort (*vīrya-*). The fourth consists of concentration of analysis (*mīmāṃsa-*). These four form a part of the thirty-seven aids to enlightenment (see entry).

four contemplations (*dhyāna*). The first contemplation is the attainment of the joy and bliss (*prītisukha*) arising from solitude and freedom from desires and sins. The second is the attainment of the joy and bliss arising from the cessation of discursive thought. The third is the attainment of equanimity, with mindfulness, awareness, and physical ease, and beyond any feeling of joy. The fourth is the utter purity of awareness of equanimity, without pleasure or pain, elation or depression. These four contemplations combine with the four absorptions (see entry) and the final state of utter cessation to form the nine sequential states (*anupūrvavihāra*) leading to the highest liberation.

four continents (*dvīpa*). These are the four continents of the flat earth of early Buddhist cosmology, which conformed to the prevailing world view of India at that time: Purvavideha in the east, Jambudvīpa (equivalent to our earth then) in the south, Aparacamara in the west, and Uttarakuru in the north.

four epitomes of the Dharma. See "four insignia."

four fearlessnesses (*vaiśāradya*). The Buddha has four fearlessnesses, as do the bodhisattvas. The four fearlessnesses of the Buddha are: fearlessness regarding the realization of all things; fearlessness regarding knowledge of the exhaustion of all impurities; fearlessness of foresight through ascertainment of the persistence of obstructions; and fearlessness in the rightness of the path leading to the attainment of the supreme success. The fearlessnesses of the bodhisattva are: fearlessness in teaching the meaning he has understood from what he has learned and practiced; fearlessness resulting from the successful maintenance of purity in physical, verbal, and mental action—without relying on others' kindness, being naturally flawless through his understanding of selflessness; fearlessness resulting from freedom from obstruction in virtue, in teaching, and in delivering living beings, through the perfection of wisdom and liberative technique and through not forgetting and constantly upholding the teachings; and fearlessness in the ambition to attain full mastery of omniscience—without any deterioration or deviation to other practices—and to accomplish all the aims of all living beings.

four foci of mindfulness (*smṛtyupasthāna*). These are the stationing, or focusing, of mindfulness on the body, sensations, the mind, and things. These four form a part of the thirty-seven aids to enlightenment (see entry).

fourfold community (*catuṣpariṣad*). This consists of monks (*bhikṣu*), nuns (*bhikṣuṇi*), laymen (*upāsaka*), and laywomen (*upāsikā*).

Four Holy Truths (*āryasatya*). The holy truths of suffering (*duḥkha*), its origin (*samudaya*), cessation (*nirodha*), and the path (*mārga*) to its cessation.

four immeasurables (*apramāṇa*). The immeasurable of love: wishing all living beings to have happiness and the cause of happiness. The immeasurable of compassion: wishing all living beings to be free of suffering and the cause of suffering. The immeasurable of joy: wishing all living beings not to be apart from supreme happiness of liberation. The immeasurable of impartiality: being free of affection and aversion. See Chap. 1, n. 48.

four insignia (or epitomes) of the Dharma (*dharmamudrā* or *dharmoddāna*). The four are as follows: All compounded things are impermanent (*anityāḥ sarvasaṃskārāḥ*). All defiled things are suffering (*duḥkhāh sarvasāsravāḥ*). All things are selfless (*anātmanāḥ sarvadharmāḥ*). Nirvāṇa is peace (*śāntaṃ nirvāṇaṃ*).

four Mahārājas. Great kings of the quarters, also called Lokapālas. Although these four are usually mentioned as a group, they may be identified as King Dhṛtarāṣtra in the east, King Virūḍhaka in the south, King Virūpākṣa in the west, and King Vaiśravana (or Kuvera) in the north.

four main elements (*mahābhūta*). These are earth (*pṛthivī*), water (*ab*), fire (*teja*), and air (*vāyu*).

four Māras. These are afflictive (*kleśamāra*), aggregative (*skandhamāra*), death (*mṛtyumāra*), and heavenly demons (*devaputramāra*).

four means of unification (*saṃgrahavastu*). This is a classification of the four ways in which a bodhisattva forms a group of people united by the common aim of practicing the Dharma: giving (*dāna*); pleasant speech (*priyavaditā*); accomplishment of the aims (of others) by teaching Dharma (*arthacaryā*); and consistency of behavior with the teaching (*samānārthatā*).

four misapprehensions (*viparyāsa*). These consist of mistaking what is impermanent for permanent; mistaking what is selfless for self-possessing; mistaking what is impure for pure; and mistaking what is miserable for happy.

four reliances (*pratisāraṇa*). To attain higher realizations and final enlightenment, the bodhisattva should rely on the meaning (of the teaching) and not on the expression (*arthapratisāraṇena bhavitavyaṃ na vyañjanapratisāraṇena*); on the teaching and not on the person (who teaches it) (*dharmapratisāraṇena bhavitavyaṃ na pudgalapratisāraṇena*); on gnosis and not on normal consciousness (*jñānapratisāraṇena bhavitavyaṃ na vijñānapratisāraṇena*); and on discourses of definitive meaning and not on discourses of interpretable meaning (*nītārthasūtrapratisāraṇena bhavitavyaṃ na neyārthasūtrapratisāraṇena*) according to the order in this sūtra. The usual order, "teaching-reliance," "meaning-reliance," definitive-meaning-discourse-reliance," and "gnosis-reliance," seems to conform better to stages of practice.

four right efforts (*samyakprahāṇa*). These are effort not to initiate sins not yet arisen; effort to eliminate sins already arisen; effort to initiate virtues not yet arisen; and effort to consolidate, increase, and not deteriorate virtues already arisen. For my use of "effort" instead of lit. "abandonment," see Dayal, p. 102 ff. These four form a part of the thirty-seven aids to enlightenment (see entry).

five basic precepts (*sikṣāpada*). These are binding on all Buddhists, monks and layman alike; not to kill, not to steal, not to engage in illicit sexual intercourse, not to lie, and not to use intoxicants.

five compulsive aggregates (*upādānaskandha*). These are the aggregates of matter (*rūpa*), sensation (*vedanā*), intellect (*samjñā*), motivation (*saṃskāra*), and consciousness (*vijñāna*), which, associated together, make up most living beings.

five corruptions (*kaṣāya*). The five negative attributes of our difficult age, namely, the corruptions of life span (*āyuḥ*), views (*dṛṣṭi*), passions (*kleśa*), living beings (*sattva*), and cosmic era (*kalpa*).

five deadly sins (*ānantarya*) (lit. "sins of immediate retribution [after death]"). These five, all of which cause immediate rebirth in hell, are killing one's father, killing one's mother, killing a saint, breaking up the Saṅgha, and causing, with evil intent, the Tathāgata to bleed.

five eyes (*cakṣu*). These consist of five different faculties of vision: the physical eye (*māṃ-*

sacakṣu), the divine eye (*dīvya-*), the wisdom eye (*prajñā-*), the Dharma-eye (*dharma-*), and the Buddha-eye (*buddha-*).

five impediments (*nīvaraṇa*). These are five mental impediments that hinder meditation: impediments of desire (*kāmacchanda*), malice (*vyāpāda*), depression and sloth (*styānamiddha*), wildness and excitement (*auddhatyakaukṛtya*), and doubt, or perplexity (*vicikitsa*).

five obscurations. Variant expression for "five impediments."

five passions (*kleśa*). The number five here is somewhat arbitrary, as there are "three," "six," and even "twenty" in other texts. In the Tantras, the following five correspond to the five Tathāgata-families: pride (*abhimāna*), envy (*īrṣya*), desire (*kāma*), hatred (*dveṣa*), and folly (*moha*).

five paths (*mārga*). These represent the stages of development of any practitioner of Buddhism, who progresses from one to another gradually. They are the paths of accumulation (*saṃbhāramārga*), application (*prayogamārga*), insight (*darśanamārga*), meditation (*bhāvanāmārga*), and mastery (*aśaikṣamārga*).

five pure aggregates (*dharmaskandha*). The five aggregates (metaphorically) of the Dharmakāya of a Buddha: morality (*śīla*), concentration (*samādhi*), wisdom (*prajñā*), liberation (*vimukti*), and knowledge and vision of liberation (*vimuktijñānadarśana*).

five spiritual faculties (*indriya*). These are called "faculties" (*indriya*) by analogy, as they are considered as capacities to be developed: the spiritual faculties for faith (*śraddhā*), effort (*vīrya*), mindfulness (*smṛti*), concentration (*samādhi*), and wisdom (*prajñā*). These are included in the thirty-seven aids to enlightenment.

five states of existence (*gati*). These refer to the categories of living beings, more often divided into six: hell-denizen (*naraka*), ghost (*preta*), beast (*tiryañca*), human (*manuṣya*), titan (*asura*), and deity (*deva*). Five are obtained from six by including the titanic within the divine.

five powers (*bala*). These are the same as the five spiritual faculties, at a further stage of development.

five superknowledges (*abhijñā*). These are more often listed as six: divine eye or vision *divyacakṣu*), divine hearing (*divyaśrotra*), telepathy (*paracittajñāna*), knowledge of former (and future) lives (*pūrva*[*para*]*nivāsānusmṛtijñāna*), knowledge of magical operations (*ṛddhividhijñāna*), and knowledge of the termination of defilements (*āsravakṣayajñāna*). Scholars generally agree that five are obtained by eliminating knowledge of magical operations from the classification.

six heterodox teachers (*tīrthikaśāstṛ*). These six sought to rival the Buddha in his day: Purāṇa Kāśyapa, who negated the effects of action, good or evil; Māskārin Gośāliputra, who taught a theory of randomness, negating causality; Saṃjāyin Vairaṭiputra, who was agnostic in refusing to maintain any opinion about anything; Kakuda Kātyāyana, who taught a materialism in which there was no such thing as killer or killed, but only transformations of elements; Ajita Keśakambala, who taught a more extreme nihilism regarding everything except the four main elements; and Nirgrantha Jñātiputra, otherwise known as Mahāvīra, the founder of Jainism, who taught the doctrine of indeterminism (*syādvāda*), considering all things in terms of "maybe."

six remembrances (*anusmṛti*). These are six things to keep in mind: the Buddha, the Dharma, the Saṅgha, morality (*śīla*), generosity (*tyāga*), and deities (*devatā*).

six sense-faculties (*indriya*). These are eye (*cakṣu*), ear (*śrotra*), nose (*ghrāṇa*), tongue (*jihvā*), body (*kāya*), and mind (*manas*).

six sense-media (*āyatana*). These occur as the fifth member of the twelve links of dependent origination (see entry). They actually include all eighteen elements (see entry) in the Abhidharmic classification, which treats each of the six senses as threefold (comprising faculty, object, and consciousness).

six sense-objects (*viṣaya*). These are color/form (*rūpa*), sound (*śabda*), scent (*gandha*), tastes (*rasa*), textures (*spraṣṭavya*), and phenomena (*dharma*).

six superknowledges (*abhijñā*). See "five superknowledges."

six transcendences (*pāramita*). These are the main categories of the bodhisattva's activities: giving (*dāna*), morality (*śīla*), tolerance (*kṣānti*), effort (*vīrya*), meditation (*dhyāna*), and wisdom (*prajñā*).

seven abodes of consciousness (*vijñānasthiti*). This refers to the seven categories of living beings, as enumerated in the *Abhidharmakośa*, III, v. 5–6a. The seven abodes of consciousness consist of beings who differ physically and intellectually; beings who differ physically but are similar intellectually; beings similar physically but who differ intellectually; beings similar physically and intellectually; and three types of immaterial beings (*nānātvakāyasaṃjñāś ca nānākāyaikasaṃjñinaḥ / viparyayāc caikakāyasaṃjñāś cārūpiṇas trayaḥ // vijñānasthitayaḥ sapta*. . .). According to Vasubandhu the first category consists of men, the six types of gods of the desire-realm, and the gods of the first realm of contemplation (*brahmavihāra*) except those fallen from higher realms (*prathamābhinirvṛta*); the second category consists of those fallen (*prathamābhiniṛvṛta*) gods who have different bodies but whose intellects are single-mindedly aware of the idea of being created by Brahmā; the third category consists of the gods of the second realm of contemplation —the *abhāsvara* (clear-light) gods, the *parīṭṭābha* (radiant) gods, and the *apramāṇābha* (immeasurably luminous) gods—who have similar luminous bodies but differ in their thoughts, which are bent on the experiences of pleasure and numbness; the fourth category consists of the *śubhakṛtsna* (pure-wholeness) gods, whose intellects are united in concentration on bliss; the fifth category consists of the immaterial beings who reside in the realm of infinite space; the sixth category consists of the immaterial beings who reside in the realm of infinite consciousness; and the seventh category consists of the immaterial beings who reside in the realm of nothingness. (See also Mvy, Nos. 2289–2295.)

seven factors of enlightenment (*saṃbodhyaṅga*). These are the factors of remembrance (*smṛti*), discrimination between teachings (*dharmapravicaya*), effort (*vīrya*), joy (*prīti*), ecstasy (*praśrabdhi*), concentration (*samādhi*), and equanimity (*upekṣā*). These seven form a part of the thirty-seven aids to enlightenment (see entry).

eight adversities (*akṣaṇa*). These are special types of adversity that prevent the practice of the Dharma; when they are absent, one has the "jewel of a human body endowed with leisure" (for cultivation of the mind through the Dharma). They are rebirth in hell, rebirth in the brute-world, rebirth in the ghost-world, rebirth among the long-lived gods, rebirth in an uncivilized country, rebirth with deficient faculties, adherence to false views, and life in a realm wherein there is no Tathāgata.

eight branches of the holy path (*āryamārgasya aṣṭāngāni*). These are the well-known right view (*samyagdṛṣṭi*), right consideration (*samyaksaṃkalpa*), right speech (*samyakvāk*), right terminal action (*samyakkarmānta*), right livelihood (*samyagājīva*), right effort (*samyagvyāyāma*), right remembrance (*samyaksmṛti*), and right concentration (*samyaksamādhi*). They are variously defined in the different Buddhist schools. These eight form a part of the thirty-seven aids to enlightenment (see entry).

eight false paths of perversion (*mithyatva*). These consist of the exact opposites of the eight branches of the holy path.

eightfold path (*aṣṭāngikamārga*). See entry "eight branches of the holy path."

eightfold peace (*aṣṭāngaśānta*). This refers to the eightfold path, which, for the bodhisattva practicing the yoga of nonperception (*anupalabdhi*) or endowed with the inconceivable liberation, is peace in itself in all its branches.

eight liberations (*vimokṣa*). The first consists of the seeing of form by one who has form; the second consists of the seeing of external form by one with the concept of internal formlessness; the third consists of the physical realization of pleasant liberation and its successful consolidation; the fourth consists of the full entrance to the infinity of space through transcending all conceptions of matter, and the subsequent decline of conceptions of resistance and discredit of conceptions of diversity; the fifth consists of full entrance into the infinity of consciousness, having transcended the infinity of space; the sixth consists of the full entrance into the sphere of nothingness, having transcended the sphere of the infinity of consciousness; the seventh consists of the full entrance into the sphere of neither consciousness nor unconsciousness, having transcended the sphere of nothingness; the eighth consists of the perfect cessation of suffering, having transcended the sphere of neither consciousness nor unconsciousness. Thus the first three liberations form specific links to the ordinary perceptual world; the fourth to seventh are equivalent to the four absorbtions; and the eighth represents the highest attainment.

nine causes of irritation (*āghātavastu*). These consist of various mental distractions caused by the nine considerations "He has caused, causes, will cause wrong to me. He has caused, causes, will cause wrong to one dear to me. He has served, serves, will serve my enemies."

nine sequential states (*anupūrvavihāra*). See "four contemplations."

ten directions (*daśadik*). These consist of the eight points of the compass, straight up, and straight down. As a conventional formula, it is tantamount to "all directions."

ten powers (*bala*). There are two different sets of ten powers, those of the Buddha and those of bodhisattvas. Those of the Buddha consist of power from knowing right from wrong (*sthānāsthānajñānabala*); power from knowing the consequences of actions (*karmavipākajñāna-*); power from knowing the various inclinations (of living beings) (*nānādhimuktijñāna-*); power from knowing the various types (of living beings) (*nānādhātujñāna-*); power from knowing the degree of the capacities (of living beings) (*indriyavarāvarajñāna-*); power from knowing the path that leads everywhere (*sarvatragāminīpratipatjñāna-*); power from knowing the obscuration, affliction, and purification of all contemplations, meditations, liberations, concentrations, and absorptions (*sarvadhyānavimokṣasamādhisamāpattisaṃkleśavyavadānavyutthānajñāna-*); power from knowing his own former lives (*pūrvanivāsānusmṛtijñāna-*); power from knowing deaths and future lives (*cyutyutpattijñāna-*); and power from knowing the exhaustion of defilements (*āsravakṣayajñāna-*). The latter set consists of the bodhisattva's power of positive thought (*āśayabala*); power of high resolve (*adhyāśaya-*); power of application (*prayoga-*); power of wisdom (*prajñā-*); power of prayer (*praṇidhāna-*); power of vehicle (*yāna-*); power of activities (*caryā-*); power of emanations (*vikurvaṇa-*); power of enlightenment (*bodhi-*); and power of turning the wheel of the Dharma (*dharmacakrapravartaṇa-*).

ten sins (*akuśala*). These are the opposite of the ten virtues, and consist of killing, stealing, sexual misconduct, lying, harsh speech, backbiting, frivolous speech, covetousness, malice, and false views.

ten stages (*bhūmi*). These are the ten stages through which the bodhisattva ascends on his way to Buddhahood: the Joyous (*pramuditā*), the Immaculate (*vimalā*), the Brilliant (*prabhākāri*), the Radiant (*arciṣmatī*), the Invincible (*sudurjayā*), the Confronting (*abhimukhī*), the Far-reaching (*durāṃgama*), the Immovable (*acalā*), the Positively Intelligent (*sādhumatī*), and the Cloud of Dharma (*dharmameghā*). These ten stages are elaborated in various Mahāyāna Scriptures, and each stage is associated with the practice of a particular transcendence. The attainment of Buddhahood itself is sometimes referred to as the eleventh stage.

ten transcendences (*pāramitā*). These consist of the six transcendences, with the addition of skill in liberative technique (*upāyakauśalya*); prayer, or commitment (*praṇidhāna*); power (*bala*); and gnosis (*jñāna*).

ten virtues (*kuśala*). These are the opposite of the ten sins, i.e., refraining from engaging in activities related to the ten sins and doing the opposite. There are three physical virtues: saving lives, giving, and sexual propriety. There are four verbal virtues: truthfulness, reconciling discussions, gentle speech, and religious speech. There are three mental virtues: loving attitude, generous attitude, and right views. The whole doctrine is collectively called the "tenfold path of good action" (*daśakuśalakarmapatha*).

twelve ascetic practices (*dhūtaguṇa*). These consist of (1) wearing rags (*pāṃśukūlika*), (2) (in the form of only) three religious robes (*traicīvarika*), (3) (coarse in texture as) garments of felt (*nāma[n]tika*), (4) eating by alms (*paiṇḍapātika*), (5) having a single mat to sit on (*aikāsanika*), (6) not eating after noon (*khalu paśċād bhaktika*), (7) living alone in the forest (*āraṇyaka*), (8) living at the base of a tree (*vṛkṣamūlika*), (9) living in the open (not under a roof) (*ābhyavakāśika*), (10) frequenting burning grounds (Indian equivalent of cemeteries) (*śmāśānika*), (11) sleeping sitting up (in meditative posture) (*naiṣadika*), and (12) accepting whatever seating position is offered (*yāthāsaṃstarika*).

twelve links of dependent origination (*nidāna*). These are ignorance (*avidyā*), synthetic activity (*samṣkāra*), consciousness (*vijñāna*), name-matter (*nāmarūpa*), six sense-media (*ṣadāyatana*), contact (*sparśa*), sensation (*vedanā*), craving (*tṛṣṇa*), function (*upādāna*), existence (*bhāva*), birth (*jāti*), and old age, death, etc. (*jaramaraṇa*).

twelve sense-media (*āyatana*). They are eye-medium (*cakṣurāyatana*), form-medium (*rūpa-*), ear-medium (*śrotra-*), sound-medium (*śabda-*), nose-medium (*ghrāṇa-*), scent-medium (*gandha-*), tongue-medium (*jihvā-*), taste-medium (*rasa-*), body-medium. (*kāya-*), texture-medium (*spraṣṭavya-*), mental-medium (*mana-*), and phenomena-medium (*dharmāyatana*). The word *āyatana* is usually translated as "base," but the Skt., Tib., and Ch. all indicate "something through which the senses function" rather than a basis from which they function; hence "medium" is suggested.

eighteen elements (*dhātu*). These introduce the same six pairs as the twelve sense-media, as elements of experience, adding a third member to each set: the element of consciousness (*vijñāna*), or sense. Hence the first pair gives the triad eye-element (*caksurdhātu*), form-element (*rūpadhātu*), and eye-consciousness-element, or eye-sense-element (*caksurvijñānadhātu*)—and so on with the other five, noting the last, mind-element (*manodhātu*), phenomena-element (*dharmadhātu*), and mental-sense-element (*manovijñānadhātu*).

eighteen special qualities of a bodhisattva (*āveṇikabodhisattvadharma*). These consist of the bodhisattva's natural (uninstructed) possession of generosity, morality, tolerance, effort, meditation, and wisdom; of his uniting all beings with the four means of unification, knowing the method of dedication (of virtue to enlightenment), exemplification, through skill in liberative technique, of the positive results of the Mahāyāna, as suited to the (various) modes of behavior of all living beings, his not falling from the Mahāyāna, showing the entrances of saṃsāra and nirvāṇa, skill in the technique of reconciliation of dichotomies, impeccable progress in all his lives, guided by wisdom without any conditioned activities, possession of ultimate action of body, speech, and mind directed by the tenfold path of good action, nonabandonment of any of the realms of living beings, through his assumption of a body endowed with tolerance of every conceivable suffering, manifestation of that which delights all living beings, inexhaustible preservation of the mind of omniscience, as stable as the virtue-constituted tree of wish-fulfilling gems, (even) in the midst of the infantile (ordinary persons) and (narrow-minded) religious disciples, however trying they might be, and adamant irreversibility from demonstrating the quest of the Dharma of the Buddha, for the sake of the attainment of the miraculous consecration conferring the skill in liberative technique that transmutes all things.

eighteen special qualities of the Buddha (*āveṇikabuddhadharma*). They are as follows: He never makes a mistake; he is never boisterous; he never forgets; his concentration never falters; he has no notion of diversity; his equanimity is not due to lack of consideration; his will never falters; his energy never fails; his mindfulness never falters; he never abandons his concentration; his wisdom never decreases; his liberation never fails; all his physical actions are preceded and followed by wisdom; all his verbal actions are preceded and followed by wisdom; all his mental actions are preceded and followed by wisdom; his knowledge and vision perceive the past without any attachment or hindrance; his knowledge and vision perceive the future without any attachment or hindrance; and his knowledge and vision perceive the present without any attachment or hindrance.

thirty-two signs of the great being (*mahāpuruṣalakṣaṇa*). They are as follows: His head has a turban-shaped protrusion on the crown; his hair curls to the right; his forehead is broad and even; he has a white hair between his eyebrows; his eyes are very dark, with lashes like a cow; he has forty teeth; his teeth are even, without gaps, and very white; he has a keen sense of taste; he has a lion's jaw; his tongue is long and slender; he has an excellent voice; his shoulders are round and even; the back of his body has seven round curves (buttocks, thighs, shoulders, and back); his trunk is thick; his skin is smooth and golden-hued; his arms reach his knees when he stands straight up; his torso is like a lion's; his body has the proportions of a banyan tree (height equal to armspan); his bodily hairs curl to the right; they stand straight up; his penis is concealed in a sheath; his thighs are well-rounded; his ankle-bones do not protrude; the palms of his hands and feet are soft and delicate; he has webbed fingers and toes; he has long fingers; he has wheel-signs on the palms of his hands and feet; his feet are well set (upon the ground); his arches are broad and high; and his calves are like an antelope's.

thirty-seven aids to enlightenment (*bodhipakṣikadharma*). These consist of the four foci of mindfulness, the four right efforts, the four bases of magical powers, the five spiritual faculties, the five powers, the seven factors of enlightenment, and the eight branches of the holy path.

sixty-two convictions (views) (*dṛṣṭigata*). These are enumerated in the *Brahmajālasūtra* and in the *Dighanikāya* and consist of all views other than the "right view" of selflessness. All sixty-two fall into either one of the two categories known as the "two extremisms": "eternalism" (*śāśvatavāda*) and "nihilism" (*ucchedavāda*).

eighty marks (of the great being) (*anuvyañjana*). These accompany the thirty-two signs and consist of fingernails the color of brass, shiny and long; round fingers; tapered fingers; fingers wide-spreading; veins not protruding, and without tangles; slender ankles; feet not uneven; lion's gait; elephant's gait; swan's gait; bull's gait; gait tending to the right; graceful gait; steady gait; his body is well-covered, clean, well-proportioned, pure, soft, and perfect; his sex organs are fully developed; his thighs are broad and knees round; his steps are even; his complexion is youthful; his posture is not stooped; his bearing is expansive, yet extremely poised; his limbs and fingers and toes are well-defined; his vision is clear and unblurred; his joints are not protruding; his belly is relaxed, symmetrical, and not fat; his navel is deep and wound to the right; he is completely handsome; he is clean in all acts; he is free of spots or discolorations of the skin; his hands are soft as cotton; the lines of his palms are clear, deep, and long; his face is not overlong and is bright as a mirror; his tongue is soft, long, and red; his voice is like an elephant's trumpet or like thunder, yet sweet and gentle; his teeth are rounded, sharp, white, even, and regularly arranged; his nose is long and straight; his eyes are clear and wide; his eyelashes are thick; the pupils and white of his eyes are clearly defined, and the irises are like lotus petals; his eyebrows are long, soft, evenly haired, and gently curved; his ears are long-lobed and symmetrical; his hearing is acute; his forehead is high and broad; his head is very large; his hair is as black as a bee, thick, soft, untangled, not unruly, and fragrant; and his feet and hands are marked with lucky signs. (This follows Mvy, nos. 269–348; there is some variation in this list from text to text.)

Technical Terms

absorption (*samāpatti*). The four absorptions are listed in the Glossary 2. "Absorption" has been translated as "meditation," "contemplation," "attainment," etc., and any of these words might serve. The problem is to establish one English word for each of the important Sanskrit words *samāpatti*, *dhyāna*, *samādhi*, *bhāvanā*, etc., so as to preserve a consistency with the original. Therefore, I have adopted for these terms, respectively, "absorption," "contemplation," "concentration" and "realization" or "cultivation," reserving the word "meditation" for general use with any of the terms when they are used not in a specific sense but to indicate mind-practice in general.

aggregate (*skandha*). This translation of *skandha* is fairly well established, although some prefer the monosyllabic "group." It is important to bear in mind that the original *skandha* has the sense of "pile," or "heap," which has the connotation of utter lack of internal structure, of a randomly collocated pile of things; thus "group" may convey a false connotation of structure and ordered arrangement. The five "compulsive" (*upādāna*) aggregates are of great importance as a schema for introspective meditation in the Abhidharma, wherein each is defined with the greatest subtlety and precision. In fact, the five terms *rūpa*, *vedanā*, *samjñā*, *saṃskāra*, and *vijñāna* (see Glossary 2, under "five compulsive aggregates") have such a particular technical sense that many translators have preferred to leave them untranslated. Nevertheless, in the sūtra context, where the five are meant rather more simply to represent the relative living being (in the desire-realm), it seems preferable to give a translation—in spite of the drawbacks of each possible term—in order to convey the same sense of a total categorization of the psychophysical complex. Thus, for *rūpa*, "matter" is preferred to "form" because it more concretely connotes the physical and gross; for *vedanā*, "sensation" is adopted, as limited to the aesthetic; for *samjñā*, "intellect" is useful in conveying the sense of verbal, conceptual intelligence. For *saṃskāra*, which covers a number of mental functions as well as inanimate forces, "motivation" gives a general idea. And "consciousness" is so well established for *vijñāna* (although what we normally think of as consciousness is more like *samjñā*, i.e., conceptual and notional, and *vijñāna* is rather the "pure awareness" prior to concepts) as to be left unchallenged.

birthlessness (*anutpādatva*). This refers to the ultimate nature of reality, to the fact that, ultimately, nothing has ever been produced or born nor will it ever be because birth and production can occur only on the relative, or superficial, level. Hence "birthlessness" is a synonym of "voidness," "reality," "absolute," "ultimate," "infinity," etc.

concentration (*samādhi*). See "absorption."

conception of the spirit of enlightenment (*bodhicittotpāda*). This can also be rendered by "initiation of . . ." because it means the mental event occurring when a living being, having been exposed to the teaching of the Buddha or of his magical emanations (e.g., Vimalakīrti), realizes simultaneously his own level of conditioned ignorance, i.e., that his habitual stream of consciousness is like sleep compared to that of one who has awakened from ignorance; the possibility of his own attainment of a higher state of consciousness; and the necessity of attaining it in order to liberate other living beings from their stupefaction. Having realized this possibility, he becomes inspired with the intense ambition to attain, and that is called the "conception of the spirit of enlightenment." "Spirit" is preferred to "mind" because the mind of enlightenment should rather be the mind of the Buddha, and to "thought" because a "thought of enlightenment" can easily be produced without the initiation of any sort of new resolve or awareness. "Will" also serves very well here.

conceptualization (*vikalpa*). This brings up another important group of words that has never been treated systematically in translation: *vikalpa*, *parikalpa*, *samāropa*, *adhyāropa*, *kalpanā*, *samjñā*, and *prapañca*. All of these refer to mental functions that tend to superimpose upon reality, either relative or ultimate, a conceptualized reality fabricated by the subjective mind. Some translators have tended to lump these together under the rubric "discursive thought," which leads to the misleading notion that all thought is bad, something to be eliminated, and that sheer "thoughtlessness" is "enlightenment," or whatever higher state is desired. According to Buddhist scholars, thought in itself is simply a function, and only thought that is attached to its own content over and above the relative object, i.e., "egoistic" thought, is bad and to be eliminated. Therefore we have chosen a set of words for the seven Skt. terms: respectively, "conceptualization," "imagination," "presumption," "exaggeration," "construction," "conception" or "notion," and "fabrication." This does not mean that these words are not somewhat interchangeable or that another English word might not be better in certain contexts; it only represents an attempt to achieve consistency with the original usages.

conscious awareness (*apramāda*). This denotes a type of awareness of the most seemingly insignificant aspects of practical life, an awareness derived as a consequence of the highest realization of the ultimate nature of reality. As it is stated in the *Anavataptaparipṛcchasūtra*: "He who realizes voidness, that person is consciously aware." "Ultimate realization," far from obliterating the relative world, brings it into highly specific, albeit dreamlike, focus.

consciousness (*vijñāna*). See "aggregate."

contemplation (*dhyāna*). See "absorption."

construction, mental (*kalpanā*, or *vikalpa*). See "conceptualization."

dedication (*pariṇāmana*). This refers to the bodhisattva's constant mindfulness of the fact that all his actions of whatever form contribute to his purpose of attaining enlightenment for the sake of himself and others, i.e., his conscious deferral of the merit accruing from any virtuous action as he eschews immediate reward in favor of ultimate enlightenment for himself and all living beings.

definitive meaning (*nītārtha*). This refers to those teachings of the Buddha that are in terms of ultimate reality; it is opposed to those teachings given in terms of relative reality, termed "interpretable meaning," because they require further interpretation before being relied on to indicate the ultimate. Hence definitive meaning relates to voidness, etc., and no statement concerning the relative world, even by the Buddha, can be taken as definitive. This is especially important in the context of the Mādhyamika doctrine, hence in the context of Vimalakīrti's teachings, because he is constantly correcting the disciples and bodhisattvas who accept interpretable expressions of the Tathāgata as if they were definitive, thereby attaching themselves to them and adopting a one-sided approach.

designation (*prajñapti*). This occurs in the axiomatic Mādhyamika description of all things as existent by virtue of "mere designation" (*prajñaptimātra*).

determination. See "ultimate determination."

dichotomy (*yamakavyatyasta*). A "contrasted pair." One who is neither attached nor averse to words may live by the "reconciliation of dichotomies." This possibility is inherent in the fact that the dualism of verbalization and its consequent perceptual habits do not accurately correspond with reality since, once beyond the narrow prison of verbal categories, anything is possible.

duality, dualism (*dvaya*, *dvayagrāha*). "Duality" is largely self-explanatory. To be pointed out here is the connection between the mental habit of dualism and verbalization, insofar as dualism is inherent in the structure of language, in which things are presented in terms of opposites. Vimalakīrti unmistakably points this out, with the help of Mañjuśrī, by his famous silence on the subject of nonduality.

egoistic views (*satkāyadṛṣṭi*). This consists of twenty varieties of false notion, consisting basically of regarding the temporally impermanent and ultimately insubstantial as "I" or "mine." The five compulsive aggregates are paired with the self, giving the twenty false notions. For example, the first four false notions are that (1) matter is the self, which is like its owner (*rūpaṃ ātmā svāmivat*); (2) the self possesses matter, like its ornament (*rūpavān ātmā alaṇkāravat*); (3) matter belongs to the self, like a slave (*ātmīyaṃ rūpaṃ bhṛtyavat*); and (4) the self dwells in matter as in a vessel (*rūpe ātmā bhajanavat*). The other four compulsive aggregates are paired with the self in the same four ways, giving sixteen more false notions concerning sensation, intellect, motivation, and consciousness, hypostatizing an impossible relationship with a nonexistent, permanent, substantial self.

emanated incarnation (*nirmāṇa*). This refers to the miraculous power of the Buddha and bodhisattvas of a certain stage to emanate apparently living beings in order to develop and teach living beings. This power reaches its culmination in the *nirmāṇakayā*, the "incarnation body," which is one of the three bodies of Buddhahood and includes all physical forms of all Buddhas, including Śākyamuni, whose sole function as incarnations is the development and liberation of living beings.

emptiness (*śūnyatā*). This Skt. term is usually translated by "voidness" because that English word is more rarely used in other contexts than "emptiness" and does not refer to any sort of ultimate nothingness, as a thing-in-itself, or even as the thing-in-itself to end all things-in-themselves. It is a pure negation of the ultimate existence of anything or, in Buddhist terminology, the "emptiness with respect to personal and phenomenal selves," or "with respect to identity," or "with respect to intrinsic nature," or "with respect to essential substance," or "with respect to self-existence established by intrinsic identity," or "with respect to ultimate truth-status," etc. Thus emptiness is a concept descriptive of the ultimate reality through its pure negation of whatever may be supposed to be ultimately real. It is an absence, hence not existent in itself. It is synonymous therefore with "infinity," "absolute," etc.—themselves all negative terms, i.e., formed etymologically from a positive concept by adding a negative prefix (in + finite = not finite; ab + solute = not compounded, etc.). But, since our verbally conditioned mental functions are habituated to the connection of word and thing, we tend to hypostatize a "void," analogous to "outer space," a "vacuum," etc., which we either shrink from as a nihilistic nothingness or become attached to as a liberative nothingness; this great mistake can be cured only by realizing the meaning of the "emptiness of emptiness," which brings us to the tolerance of inconceivability (see "tolerance").

enlightenment (*bodhi*). This word requires too much explanation for this glossary because, indeed, the whole sūtra—and the whole of Buddhist literature—is explanatory of only this. Here we simply mention the translation equivalent.

gnosis (*jñāna, āryajñāna*). This is knowledge of the nonconceptual and transcendental which is realized by those attaining higher stages.

grace (*adhiṣṭhāna*). The "supernatural power" with which the Buddhas sustain the bodhisattvas in their great efforts on behalf of living beings.

great compassion (*mahākaruṇā*). This refers to one of the two (see "enlightenment" entry) central qualities of a Buddha or high bodhisattva: his feeling born of the wish for all living beings to be free of suffering and to attain the supreme happiness. It is important to note that this great compassion has nothing to do with any sentimental emotion such as that stimulated by such a reflection as "Oh, the poor creatures! How they are suffering!" On the contrary, great compassion is accompanied by the clear awareness that ultimately there are no such things as living beings, suffering, etc., in reality. Thus it is a sensitivity that does not entertain any dualistic notion of subject and object; indeed, such an unlimited sensitivity might best be termed "empathy."

high resolve (*adhyāśaya*). This is a stage in the conception or initiation of the spirit of enlightenment. It follows upon the positive thought, or aspiration to attain it, wherein the bodhisattva becomes filled with a lofty determination that he himself should attain enlightenment, that it is the only thing to do to solve his own problems as well as those of all living beings. This high resolve reaches its most intense purity when the bodhisattva simultaneously attains the Path of Insight and the first bodhisattva-stage, the Stage of Joy. The translation follows Lamotte's happy coinage "*haute résolution*."

identity and identitylessness (*svabhāva, niḥsvabhāvatā*). *Svabhāva* is usually rendered as "self-nature," sometimes as "own-being," both of which have a certain literal validity. However, neither artificial term has any evocative power for the reader who has no familiarity with the original, and a term must be found that the reader can immediately relate to his own world to fulfill the function the original word had in its world. In our world of identities (national, racial, religious, personal, sexual, etc.), "identity" is a part of our makeup; thus, when we are taught the ultimate absence of identity of all persons and things, it is easy to "identify" what is supposedly absent and hence to try to understand what that entails.

incantation (*dhāraṇī*). This is literally a formulaic spell, a series of potent sounds that, in the enunciation of the adept, creates a certain effect because it contains the essence of profound experience and knowledge in a psychic seed-form, as it were. A bodhisattva of a certain stage uses spells to accomplish his work of developing living beings and hence is said to have the power of incantations. They are particularly useful for anchoring the bodhisattva's memory of the teachings, and of his previous realizations of them.

incarnation (*nirmāna*). See "emanated incarnation."

incomprehensibility (*anupalabdhatva*). This refers to the ultimate nature of things, which cannot be comprehended, grasped, etc., by the ordinary, conditioned, subjective mind. Hence it is significant that the realization of this nature is not couched in terms of understanding, or conviction, but in terms of tolerance (*kṣānti*, see "tolerance"), as the grasping mind cannot grasp its ultimate inability to grasp; it can only cultivate its tolerance of that inability.

inconceivability (*acintyatā*) (lit. "unthinkability," on the part of a mind whose thinking is conditioned and bound by conceptual terms). This is essentially synonymous with "incomprehensibility" (see entry).

instinct (*vāsanā*). The subconscious tendencies and predilections of the psychosomatic conglomerate. This most obvious word is seldom used in this context because of the hesitancy of scholars to employ "scientific" terminology.

intellect (*samjñā*). See "aggregate."

interpretable meaning (*neyārtha*). See "definitive meaning."

liberative technique (*upāya*). This is the expression in action of the great compassion of the Buddha and the bodhisattvas—physical, verbal, and mental. It follows that one empathetically aware of the troubles of living beings would, for his very survival, devise the most potent and efficacious techniques possible to remove those troubles, and the troubles of living beings are removed effectively only when they reach liberation. "Technique" was chosen over the usual "method" and "means" because it has a stronger connotation of efficacy in our technological world; also, in Buddhism, liberative technique is identified with the extreme of power, energy, and efficacy, as symbolized in the *vajra* (adamantine scepter): The importance of this term is highlighted in this sūtra by the fact that Vimalakīrti himself is introduced in the chapter entitled "Inconceivable Skill in Liberative Technique"; this indicates that he, as a function of the *nirmāṇakāya* (incarnation-body), just like the Buddha himself, is the very incarnation of liberative technique, and every act of his life is therefore a technique for the development and liberation of living beings. The "liberative" part of the translation follows "*salvifique*" in Lamotte's phrase "*moyens salvifique.*"

life (*saṃsāra*). This term is natural, instead of either "transmigration" or "the round," because it conveys well the sense of the transformations of living things; it also connotes to all modern readers the whole span and scope of the world of living things. Sometimes "world" suffices, sometimes "evolution" is intriguing.

Lord (*Bhagavān*). "Lord" is chosen to translate the title *bhagavān* because it is the term of greatest respect current in our "sacred" language, as established for the Deity in the Elizabethan version of the Bible. Indeed, the Skt. *Bhagavān* was given as a title to the Buddha, although it also served the non-Buddhist Indians of the day and, subsequently, it served as an honorific title of their particular deities. As the Buddha is clearly described in the Scriptures as the "Supreme Teacher of Gods and Men," there seems little danger that he may be confused with any particular deity through the use of this term [as indeed in Buddhist Scriptures various deities, creators, protectors, etc., are shown in their respective roles]. Thus I feel it would compromise the weight and function of the original *Bhagavān* to use any less weighty term than "Lord" for the Buddha.

matter (*rūpa*). See "aggregate."

mental quiescence, or trance (*śamatha*). "Mental quiescence" is a general term for all types of mind-practice, meditation, contemplation, concentration, etc., that cultivate one-pointedness of mind and lead to a state of peacefulness and freedom from concern with any sort of object. It is paired with "transcendental analysis" or "insight," which combines the analytic faculty with this one-pointedness to reach high realizations such as selflessness (see "transcendental analysis"). "Mental quiescence" and "transcendental analysis" were coined by E. Obermiller in his invaluable study "Prajña Pāramitā Doctrine, as Exposed in the Abhisamayālaṃkāra of Maitreya" (*Acta Orientalia*, Vol. XI [Heidelberg, 1932], pp. 1–134).

motivation (*saṃskāra*). See "aggregate."

nonapprehension (*anupalambha*); equivalent to "nonperception." This refers to the mental openness cultivated by the bodhisattva who has reached a certain awareness of the nature of reality, in that he does not seek to apprehend any object or grasp any substance in anything; rather, he removes any static pretension of his mind to have grasped at any truth, conviction, or view (see "incomprehensibility").

nonduality (*advayatvā*). This is synonymous with reality, voidness, etc. But it must be remembered that nonduality does not necessarily mean unity, that unity is only one of the pair unity-duality; hence nonduality implies nonunity as well. This point is obscured by designating this nondual philosophy as "monism," as too many modern scholars have done. See Introduction.

nonperception (*anupaladhi*). See "nonapprehension."

omniscience (*sarvajñatā*). This refers to the gnosis of the Buddha, with which there is nothing he does not know. However, not to confuse "omniscience" with the theistic conception of an omniscient god, the "everything" here is specifically everything about the source of the predicament of worldly life and the way of transcendence of that world through liberation. Since "everything" is only an abstract term without any particular referent, once we are clear about the implications of infinity, it does not refer to any sort of ultimate totality, since a totality can only be relative, i.e., a totality within a particular frame of reference. Thus, as Dharmakīrti has remarked, "it is not a question of the Buddha's knowing the number of fish in the ocean," i.e., since there are infinity of fish in infinity of oceans in infinity of worlds and universes. The Buddha's omniscience, rather, knows how to develop and liberate any fish in any ocean, as well as all other living beings.

positive thought (*āśaya*). This is the first stirring in the bodhisattva's mind of the inspiration to attain enlightenment (see "high resolve"). See Lamotte, *Appendice*, Note II.

reality-limit (*bhūtakoṭi*). A synonym of the ultimate reality. In the Mahāyāna Scriptures, it has a somewhat negative flavor, connoting the Hinayāna concept of a static nirvāṇa. Sthiramati glosses the term as follows: "'Reality' means undistorted truth. 'Limit' means the extreme beyond which there is nothing to be known by anyone" (*bhūtaṃ satyam aviparītamityarthaḥ / koṭiḥ paryanto yataḥ pareṇa-anyajjñeyaṃ nāsti . . /*).

reincarnation (*punarjāti, punarbhāva*). It is well to make a distinction between "rebirth" and "reincarnation." The former is the normal process following the death of a normal living being; the latter is the conscious and voluntary descent into a physical body of a bodhisattva or Buddha who, because of his transcendence of the bonds of action and passions, is not compelled but incarnates in order to develop and liberate other living beings.

relativity (*pratītyasamutpāda*). This Skt. term is usually translated as "dependent origination," which serves in certain contexts. However, in the Mādhyamika context, which is an important context in this Scripture, *pratītyasamutpāda* describes ultimate reality. It is equated to *śūnyatā*, voidness, the nature of birthlessness; thus "origination" is somewhat out of place, since ultimately nothing originates. "Relativity," which T. Stcherbatski (in *Central Conception of Buddhist Nirvāṇa* [Leningrad, 1927] and other works) used by extension for "voidness" (*śūnyatā*) itself, seems ideal to convey the sense that nothing exists independent of relation with something else; therefore there is no absolute, permanent, independent self-substantial thing—only things that exist conventionally, dependent on their verbal and intellectual designations.

saint (*arhat*). This term seems appropriate to translate the title *arhat* because an *arhat* is one who has become pure from taints of the passions, etc., and "saint" is etymologically (Latin: *sanus*) connected with "cleanness" and "purity."

self (*ātma*). It is crucial to understand what is meant by "self," before one is able to realize the all-important "selflessness." Before we can discover an absence, we have to know what we are looking for. In Mahāyāna, there is a self of persons and a self of things, both presumed habitually by living beings and hence informative of their perceptions. Were these "selves" to exist as they appear because of our presumption, they should exist as substantial, self-subsistent entities within things, or as the intrinsic realities of things, or as the intrinsic identities of things, all permanent, unrelated and unrelative, etc. The nondiscovery of such "selves" within changing, relative, interdependent persons and things is the realization of ultimate reality, or selflessness.

selflessness (*anātmatā*, or *nairātmya*). This describes actual reality, as finally there is no enduring person himself or thing itself, since persons and things exist only in the relative, conventional, or superficial sense, and not in any ultimate or absolute sense. To understand Buddhist teaching correctly, we must be clear about the two senses (conventional/ultimate, or relative/absolute), since mistaking denial of ultimate self as denial of conventional self leads to nihilism, and mistaking affirmation of conventional self as affirmation of ultimate self leads to absolutism. Nihilism and absolutism effectively prevent us from realizing our enlightenment, hence are to be avoided.

signlessness (*animittatā*). In ultimate reality, there is no sign, as a sign signals or signifies something to someone and hence is inextricably involved with the relative world. We are so conditioned by signs that they seem to speak to us as if they had a voice of their own. The letter "A" seems to pronounce itself to us as we see it, and the stop-sign fairly shouts at us. However, the configuration of two slanted lines with a crossbar has in itself nothing whatsoever to do with the phenomenon made with the mouth and throat in the open position, when expulsion of breath makes the vocal cords resonate "ah." By extending such analysis to all signs, we may get an inkling of what is meant by "signlessness," which is essentially equivalent to voidness, and to "wishlessness" (see entry). Voidness, signlessness, and wishlessness form the "Three Doors of Liberation" (see Glossary 2).

tolerance (*kṣānti*). This is itemized under the "six transcendences" (see Glossary 2). Here we are concerned with the "intuitive tolerance of the birthlessness (or incomprehensibility) of all things" (*anutpattikadharmakṣānti* or *anupalabdhidharmakṣānti*). To translate *kṣānti* as "knowledge" or "conviction" defeats entirely the Skt. usage and its intended sense: In the face of birthlessness or incomprehensibility (i.e., the ultimate reality), ordinary knowledge and especially convictions are utterly lost; this is because the mind loses objectifiability of anything and has nothing to grasp, and its process of coming to terms may be described only as a conscious cancellation through absolute negations of any false sense of certainty about anything. Through this tolerance, the mind reaches a stage where it can bear its lack of bearings, as it were, can endure this kind of extreme openness, this lack of any conviction, etc. There are three degrees of this tolerance—verbal (*ghoṣānugā*), conforming (*anulomikī*), and complete. See Lamotte, *Appendice*, Note III.

transcendental analysis (*vipaśyana*). This is paired with "mental quiescence" (see entry). In general "meditation" is too often understood as only the types of practices categorized as "quietistic"—which eschew objects, learning, analysis, discrimination, etc., and lead only to the attainment of temporary peace and one-pointedness. However, in order to reach any high realization, such as personal selflessness, phenomenal selflessness, or voidness, "transcendental analysis," with its analytical penetration to the nature of ultimate reality, is indispensable. The analysis is called "transcendental" because it does not accept anything it sees as it appears. Instead, through analystic examination, it penetrates to its deeper reality, going ever deeper in infinite penetration until tolerance is reached. All apparently self-sufficient objects are seen through and their truth-status is rejected—first conceptually and finally perceptually, at Buddhahood. Thus "meditation," to be efficacious, must include both mental quiescence (*śamatha*), and transcendental analysis (*vipaśyana*) in integrated combination.

ultimate (*paramārtha*). "Ultimate" is preferable to the usual "absolute" because it carries fewer connotations than "absolute"—which, however, when understood logically, is also correct. It is contrasted with "superficial" (*vyavahāra*) or "relative" (*samvṛtti*) to give the two types, or "levels," of truth. It is synonymous with ultimate reality, the uncompounded, voidness, reality, limit of reality, absolute, nirvāṇa, ultimate liberation, infinity, permanence, eternity, independence, etc. It also has the soteriological sense of "sacred" as opposed to "profane" as is conveyed by its literal rendering "supreme" (*parama*) "object" (*artha*).

ultimate determination (*niyāma, samyaktvaniyata*). This is the stage attained by followers of the Hinayāna wherein they become determined for the attainment of liberation (nirvāṇa, i.e., the ultimate for them) in such a way as never to regress from their goals, and by bodhisattvas when they attain the holy path of insight. (See "five paths" entry, Glossary 2.)

ultimate realm (*dharmadhātu*). This compound is actually metaphorical in sense, with (at least) two interpretations possible because of ambiguities in the word *dhātu*. *Dhātu* as in the expression *kāmadhātu* (desire-realm), may mean "realm"; or it may mean "element," as in the eighteen elements (see entry), where it is explained as analogous to a mineral such as copper. Thus the realm of the Dharma is the Dharmakāyā, the pure source and sphere of the Dharma. And the element of the Dharma is like a mine from which the verbal Dharma, the buddha-qualities, and the wisdoms of the saints and bodhisattvas are culled. This is metaphorical, as Vimalakīrti would remind us, because the Dharma, the ultimate, is *ultimately* not a particular place; it is immanent in all places, being the actuality and ultimate condition of all things and being relatively no one thing except, like voidness, the supremely beneficent of concepts.

view (*dṛṣṭi*). This means a mental conviction or opinion that conditions the mind and determines how it sees reality.

voidness (*śūnyatā*). See "emptiness."

wishlessness (*apraṇihitatā*). Third of the Three Doors of Liberation (see Glossary 2). Objectively, it is equivalent to voidness; subjectively, it is the outcome of the holy gnosis of voidness as the realization of the ultimate lack of anything to wish for, whether voidness itself, or even Buddhahood. See "emptiness."